Ralph A. Ricci

# AFVs IN IRISH SERVICE SINCE 1922

## From the National Army to the Irish Defence Forces

*Dedication*
*To the men and women of the Irish Cavalry Corps who have served Ireland*
*with honor through the years.*

STRATUS

# Picture Credits

Published in Poland in 2011
by STRATUS s.c.
Po. Box 123,
27-600 Sandomierz 1, Poland
e-mail: office@mmpbooks.biz
for
Mushroom Model Publications,
3 Gloucester Close,
Petersfield,
Hampshire GU32 3AX
e-mail: rogerw@mmpbooks.biz

© 2010 Mushroom Model
Publications.
http://www.mmpbooks.biz

All rights reserved. Apart from any fair dealing for the purpose of private study, research, criticism or review, as permitted under the Copyright, Design and Patents Act, 1988, no part of this publication may be reproduced, stored in a retrieval system, or transmitted in any form or by any means, electronic, electrical, chemical, mechanical, optical, photocopying, recording or otherwise, without prior written permission. All enquiries should be addressed to the publisher.

**ISBN
978-83-61421-19-1**

*Editor in chief*
Roger Wallsgrove

*Editorial Team*
Bartłomiej Belcarz
Robert Pęczkowski
Artur Juszczak

*Scale plans*
Rodolfo Ciuffoletti

*DTP*
Robert Pęczkowski
Bartłomiej Belcarz

*Printed by*
Drukarnia Diecezjalna,
ul. Żeromskiego 4,
27-600 Sandomierz
tel. +48 (15) 832 31 92
fax +48 (15) 832 77 87
www.wds.pl
marketing@wds.pl

PRINTED IN POLAND

| | |
|---|---|
| BAE OMC | BAE Land Systems OMC, Benoni, South Africa |
| Sue Bryant | Sue Bryant, Canada |
| Bob Cantwell | Cpl Bob Cantwell, 31 Reserve Cavalry Squadron, Clonmel, Ireland |
| Curragh History Group | Curragh History Group, Ireland |
| David Dunne | David Dunne, Donaghadee, County Down |
| James Hayle | Sgt James Hayle, Irish Defence Forces Ret'd |
| Howth | National Transport Museum, Howth, Ireland |
| IWM | Imperial War Museum, London |
| Karl Martin | Karl Martin, Dublin, Ireland |
| MA | Military Archives, Cathal Brugha Barracks, Rathmines, Dublin, Ireland |
| Mats Hjorter | Mats Hjorter, Strangnas, Sweden |
| Denis McCarthy | Denis McCarthy, Dalkey, Ireland |
| Matt McNamara | Matt McNamara, Curragh History Group, Ireland |
| Mayo County Library | Mayo County Library, County Mayo, Ireland |
| Mowag | Mowag GMBH, Kreuzlingen, Switzerland |
| Sgt David Nagle | Sgt David Nagle, Editor, An Cosantoir, Dublin |
| NLI/NPA | National Library of Ireland, National Photographic Archive, Dublin |
| Paul McMenamin | Paul McMenamin, Ireland |
| Paul Murphy | Paul Murphy, Clonmel, Ireland |
| Peter Leslie | Peter Leslie, Staffordshire, England |
| Pignato | Dott. Nicola Pignato, Rome, Italy |
| Preston Isaac | Preston Isaac, Cobbaton Combat Collection, Devon, England |
| Roy Kinsella | Roy Kinsella, Glengeary, County Dublin, Ireland |
| Sean O'Sullivan | Sean O'Sullivan, Hospital, County Limerick, Ireland |
| Brian Quinn | Brian Quinn, Galway, Ireland |
| SISU | SISU Defence (Patria Group), Karjaa, Finland |
| Terry Ward | Terry Ward, Dublin, Ireland |
| Thompson | Thompson Engineering (formerly Thomas Thompson and Son), Carlow, Ireland |
| TMB | Tank Museum Bovington, Dorset, England |
| UFTM | Ulster Folk and Transport Museum, Cultra, Holywood, County Down (Northern Ireland) |
| UN | United Nations Photo Library |

**Get in the picture!**

Do you have photographs of historical aircraft, airfields in action, or original and unusual stories to tell? MMP would like to hear from you! We welcome previously unpublished material that will help to make MMP books the best of their kind. We will return original photos to you and provide full credit for your images. Contact us before sending us any valuable material: rogerw@mmpbooks.biz

*On title page: Rolls-Royce Admiralty Pattern armoured car. (TMB 37/B/2)*

# Table of contents

Picture Credits .................................................................................................................. 2
Introduction ..................................................................................................................... 5
Acknowledgements......................................................................................................... 5
Selected Irish Terminology ............................................................................................ 8
Technical Notes ............................................................................................................... 8
**Origins of Armour in Ireland** ..................................................................................... 9
**1922: Armour During the Civil War**........................................................................ 24
Free State (National Army) Armoured Operations.................................................. 24
Republican Armoured Operations............................................................................. 34
**Organization of Irish Armoured Units** ................................................................... 40
Cavalry Organization: .................................................................................................. 40
World War II Organization: ........................................................................................ 46
    1st Armoured Car Squadron............................................................................... 48
    2nd Armoured Car Squadron............................................................................. 49
    3rd Armoured Car Squadron............................................................................. 50
    4th Armoured Car Squadron ............................................................................. 50
    Carrier Squadron .................................................................................................. 51
    1 Motor Squadron ............................................................................................... 51
    2 Motor Squadron ............................................................................................... 52
    3 Motor Squadron ............................................................................................... 53
    4 Motor Squadron ............................................................................................... 54
    5 Motor Squadron ............................................................................................... 54
    6 Motor Squadron ............................................................................................... 54
    7 Motor Squadron ............................................................................................... 55
    11 Cavalry Squadron (FCA) ................................................................................ 55
Post World War II and Current Organization ......................................................... 56
    1st Tank Squadron............................................................................................... 57
    1st Armoured Cavalry Squadron ....................................................................... 57
    1st Cavalry Squadron .......................................................................................... 57
    2nd Cavalry Squadron ........................................................................................ 57
    4th Cavalry Squadron.......................................................................................... 57
    31 Reserve Cavalry Squadron ............................................................................ 58
    54 Reserve Cavalry Squadron ............................................................................ 58
    62 Reserve Cavalry Squadron ............................................................................ 58
    Non-Cavalry Armour Assignments................................................................... 58
    3rd Infantry Battalion (The Bloods) ................................................................. 58
    27th Infantry Battalion ........................................................................................ 58
    28th Infantry Battalion ........................................................................................ 58
    29th infantry Battalion ........................................................................................ 58
**Armour in Support of Irish Peacekeeping Contingents Abroad**....................... 59
ONUC – Congo............................................................................................................ 59
UNFICYP – Cyprus...................................................................................................... 61
UNIFIL - Lebanon ....................................................................................................... 62
UNOSOM II - Somalia ................................................................................................ 64
KFOR - Kosovo ............................................................................................................ 65
UNMEE - Eritrea ......................................................................................................... 65
UNMIL - Liberia .......................................................................................................... 65
EUFOR - Chad/Central African Republic) ............................................................. 66

**Armoured Vehicles in Irish Service 1922-2010** ................................................................. 67
Rolls-Royce 1920 Pattern Armoured Car .................................................................................. 67
Peerless Armoured Car (1919 Pattern) ..................................................................................... 72
Lancia Armoured Troop Carriers .............................................................................................. 74
Fiat armoured cars .................................................................................................................... 79
Partially armoured vehicles ...................................................................................................... 79
Leyland Armoured Car ............................................................................................................. 79
Landsverk L 180 Armoured Car ............................................................................................... 83
GSR Morris and GSR Ford Mk IV Armoured Cars ................................................................. 88
Ford Mk V Armoured Car ........................................................................................................ 90
Ford Mk VI Armoured Car ....................................................................................................... 92
Dodge Mk VII and Dodge Mk VIII Armoured Cars ................................................................ 97
Beaverette Light Armoured Car Scout Car ............................................................................... 99
Ferret Mk II Armoured Car ..................................................................................................... 103
Scania SKPF m/42 APC .......................................................................................................... 105
Humber Mk I (FV 1611) Pig ................................................................................................... 108
Panhard AML 245 Armoured Cars (H60 and H90 Series) ..................................................... 110
Landsverk Unimog Scout Car ................................................................................................. 131
Panhard M3 VTT Armoured Personnel Carrier ..................................................................... 134
Timoney Mk I APC .................................................................................................................. 139
Timoney Mk II APC ................................................................................................................ 139
Timoney Mk III APC ............................................................................................................... 140
Timoney Mk IV APC ............................................................................................................... 142
Timoney Mk VI APC ............................................................................................................... 144
SISU XA-180 APC .................................................................................................................. 148
RG-31 Mk 3 Nyala .................................................................................................................. 153
MOWAG Piranha III H Armoured Personnel Carrier/Armoured Infantry
Fighting Vehicle ...................................................................................................................... 154
BAE RG 32M LTV Light Tactical Vehicle (LTV) ................................................................. 164
Vickers Mk D Tank ................................................................................................................. 167
Landsverk L60 Light Tank ...................................................................................................... 169
Universal Carrier (Bren Gun Carrier) ..................................................................................... 173
Churchill Mk VI Tank ............................................................................................................. 176
Comet A34 Tank ..................................................................................................................... 181
M113 APC ............................................................................................................................... 186
Alvis Scorpion CVR(T) ........................................................................................................... 187
Appendix 1: **Colour Equivalents for Modelers** ................................................................. 191
Appendix 2: Irish Cavalry Corps Unit Designations .............................................................. 192
Appendix 3: Cavalry Corps Unit Insignia .............................................................................. 196
Appendix 4: Markings and Colours ........................................................................................ 198
Appendix 5: Vehicle Registration Numbers ........................................................................... 202
Appendix 6: Vehicle Service Dates ........................................................................................ 202
Appendix 7: Weapon Characteristics ..................................................................................... 204
Appendix 8: Preserved Vehicles ............................................................................................. 204
Bibliography ............................................................................................................................ 222

# Introduction

It is somewhat surprising that the Irish, who are universally recognised as perhaps the most adept of storytellers, known for their turns of phrase that range from the eloquent to the comically ribald, and who likewise are firmly rooted to their past history, have given scant attention to the history and accomplishments of their armed forces in the form of published works. The number of books dealing with the Irish Army (that of the Republic of Ireland) can be counted on the fingers of one hand, still leaving a few to spare (Karl Martin, Irish Army Vehicles: Transport and Armour Since 1922, and Donal MacCarron, Step Together: Ireland's Emergency Army 1939-46 As Told By Its Veterans). There is also one excellent work on vehicles in service in Northern Ireland (David Dunne, Armoured and Heavy Vehicles of the RUC 1922-2001), but there seems to have been no attempt to publish a more or less complete chronicle of the history of the Irish Army since its inception in 1922 as the National Army of the Provisional Government, or of any of its various corps. This book is an attempt to address the history of the use of armoured vehicles by Irish forces since 1922 (although it actually begins with a brief look at the use of armoured vehicles by British forces between 1916 and 1922) to the extent possible given the limitations imposed by working with the sources available, and relying on the generosity and good grace of a number of truly unselfish and enthusiastic individuals, mostly in Ireland. In addition to describing the vehicles themselves, the history and organization of the Cavalry Corps is portrayed, probably imperfectly, for what is believed to be the first time in a published work.

# Acknowledgements

Although it is my name that appears on the cover of this book as the author, in reality this book has been, in my estimation, very much of a cooperative effort, as I have relied on the institutional memory, knowledge, and at times, just plain common sense of a small group of individuals (David Fletcher, Karl Martin, Paul Murphy, Peter Leslie, and Paul V. Walsh) whose in-depth knowledge of the subject, accumulated over many years that they have dedicated to the study and analysis of armour in general and in the case of Martin and Walsh, of armour in Irish service in particular. I am greatly indebted to these experts (whether or not they like to be referred to as such), for ultimately, this book would not have been possible without their assistance, patience, and generosity.

**David Fletcher**, Historian, The Tank Museum, Bovington, Dorset, England, has been a sage adviser from the time I initially broached the subject about writing something on Irish armour. He was most encouraging, and is solely responsible for urging me to tackle a much larger project than I had originally envisioned. Over the course of countless E-mails and telephone calls he answered dozens, if not hundreds, of questions I had, at times reaching deep down into his pool of knowledge to provide some obscure bit of trivia that I absolutely had to have. Throughout this correspondence, his unceasing wit and acerbic comments often brought me back to reality. He will, of course, deny that most, if any, of this is true, and likely will find it as an excuse to repair to the nearest pub to quaff a beer in order to drown out the memories of an American who sometimes just doesn't understand.

**Karl Martin**, the preeminent author on Irish Army vehicles, has been unbelievably generous and forthcoming not only with information and personal photographs, but has also offered advice, constructive criticism, and insights I could not have obtained elsewhere. His books have set the standard for others to emulate with respect to the subject, and I can only hope that my efforts have been useful in complementing his work.

**Paul Murphy**, formerly a Sergeant with 31 Reserve Cavalry Squadron, has been a major source of photographs as well as of information on a number of specific details such as vehicle colours, location of preserved vehicles, and unit designations and markings. He has also been incredibly generous and helpful in contacting friends and colleagues for additional photographs. During a protracted period of intense E-mail exchanges, Paul continued to offer encouragement and advice, suggesting several additional sources of information as well as thoughts on how to improve certain aspects of the book. His enthusiasm for this project was boundless.

**Roy Kinsella**, who in addition to providing many unique photographs and information on Irish Army vehicle colours, also offered to drive me to Curragh Camp during my visit to Ireland in May 2009, making what otherwise would have been impossible a reality.

**Peter Leslie**, who has long been addicted to the study of armoured vehicles, with a sharp focus on certain aspects of their use in Irish service, has provided details on a number of aspects that otherwise would have been virtually impossible to find. Peter and I seem to share the same irrational fascination with the subject of the Lancia armoured troop carriers in Ireland, as well as sharing the frustration in attempting to come to some conclusion relating to the number built for service in Ireland.

**Paul V. Walsh**, whose research on the use of armoured vehicles during the Irish Civil War, and scholarly writings on the subject are truly impressive, and who was unstinting in sharing information and who was always willing to provide critical comment on my logic, reasoning, and conclusions regarding armoured operations during the Civil War period.

**David Dunne**, who shared his knowledge relating to the location and disposition of vehicles in Northern Ireland during the period immediately following the Civil War, and who also took extraordinary pains to identify the locations where vintage photographs were taken.

**Sean F. O'Sullivan, Terry Ward, and Bob Cantwell**, whose efforts to take or find photographs of armoured vehicles went well above and beyond the call of duty, and whose contributions added significantly to the variety of new images presented in this book.

**Ray Broe**, who virtually in the final stages of preparation of the manuscript, graciously provided a treasure trove of previously unpublished photographs from his grandfather George Pierce's collection, and who along with his mother, Mrs. Janice Pierce Broe, walked me through several of the sites that figured prominently during the fighting at the Four Courts and The Block in Dublin.

**Lt Col Eamonn J. Cullagh**, School Commandant, Cavalry School, Combat Support College, Curragh Camp, who not only generously and patiently provided much information over the course of many phone conversations, and who commented on several versions of my draft manuscripts, but who most graciously hosted a visit to Curragh Camp in May 2009 during which he provided valuable background and insights, and enabled me to take a number of interesting and useful photographs.

**Nicola Pignato** has been very much a mentor to me in my previous works on Italian armour, so it was natural that I turn to him for otherwise unobtainable information on the Lancia armoured cars used in Ireland.

**Captain Padraic Kennedy**, Defence Forces Information Officer, who graciously granted permission to use many excellent Defence Forces photographs, and **Sergeant David Nagle**, Irish Defence Forces, Editor of An Cosantoir, Dublin, Ireland, who has been instrumental in finding, obtaining, and sharing information from the outset of my research, as well as providing photographic documentation not available elsewhere.

**Rodolfo Ciuffoletti** for his willingness to tackle the job of providing line drawings of a quality unseen of vehicles in Irish service.

It would be totally remiss of me if I did not give sincere thanks to Roger Wallsgrove of Mushroom Model Publications for his willingness to take on what certainly is an underreported niche of military history. Thanks likewise are in order for the Robert Pęczkowski and staff at STRATUS for their part in making this book a reality.

I am likewise indebted to the following individuals and organizations for their assistance, and very often, for their patience in dealing with my requests, not to mention having to cope with my American accent.

Andrew Berg, Ray Broe, Janice Pierce Broe, Eamon Browne (Kerry Archaeological and Historical Society), Sue Bryant, Paddy Byrne and Lt. Sharon Crean (Army Equitation School), Pat Clemens (Curator, Collins Barracks Military Museum, Cork), Deirdre Condon (Southside Coal Company, Cork, Ireland), Michael Corcoran (National Transport Museum Howth), Comdt Robert Duggan (Officer in Charge, Combined Vehicles Base Workshop, Defence Forces Logistics Base), Clive Elliot, Elizabeth Evensen and Labhras Joye (National Museum of Ireland), Hugh Forrester (Curator, PSNI Museum, Belfast), Reverend Father J. Anthony Gaughan, Philip Hall (The Sir Henry Royce Memorial Foundation, Paulerspury, Northants, England), Ivor Hamrock (Mayo County Library), Lt Col Billy Harrington and Capt Padraic Kennedy (Defence Forces Information Office, Irish Defence Forces), RSM Terry Hall, Mats Hjorter, Preston Isaac (Cobbaton Combat Collection), Bronach Joyce (Clew Bay Heritage Centre), Mark Kennedy and Alan McCartney (Ulster Folk and Transport Museum, National Museums Northern Ireland), Squadron Quartermaster Sergeant Francis "Buddy Kertin", CPL Mark Buckley, CPL Bob Cantwell, and CPL Cormac O'Keeffe (31 Reserve Cavalry Squadron, Clonmel), Sgt Paddy King (62 Reserve Cavalry Squadron), Roy Kinsella, Daniela Leo (MOWAG GmbH, Kreuzlingen, Switzerland), Anthony Leonard, Bidey Leonard, Patrick Lynch, Kevin MacBride, Donal MacCarron, John Malamatenios, Denis McCarthy, Shirley McCormack (Irish National Stud, Kildare), Sandra McDermott and Anne O'Donoghue (Reader Services, Rights and Reproductions, National Library of Ireland), Paul McMenamin, Liz McEvoy (Irish National Archives), Karen Millward (Karen Millward Books, Bantry, County Cork, Ireland), Natalie Milne (RTÉ Stills Library, Donnybrook), Military Archives Staff, Dublin (Comdt Victor Laing, Hugh Beckett, Lisa Dolan, and Noelle Grothier), Professor Richard M. Ogorkiewicz, Risto Paloposki, (Patria, Finland), Flight Sergeant James G. Perkins, Natasha Pheiffer (BAE Systems Land Systems South Africa), Brian Quinn, Fintan Quinn (National Library of Ireland), Richard Slattery, Sara Smyth (Photographic Archives, National Library of Ireland), Paddy Thomas, and Eileen Jordan (Thomas Thompson and Sons, Carlow, Ireland), Jochen Vollert (Tankograd Publishing), Terry Ward, Bob Webster.

A special thanks to my wife, Charlene, who encouraged and supported this project from its inception, and who spent countless hours proofreading the text and offered suggestions for stylistic improvements.

# SELECTED IRISH TERMINOLOGY

The period from January to December 1922 was a chaotic period in Irish history. Ireland was in the throes of establishing its independence from Britain, as well as fighting a civil war internally. Ireland established a Provisional Government on 14 January, 1922, but it was not until 6 December, 1922, that the Free State of Ireland was established. During the period of conflict in 1922-23 between opposing factions of the Irish Republican Army, those in favor of the Anglo-Irish Treaty of 6 December, 1921 (which called for partition of Ireland into its present configuration, with the six northern counties of Ulster remaining part of Britain) were generally referred to as the Free State (Saorstát Éireann in Irish) or National Forces, and those opposed to it as the Republican or Irregular forces. The two sides have also been referred to simply as the pro-Treaty and anti-Treaty forces. Thus, throughout the section of this book dealing with the Irish Civil War, all of those terms may be encountered, although strictly speaking, reference to Free State forces prior to 6 December, 1922 is inaccurate, as prior to that date the forces, known as the National Army, belonged to the Provisional Government rather than to the Free State, which had not yet been officially established.

Especially for the American reader, a few words about Irish Provinces and Counties might be useful. Historically, Ireland is divided into four Provinces (Ulster, Leinster, Munster, and Connacht), and is further subdivided into 32 Counties. Because of the ongoing troubles in Northern Ireland, the northernmost province of Ulster is the province name most familiar to American readers. The Province of Ulster comprises nine counties; however, only six of those nine counties belong to Northern Ireland, the other three, overwhelmingly Catholic in population, having been made part of the Free State (now the Republic of Ireland).

# TECHNICAL NOTES

Wherever possible, to avoid confusion between metric tons (2204 pounds), British tons (2240 pounds, or long ton) and US tons (2000 pounds, or short ton) weights are given in pounds and kilograms.

Dimensions are provided in inches (normally rounded to the nearest inch) and millimeters (normally rounded to the nearest millimeter). Armour thicknesses generally are provided in millimeters, although a few are provided in fractions of an inch. Distances and speeds are provided in miles, or miles per hour (mph), and in kilometers, or kilometers per hour (km/h), usually rounded off to the nearest mile or kilometer.

Liquid measures (e.g. fuel capacities) are provided in Imperial gallons, US gallons, and litres.

# Origins of Armour in Ireland

In order to set the scene for the initial (and subsequent) use of armoured vehicles in Ireland, an encapsulated history of Anglo-Irish relations is appropriate. In 1169 the Normans invaded Ireland, but it was not until 1603 that a British victory over the recalcitrant Irish in the northern province of Ulster allowed Britain to completely control the island. To ensure control of the troublesome province, the British confiscated land from the Catholic Irish and settled it with Protestant Scottish farmers, laying the groundwork for the subsequent (and current) partition of Ireland. In 1801 the United Kingdom of Great Britain and Ireland was created, pleasing neither Protestant nor Catholic in Ireland. The situation remained troublesome, and in 1912 a third Home Rule Bill was introduced, and in 1914 the Third Home Rule Act was passed, but was not implemented due to the advent of the First World War. Feelings festered in Ireland, and in 1916 the Irish Republicans staged the Easter Rising (which saw the first use of armoured vehicles in Ireland). The aftermath was badly handled by the victorious British, and in January 1919 the Irish formed a Republican parliament, unilaterally declared sovereignty over the entire island, and established a provisional government. The Irish Republican Army (IRA), which was the army, or military arm, of the newly declared Irish Republic, was unwilling to negotiate any understanding with Britain short of complete independence, leading to three years of guerrilla warfare by the Irish against the British, culminating in a truce signed on 11 July, 1921. Talks between the British and Irish resulted in the Anglo-Irish Treaty of 6 December, 1921, which effectively partitioned Ireland into the 26 predominantly Catholic counties in the south and six[1] of the nine counties of the province of Ulster in the predominantly Protestant north, formally establishing the Irish Free State a year later, on 6 December, 1922.

The earliest armoured vehicles to be used in Ireland were hastily improvised vehicles built by the British in Ireland to deal with the April 1916 Easter Rising by Irish Republican forces that had taken control of a number of key buildings in Dublin. The idea for these armoured vehicles is attributed to a Colonel Portal, commanding the Curragh Mobile Column, while their actual design is credited to Colonel H.W.T Allatt, who subsequently fell during the fighting in Dublin. A small fleet of makeshift armoured trucks was hastily cobbled together, quite ingeniously, by appropriat-

---
1  *The six counties are Antrim, Armagh, Down, Fermanagh, Londonderry, and Tyrone.*

*One of the first three improvised armoured trucks built on a Daimler chassis. Note the locomotive cab roof, in addition to the body fabricated from locomotive steam boxes, clearly reflecting the railway shop provenance of these vehicles. The driver's cab was isolated from the troop compartment. (TMB 4294/E/3)*

*One of the "second series" of two Daimler lorries hastily assembled at the Inchicore shops of the GS&WR in Dublin, shown as it appeared on Batchelor's Walk, along the River Liffey near Sackville Street (now O'Connell Street) in Dublin. The body, utilizing flat plates, was radically different in style from the first three improvised vehicles using locomotive smokeboxes. (TMB 552/E/6)*

ing five Daimler three-ton shaft-driven flatbed trucks from the Guinness Brewery in Dublin, which were then taken to the Great Southern and Western Railway (GS&WR) workshops in the Inchicore area on the west side of Dublin where they were fitted with armoured bodies literally within hours. The bodies for the first three were made from four locomotive smokeboxes bolted together on the bed of the truck, with a smokebox door fitted to the open end of the rearmost segment providing access to the fighting compartment. The door also contained a rear-facing machine-gun mounting. The driver's compartment and hood were covered by steel plates, and further accenting the railroad origins of the vehicle, the driver's compartment was topped by the cab roof of a locomotive. Because the vehicles were so hastily assembled from what was immediately at hand, there were some slight variations between the three vehicles in terms of the configuration of the smokeboxes and cab roofs. The boiler plate used as armour was not proof against rifle rounds fired at close range, although the curvature of the cylinder added somewhat to the anti-ballistic effectiveness and provided at least a modicum of protection to the occupants. The body had somewhat of a mottled appearance due to firing slits cut into the boiler plate as well as to a number of false slits painted on the plate to confuse enemy snipers. The Irish snipers, however, apparently were not easily fooled, as they concentrated on the vision slots of the driver's compartment, putting the driver of the first armoured truck out of action not long after it appeared on Sackville Street (now O'Connell Street). Two other armoured trucks were built using the Daimler chassis but, except for the curved covering over the engine, used mainly flat steel plates rather than the circular boilers of the earlier vehicles. The rather large rectangular box bodies were extended far enough forward to include the driver's compartment, and access was through a door in the rear plate. All five vehicles were used in street patrols, but were also used to assault occupied buildings by backing up to the building entrance, using the machine-gun as appropriate, and then discharging the troops to storm the building. After the crisis had passed, the armoured bodies are believed to have been removed at Inchicore for use in building locomotives, and the trucks themselves returned to the Guinness brewery for use in delivering barrels of stout.

In addition to the five improvised armoured trucks quickly built to cope with the situation in Dublin, the British arranged for improvised assembly at least one armoured train, availing themselves of the facilities of the Great Northern Railway (Ireland) at Dundalk, north of Dublin, for the purpose. The train consisted of a locomotive that had been armoured with a combination of metal

*This photograph of an armoured train during the Easter 1916 period raises more questions than it answers. It appears to be a 4-4-2 tank locomotive, possibly a T1 class, built by Beyer and Peacock of Manchester, England, and belonging to the Great Northern Railway (Ireland). The locomotive would have weighed 65 tons in standard condition, prior to the addition of the armour plating, which itself is metal plate backed by an undetermined type of wooden planking. The cars themselves are 15 ton locomotive coal wagons used to move coal around the railroad yard rather than for route delivery and have loopholes cut into the side planking, as well as having a rim of metal armour around the top of the standard wooden body. The wagon's dimensions were 19'11" over the buffers, 16'6' long inside, 7'11" wide inside, and 4'6 ½" high wooden bodywork. The soldiers shown in the wagons would certainly have been standing on some sort of elevated platform inside the cars in order to be as exposed as they are. The main construction shops of the GNR(I) were located at Dundalk, where this photograph likely was taken. Although all of the personnel in the photograph are in uniform, including the individual in the locomotive cab, the train would have been driven by its regular crew. (UFTM 596.1992, via Mark Kennedy)*

*Rolls-Royce Admiralty Pattern armoured car. The Admiralty Pattern differed from the later 1920 Pattern in details such as the wire spoke wheels, the solid armoured radiator cover without louvers, and the headlights mounted on the front fenders. In this example, a stock photograph of a machine in England, the headlights themselves are missing from the headlight mounting brackets. (TMB 37/B/2)*

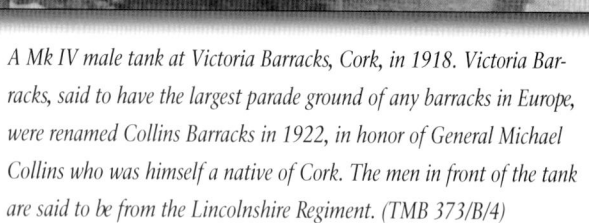

*A Mk IV male tank at Victoria Barracks, Cork, in 1918. Victoria Barracks, said to have the largest parade ground of any barracks in Europe, were renamed Collins Barracks in 1922, in honor of General Michael Collins who was himself a native of Cork. The men in front of the tank are said to be from the Lincolnshire Regiment. (TMB 373/B/4)*

*An Austin Model 1918 named "May", assigned to 17 Armoured Car Battalion, Tank Corps, stationed in Ireland in 1919. The car is painted in a two-tone camouflage scheme. The number 2201 or 2207 is visible behind the Lance Corporal standing on the right-hand running board. (TMB 4294/F/4)*

*An Austin armoured car in front of Mountjoy Jail, Dublin, during the April 1920 hunger strike by inmates. Although vehicle crews habitually adorn their vehicles with pet names, this crew seems rather to have expressed their feelings concerning the Irish insurgents somewhat succinctly by chalking the uncomplimentary slogan "Up Sinn Fein" on the storage box. (NLI/NPA IND H 0439, Courtesy of the National Library of Ireland)*

plates backed by wooden planking, and two coal wagons that had been partially armoured. The GNR(I) operated mainly northeast of Dublin and did in fact serve Dublin, as well as other important cities and towns such as Belfast, Londonderry, Armagh, Portadown, and Omagh. Whether this was the only such train to have been improvised by the British during the Easter Rising is open to question, as is what use, if any, was ever made of the train.

The first military armoured vehicles sent to Ireland by the British seem to have been seven Rolls-Royce Admiralty Pattern armoured cars sent to Dublin in May 1916, shortly after the Easter Rising, to help deal with the internal security situation that had developed. These seven cars were assigned to mobile detachments organized to counter predatory attacks on police stations by armed Irish insurgents. The detachments generally consisted of one or two companies of infantry, a horse-mounted cavalry squadron, an 18-pdr gun, and one armoured car; detachments were stationed in Athlone, Castlebar, Cork, Kilkenny and Limerick, as well as Dublin.

The Rolls-Royce armoured car was developed in 1914 for the Royal Naval Air Service and was based on the Rolls-Royce Silver Ghost touring car chassis. The design of this vehicle dates to October 1914, with initial deliveries beginning in December 1914. These cars, marked by an enclosed turret fitted with a Vickers .303 in. machine-gun, wire spoke wheels, and an open rear deck containing side-mounted tool and storage boxes, were known as the Admiralty Pattern. Entry into and exit from the car was through a door in the rear of the turret; there were no side doors on the car. This version was modernized in 1920, resulting in the 1920 Pattern car which featured armoured hood louvers and disc wheels replacing the earlier wire spoke wheels; the headlights were also repositioned from on top of the fenders to being mounted in front of the hood louvers. The Rolls-Royce 6-cylinder gasoline engine developed 80 HP and enabled the car to reach a top speed of 50 mph on paved roads which, for the times, represented an extremely fast vehicle.[2] In British service in Ireland, in addition to the Vickers armament, a Hotchkiss machine-gun was also carried in the car as a backup weapon. In Ireland the Rolls-Royce (both Admiralty and 1920 Patterns) figured prominently in British service up to withdrawal in 1922, and in Irish Free State service from 1922 until their retirement from active service in 1954. In British service, it was considered a workhorse, being more reliable, agile, and overall more mission-capable than the other types of armoured cars that were, or had been, stationed in Ireland.

For several years the seven Rolls-Royces were the only armoured vehicles supporting British forces in Ireland, but in late 1918 or early 1919, in order to cope with the insurgency being carried out by the Irish Republican Army, a company of heavy tanks (probably Mark IV) was sent to Marlborough Barracks (now McKee Barracks) in Dublin. Close on the heels of this first company, in January 1919, Britain dispatched the 17th Armoured Car Battalion from occupation duty in Germany's Rhineland to Dublin. The battalion was organized into three companies, two of which, despite the battalion's designation as an armoured car battalion, were equipped with tanks. "A" Company, stationed in Limerick, consisted of fourteen Austin armoured cars (later increased to sixteen). Battalion headquarters and the other two companies of the 17th Armoured Car Battalion were stationed at Marlborough Barracks in Dublin itself; "B" company consisted of sixteen Medium "A" tanks, and "C" Company was equipped with Mark IV (later with Mark V* and Medium "B") tanks. A photograph taken on 19 July, 1919, shows four Medium "A" tanks followed by at least three Mark V* male tanks on parade on Dame Street in Dublin.[3] The 17th was charged mainly with escort and patrol duties, which called for parceling out the tanks and armoured cars over wide areas of Ireland.

The Austin had its origins as an armoured car built by the Austin Motor Co. Ltd for the Russian Imperial Government in 1914, and soon became known as the Austin-Putilov armoured car, as they were modified at the Putilov armament works in Petrograd. Four series of the car were built;

---
2  *Although the Rolls-Royce was capable of a top speed of 50 mph, standing regulations in Ireland called for a maximum speed of no more than 20 miles per hour (William Sheehan, Fighting for Dublin, page 101).*
3  *Tim Pat Coogan and George Morrison, The Irish Civil War, photograph 64 on page 97.*
*The date given for the picture by Coogan and Morrison is 11 November, 1919.*

the fourth series, sometimes referred to as the Austin Model 1918, was ordered by Russia in 1917, but none of that series were ever delivered to Russia due to the collapse of the Czarist government. The undelivered Model 1918s, (possibly as many as 70) characterized by a strengthened chassis and double rear wheels, were taken over by the British Army, and sixteen, as previously mentioned, were sent to Ireland. As was common on Russian armoured cars, the Austin was fitted with twin machine-gun turrets, fitted with .303 in. Hotchkiss Model 1909 weapons in the British vehicles. Although the Austin cars in Ireland were considered excellent vehicles, they were gradually decommissioned, and the last of them were scrapped along with the tanks prior to the British withdrawal from Ireland in 1922.

All of the tanks deployed to Ireland had seen service in World War I, which was concluded not long before their deployment there. The Mark IV was a 1917 design, powered by a 105 HP Daimler engine. Two versions, a "Male" version armed with 6-pdr guns, and a "Female" version armed with machine-guns were produced; it is not clear if both versions of the Mark IV were sent to Ireland, although the few period photographs show the male version. The later Mark V* (1918) was similar to the Mark IV, but was considerably elongated in order to be better able to cross trenches. The Mark V* was powered by a six-cylinder Ricardo engine developing 150 HP. As with the Mark IV, the Mark V* was also built in male and female versions, but only the male version was sent to Ireland. The Medium Mark "A" tank was a somewhat lighter tank, powered by two Tylor commercial vehicle engines, moving it along at about 8 mph. Armament consisted of four Hotchkiss Model 1909 .303 in. machine-guns in a fixed raised superstructure. The Mark "A" was nicknamed the "Whippet"; this should not be confused with the Rolls-Royce armoured cars which, later in Irish service, were also referred to as "Whippets". The Medium Mark "B" was a completely different design from that of the Mark "A", and reverted to the lozenge shape of the earlier heavy tanks. It had a raised superstructure fitted with ball mountings for five Hotchkiss Model 1909 .303 in. machine-guns, as well as ball mountings on the door on each side of the vehicle. The Mark "B" was powered by a four-cylinder Ricardo engine providing a top speed of 6 mph.

*An Austin stationed in Ireland displaying a two-tone camouflage scheme. The unit and location are unknown, and the letter "T" prominently displayed on the side likewise cannot be identified with a specific unit. (TMB 7660/F/4)*

The British decision to send tanks to Ireland may have been partly as a show of force and partly due to the ready availability of the vehicles; arguably, there were no insurgent weapons or capabilities that would have dictated the deployment of tanks as a countermeasure. Operational use of tanks in Ireland seems to have been limited; anecdotal evidence suggests that the tanks, stationed in Dublin, were used to break down Republican barricades and gates or doorways to buildings occupied by the insurgents. The tanks were slow, cumbersome, and difficult to deploy anywhere outside Dublin itself where they were stationed, although at least one Mark IV was sent to Limerick in April 1919 to deal with heightened insurgent activity in that area, and at least one tank was in Cork in January 1921. Instead, it seems that there was almost total reliance on the various armoured cars and the Lancia armoured personnel carriers to provide convoy escort, carry out patrols and curfew enforcement, support occasional raids against the Irish insurgents, and to carry out other assorted security tasks. The Rolls-Royces may have been the preferred vehicles for patrols, as they were the quietest of the cars available and did not announce their presence as readily as did the other types. In practical terms, there was little need for anything more powerful than an armoured car, as the insurgent forces had no armour or anti-armour capability of their own.

Sometime in early 1919 another armoured car company arrived, equipped with two Admiralty Pattern Rolls-Royces and a number of Jeffery-Quad armoured cars (either 20 or 22, depending on the source consulted[4]), possibly diverted from India to Ireland. The Rolls-Royces remained with the company headquarters based in the Curragh, while the Jeffery-Quads were allocated to various military installations throughout the country. The Jeffery-Quad was a four-wheel drive truck with four-wheel brakes and steering on all wheels. Several thousand Jeffery-Quads were built in the United States during the First World War, their four-wheel drive making them invaluable as cargo trucks, gun tractors and ambulances, and an armoured car was soon developed on the chassis and manufactured in an appreciable quantity for the British Army. The armoured car had a single rotating turret in the center, supplemented by four small semi-circular sponsons, each with two loopholes, on the hull sides. The vehicle was equipped with a dual-drive system with driving

*A British Medium A tank pulling a lorry from the River Liffey, 17 May, 1921. This tank likely was assigned to "B" Company, 3rd Tank Battalion. (NLI/NPA HOG 175, Courtesy of the National Library of Ireland)*

---

4  David Fletcher, *War Cars, British Armoured Cars in the First World War*, page 8, cites a figure of 20, while B.T. White in *Tanks and Other Armoured Fighting Vehicles*, page 149, claims that there were 22 in Ireland in 1919.

*A British Mk V\* male tank with the Tank Section of the 2nd Battalion, Royal Berkshire Regiment in Dublin, November 1920. It is obvious that the size of the machine would limit its utility in an urban environment. (TMB 353/H/5)*

stations in raised armoured driver's cabs fore and aft of the turret; the British had pioneered the use of the dual-drive feature in World War I, and this feature later was to figure on several other armoured cars, both British as well as Swedish designs, used in Ireland. Suspension consisted of semi-elliptic leaf springs front and rear and the solid disc wheels had solid rubber tires. The Quad was powered by a 40 HP Buda four-cylinder gasoline engine that moved it along at about 20 mph. The Quads in British service normally were armed with a Vickers .303 in. machine-gun in the turret. The Quads were difficult to maintain and did not enjoy a favorable reputation in Ireland. The last of the Jeffery-Quads were broken up and scrapped sometime in 1922.

About a year later, in April 1920, the armoured car company based in the Curragh was disbanded, and in March 1920, a decision was made to eliminate the 17th Armoured Car Battalion, and on 29 May, No. 5 Armoured Car Company was formed with a reduced number of personnel from the 17th. No. 5 Armoured Car Company appears likely to have been the 17th Battalion's "A" Company renamed, as the company's equipment consisted of sixteen Austin armoured cars, complemented by eight tanks from the former "C" Company. Four Mark V* remained in Dublin at Marlborough Barracks, while Cork and Limerick each had one Mark V* and one Medium B. One Rolls-Royce section was stationed at Dublin and one Peerless section was stationed at Royal Barracks (now Collins Barracks). The remaining armoured vehicles were handed over to varying infantry battalions throughout the country.[5] From May to December 1920, the scattered detachments of the company were called on heavily to conduct escorts and patrols. The situation improved somewhat beginning in July 1920, as a number of Peerless armoured cars began to arrive to replace the Austin and Jeffery-Quad armoured cars that had seen better days. By December, 48 Peerless cars had arrived in Ireland (eventually rising to a total of 70 cars of that type). Due to some inherent limitations, the Peerless cars were used largely for convoy escort and for urban patrols. A faster, more agile armoured car was needed to replace the Austins, and accordingly in January 1921, the first Rolls-Royce 1920 Pattern armoured cars, diverted from Mesopotamia, began to arrive in Ireland. Between January and March, a total of 34 Rolls-Royce cars had arrived and were distributed, replacing the Austin and Jeffery-Quad armoured cars that had been withdrawn from service. By July 1921, there were two Rolls-Royce sections (with a total of 12 cars) and four Peerless sections (with a total of 16 cars) in the Dublin District. The Peerless cars continued in service

---

5   Charles Townshend, *The British Campaign in Ireland 1919-1921*, page 144, shows some 51 infantry battalions in 11 brigades deployed throughout Ireland as of January 1921.

*A Mark V\* tank, possibly a hermaphrodite version, in Ireland. It is somewhat curious that this tank has been named "The Rebel" while in service combating rebel forces in Ireland. Date, specific location, and unit of assignment unknown. (TMB 7660/E/2)*

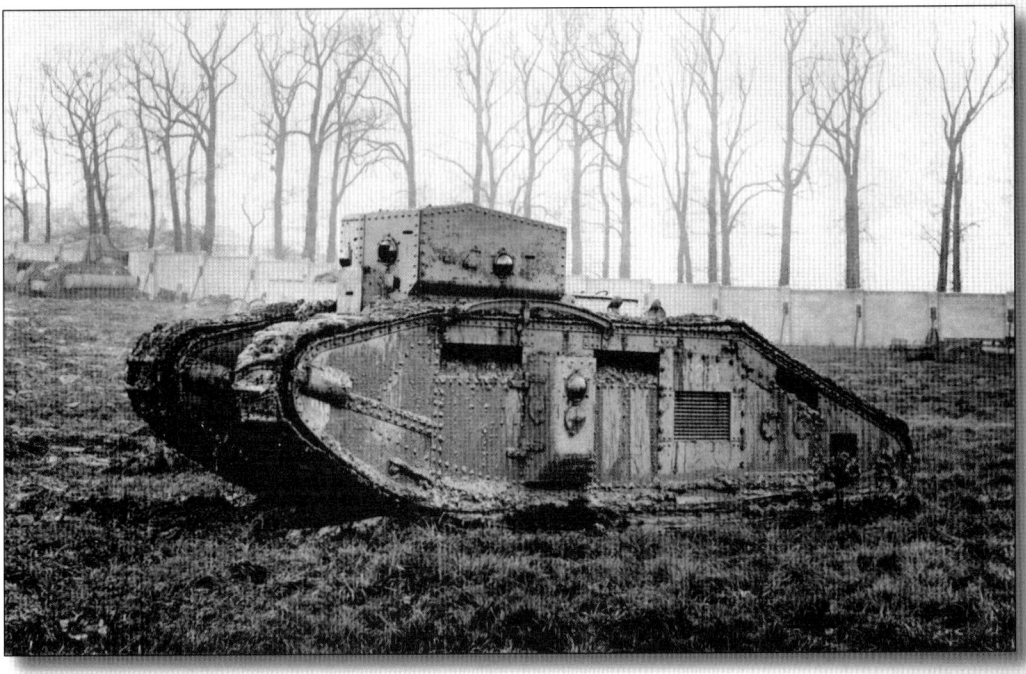

*A British Medium B tank. Unlike the Medium A tank, the Medium B reverted to the lozenge configuration of the Mk IV and Mk V\* tanks used extensively during World War I. This particular photo is of a tank in England. (TMB 351/B/5)*

mainly in urban areas, as their weight and size made them unsuitable for work on Irish country roads. One British officer whose battalion was stationed in Mullingar with two Peerless cars described them as "…very heavy, noisy, slow, and unwieldy craft, and only suitable for main roads, but occasionally I wandered on to a by-road. This invariably ended in our getting bogged."[6] The Peerless cars often were used to protect dockside loading and unloading parties in Dublin. Both the Rolls Royce and the Peerless machines were used to support Royal Irish Constabulary operations against the insurgents; interestingly, there is at least one photograph showing RIC personnel next to a Rolls Royce car, posed as though they were in fact the crew of the car.

As a note of interest, on 14 May, 1921, a small party of Irish insurgents, led by Michael Collins, can lay claim to having made the first use of an armoured car by Irish forces. Succinctly, Michael Collins drew up a very detailed plan to free Sean MacEion from Mountjoy Prison, where he was

---

6  Robert R. Money, *Flying and Soldiering*, page 173.

*A Peerless armoured car towing another Peerless in distress. Note the chain drive on the rear wheels of the leading car. The Peerless was a heavy, cumbersome armoured car ill suited to Irish roads, but for the times boasted a formidable armament consisting of two Vickers .303 machineguns. (TMB 7660/E/5)*

*A number of Jeffery Quad armoured cars in what appears to be company strength. Date and of the photograph is unknown, as is the location, which may be either England or possibly Ireland. Some 20 Jefferys served in Ireland from 1919 to 1922. (TMB)*

*A column of Rolls-Royce 1920 Pattern armoured cars delayed by a ditch cut in the road near Carrignavar, County Cork, on 10 June 1921. While the following cars have halted, the lead car is attempting to bypass the ditch. It is curious that despite what appears to be a ditching board mounted on the side of the car, with presumably a similar board on the other side, no attempt has been made to use them for their intended purpose. (IWM Q107763)*

*A combined patrol consisting of British Army and Royal Irish Constabulary in action against Irish insurgents in County Clare. Combined patrols of this sort were fairly common during the British attempt to quell the rebellion. (IWM Q107751)*

*A Crossley tender in British service with armour plate partially protecting the driver. A Lewis gun is fitted in the bed of the tender. The photograph is from 1 February 1921, and was taken in Meelin, County Cork, following a British raid in reprisal for an Irregular ambush. (NPA HOG 156, Courtesy of the National Library of Ireland)*

being held by the British. The plan called for a small group of insurgents to capture a Peerless armoured car at the Dublin Abbatoir. This in fact was achieved despite the existence of standing orders for armoured cars in Ireland that stressed the importance of being vigilant against any attempts to capture an armoured car.[7] The Irishmen then drove the car to Mountjoy Prison, stopping along the way at Hanlon's Corner to pick up Emmet Dalton and Joe Leonard, both dressed and armed as British officers. Although the car was allowed to enter the prison, the gambit failed due to an alarm having been given. However, the insurgents managed to depart the prison in the armoured car, intending to drive it to a point between Malahide and Swords where it would be hidden in a barn. However, the Peerless overheated badly and gave up the ghost, outside what is now the Clontarf Golf Club. The crew then set fire to the engine and made their way from the scene.

The Peerless armoured car was built on a three-ton TC4 4x2 truck chassis provided by the Peerless Truck and Motor Company of Cleveland, Ohio. The Peerless trucks had a reputation for being extremely sturdy and robust vehicles, and were characterized by chain drive and solid tires, with dual tires on the rear axle. The armoured car bodies were based on a design originally drawn up for the Russian Army and were built in England following World War I for the Royal Navy, to be used for "internal security duties", but later were turned over to the Army. The body consisted of an armoured cab and armoured fighting compartment fitted with two revolving machine-gun turrets; the turrets, however, were able to rotate through an arc of only 320°, their traverse being limited by the presence of the adjoining turret. The Peerless cars had an auxiliary steering arrangement at the rear of the car that enabled it to be driven in either direction at full speed. The Peerless cars were very heavy for a wheeled fighting vehicle at the time, weighing about two and a half tons more than the Rolls-Royce cars that were also serving in Ireland during the same period. The armament, consisting of two Hotchkiss .303 in. machine-guns, also made the Peerless the most powerfully armed car deployed to Ireland up to that time, and it was not until the advent of the Swedish Landsverk L 180 in 1938 that armoured cars in Ireland mounted heavier armament than that of the Peerless. An interesting historical sidelight to the Peerless company is that in 1933, faced with a depressed economy, the company's management sought a new business opportunity. Deciding to take advantage as what they saw as the rebirth of the dormant American brewing industry, they

---

7  William Sheehan, *Fighting for Dublin*, Appendix IV, *Battalion Standing Orders for Armoured Cars in Ireland*, pages 95-101.

accordingly obtained brewing rights from Carling's of Canada and converted the Peerless factory into a brewery, brewing Carling's Black Label beer, which continues to be a popular brand in the United States.

Not all armoured vehicle crews were Tank Corps personnel. While tanks and Rolls Royce armoured cars were manned by Tank Corps personnel, the Peerless crews were a mix of personnel from the cavalry, infantry and artillery, with RASC (Royal Army Service Corps) drivers.

On 8 January, 1921, the 3rd Tank battalion arrived in Dublin as a cadre unit. Its mission was to administer the various Tank Corps units, consisting of seventy Peerless and two (eventually increased to sixteen) Rolls-Royce armoured cars and ten tanks that were scattered all over Ireland. The 3rd Tank Battalion consisted of a headquarters and three companies, plus No. 5 Armoured Car Company. The battalion's "A" Company, assigned to 6th Division, was headquartered in Cork and operated in Munster; "B" Company, headquartered in the Curragh and operating in Leinster and Connacht, was assigned to the 5th Division; and "C" Company went to Belfast, assigned to the 1st Division, operating in Ulster. No. 5 Armoured Car Company remained stationed in Dublin. The primary duties of the battalion from January to the signing of the truce on 11 July 1921 consisted of escort work, curfew enforcement, and patrols. However, two sections of Rolls-Royce cars, each consisting of four cars, stationed in Dublin and Cork, were used in offensive actions, supporting raids carried out by the infamous Black and Tans. In May 1921 the Dublin section was involved in the counterattack on the Custom House which had been occupied by Irish Republican Army elements and then set ablaze. On 3 or 4 June, the IRA attacked the GHQ Motor Repair and Ordnance Depot at the Dublin Shell Factory, burning a large quantity of ordnance stores, including five Peerless armoured cars.

In April 1922 No. 12 Armoured Car Company from Wareham arrived in Ireland, taking possession of the sixteen Rolls-Royce cars that in the meantime had been brought to Dublin from Cork and the Curragh. In June, two of the company's sections were sent to the north, one to Newtownards, east of Belfast, and the other to Ballykinlar, about 25 miles southeast of Belfast, to reinforce policing of the Ulster border. No. 5 Armoured Car company had been withdrawn from Dublin sometime in 1921 and apparently relocated along the border area, presumably in either County Donegal (Belleek or Ballyshannon would seem likely, given the presence of barracks there and of the proximity to the border with County Tyrone) or County Tyrone. In early June 1922 the Rolls-Royce cars of No. 1 Section of No. 5 Armoured Car Company, on duty along the Ulster border, dispersed concentrations of insurgent raiding parties at Pettigo (4 June) and Belleek (8 June).

At this point, the number of armoured cars remaining in British service and those in Free State hands begins to become clouded. During the June-July 1922 fighting in Dublin that began with the Republican occupation of the Four Courts building complex, the Free State had already received some of the Rolls-Royce armoured cars from the British Army, and some Lancia personnel carriers from the RIC. However, some Rolls-Royces remained under British control, as there is reference to these cars performing escort duty and carrying out patrols for the protection of British troops still in Dublin. The British had in fact also developed a plan of attack against the Four Courts that called for aerial bombardment, artillery bombardment, and an assault to be led by tanks (number and type unspecified), four Rolls-Royce and four Peerless armoured cars. Clearly, then, even at that date a number of tanks and at least one section of Rolls-Royce armoured cars, as well as most if not all of the Peerless cars, remained under British control.

On 17 December, 1922, (more than ten days after formal establishment of the Free State) Group Headquarters and No. 5 Armoured Car Company (which seems to have returned from duty along the County Donegal-County Tyrone border area) left Dublin for Belfast. No. 12 Armoured Car Company, which in the meantime had been transferred to Ulster, remained in Belfast until the General Strike of 1926, leaving Belfast for Warrington in May, 1926. It is virtually certain that these units were equipped with Rolls-Royces, even though they may not have been at full establishment.

In addition to the Rolls-Royce and Peerless armoured cars built in Britain and sent to Ireland, British authorities also arranged to have some 150 armoured personnel carriers to be built in

Ireland on Italian Lancia truck chassis,[8] specifically for service with the Royal Irish Constabulary (RIC). Although sometimes erroneously referred to as armoured cars, the Lancias were not fitted with integral fixed armament, but often were armed with a .303 in. Lewis light machine-gun mounted on a tripod oriented to fire over the driver's compartment. The first of these armoured trucks appeared on the streets of Dublin in April 1921. These armoured vehicles were designed by the British War Office, and were built on two different types of Lancia chassis: the chassis variously referred to as the 1Z, Iota or Jota chassis, and the later 1920-1921 Triota chassis. The Lancia 1Z chassis was a truck chassis modified by the Italians for use as an armoured car chassis (for the Italian Lancia 1ZM car) during World War I; the Iota (referred to as Jota in Italian) chassis used the same engine and transmission of the 1Z, but the chassis dimensions were somewhat larger. It is not clear how many of each type of chassis were used as the basis for conversion to armoured troop carriers, but inasmuch as a fairly large stock of Lancia IZ/Iota trucks remained in the British vehicle fleet at the end of the war and that the Triota model did not appear until 1921, it is likely that most of the cars may have been built on the earlier IZ/Jota chassis.[9] The bodies were similar for both models and were fabricated in Ireland at the Great Southern and Western Railway's Inchicore shops in Dublin beginning in late 1920.[10] The body on the Iota chassis had an open top driving compartment and cab sides that were no higher than the body sides. The earliest version had a small hatch door in the center of the rear panel for access, while the later IZ and Triota carriers had a large door, comprising the center third of the rear plate, as an outward opening door. The body on the Triota chassis differed in that it had a full angled plate covering the front of the driving compartment; the plate had a sliding vision port for the driver and a small vision or firing port to the left of the driver's port. The front plate was surmounted by a short plate that formed a brow in front of the open troop compartment; the cab sides were slightly higher than the body sides. Other differences in detail could be encountered among and between the two versions as well, such as angle iron edging along the top edges of the armoured compartments, or different style armoured radiator plates (side opening or center opening). The armour itself, unavailable in Ireland, was supplied by an engineering firm in Scotland. The Lancia configured as an armoured carrier actually had been preceded by somewhat earlier attempts, the first of which were in July 1920, to provide a modicum of protection to troops by fitting a boxlike metal structure on the rear of an unspecified number of Crossley and Lancia trucks; the cab area, however, remained unprotected on these vehicles. Subsequently, the body was redesigned and consisted of an armoured cab and an open-topped troop compartment mounted on the Lancia chassis which were found to be more suitable to the purpose than were the Crossleys. The open-topped configuration of the cars apparently was an invitation for Republicans to toss grenades into the vehicles; consequently, anti-grenade cages, consisting of an inverted V-shaped framework with wire netting, were fitted over the open troop compartment, but the resourceful Republican forces countered by attaching hooks to the grenades so that they would cling to the cagework. Not surprisingly, the anti-grenade cages soon led to the Lancias being nicknamed "Chicken Coops". The scale of issue to the RIC suggests that the Lancias would have been deployed to many locations throughout Ireland, although no details have been unearthed.

In early 1922 all British Army armoured vehicles in Ireland (the remaining tanks, Rolls-Royce and Peerless armoured cars, as well as the remaining Jeffery-Quads) were brought together in Dublin. The Lancia APCs, however, were not part of this concentration, as they were scattered far and wide throughout Ireland, and more to the point, were not under Army jurisdiction as they were assigned to the RIC who employed them in conjunction with the Black and Tans. By

---

8  *Townshend, page 143, notes that 154 sets of armour plate had been acquired to build "armoured lorries". This would have been the plate used to build the Lancia armoured troop carriers.*

9  *A total of 2131 Jota chassis were produced between 1915 and 1920, whereas only 256 Triota chassis were built. Export figures to Britain are unavailable.*

10 *Although the consensus seems to point to fabrication of the bodies in Ireland, Peter Leslie's research indicates that some, and possibly all, may have been built at Cammell Laird shipyards in England. This remains an unresolved issue.*

December 1922 all of the British Army's armoured vehicles (essentially, the armoured cars) that had not been turned over to the Provisional Government had been evacuated to Belfast. The tanks, and possibly the Jeffery–Quads and the Austin cars, were broken up and sold for scrap. Exactly how many Lancias remained in the Free State and how many were transferred north to be added to those already stationed in Ulster with the RIC (soon to be transformed into the RUC) is far from clear.[11]

At one time or another between 1916 and 1922, the British had a total of about 175 armoured vehicles (armoured cars and tanks)[12] in Ireland, although not all were likely to have been operational at the same time. To this must be added the number of approximately 155 Lancia armoured personnel carriers, bringing the overall total of all types of armoured vehicles to about 330. Of this number, probably fewer than 100 armoured cars and armoured troop carriers were transferred to the Irish Provisional Government in 1922. The British did not provide any tanks to the new government, scrapping them instead.

*A Crossley tender in Ireland with an armour plating configuration very similar to that used on the Lancia Iota armoured troop carriers. The armour, however, is made of multiple panels rather than the larger panels used on the Lancias. The mixed group of uniformed and civilian personnel, some of whom have revolvers drawn, suggests an obviously staged and posed photograph. (TMB 7660/F/2)*

---

11 *Conventionally accepted figures are that approximately 150 Lancias were armoured in Ireland (a more precise figure might be 154, as previously noted), and that 111 were transferred to the Free State by the British. However, in an extremely detailed appendix in David Dunne's Armoured and Heavy Vehicles of the RUC, 1922-2001, 70 Lancias can definitely be accounted for as having belonged to the RUC after 1922, and an additional 67 are noted, but have no RUC records associated with them. Clearly, if there were 111 in the Free State and 70 in Ulster, considerably more than 154 Lancias were armoured. At the risk of further confusing the issue, this author believes that the appendix in Dunne's book indicating a total of 137 Lancias reflects the total number of Lancias in the Royal Irish Constabulary inventory prior to the formation of the RUC, and that the 67 Lancias unaccounted for by specific RUC records were turned over to the Free State. This belief would seem to be supported by another figure (64, close to the elusive figure of 67) that often surfaces with respect to Free State Lancias and which the author believes may be a more accurate figure than 111 for the Free State holdings. However, it is also possible that more than 154 Lancias were armoured, although there is no firm evidence to support such a supposition.*

12 *The numbers were 34 Rolls-Royce, 16 Austin, 20-22 Jeffery-Quad, and 70 Peerless armoured cars, and 32 tanks of various Marks (Medium A, Medium B, Mk IV, and Mk V*).*

# 1922: Armour During the Civil War

The signing of the Anglo-Irish Treaty on 6 December, 1921, soon led to bitter fighting between two factions that had formed within the Irish Republican Army, those favoring the treaty (the Free State, or National, faction) and those opposed to the treaty (the Republican, or Irregular forces). Fighting in Dublin, as well as throughout other parts of the south of Ireland during the so-called "conventional" phase that lasted from late June through mid-August 1922, involved several mobile operations in which armoured cars were used by both sides.

## FREE STATE (NATIONAL ARMY) ARMOURED OPERATIONS

In 1922, the Irish Republican Army possessed virtually no equipment, and there were no capabilities within Ireland to manufacture any sort of military equipment; even uniforms had to be manufactured in Britain.[1] The conditions under which British equipment was handed over to the Free State is not entirely clear from available correspondence; indeed, correspondence from the period reflects that there was a less than clear understanding between the parties themselves (the British and Free State governments) as to the terms under which equipment was to be handed over and paid for.[2] However, it appears that some equipment in situ may have been handed over without expectation of repayment, while other equipment was provided on a credit basis, and still other items were transferred to the new government on the basis of "replacement cost" payment to the British. As events were moving rather rapidly, in practice the British either "loaned" some equipment, such as artillery, to the Provisional Government, or extended credit until arrangements could be made for actual payment. Other equipment was obtained from surplus stocks awaiting disposal, probably at market value. This arrangement would seem to have benefited the British as well as the Irish, as the former could dispose of used equipment[3] and not have to worry about the cost or bother of returning worn equipment back to Britain, and the latter could equip itself with generally serviceable, if worn, equipment very quickly. A bonus for the Irish would have been the fact that any of the Irish troops who had formerly served with the British Army would have been acquainted with the operation, use, and maintenance of much of the equipment (especially small arms, and possibly to a lesser extent artillery and armoured vehicles), thus abbreviating or eliminating the learning curve. It is impossible to say how items seized by anti-treaty IRA elements were handled with respect to payment – certainly the Republicans were not about to honor any deals made by the Free State with the British.

It should be noted that in addition to a myriad of other problems such as supply, organization, training, and discipline that both opposing military organizations faced in their struggle against each other, due to the nature of Irish society at the time, practical issues such as locating soldiers qualified to drive and maintain the vehicles also had to be faced. Today, when we accept it as normal that virtually every young person has access to and knows how to drive a motor vehicle, it may be hard to imagine that in 1922 the pool of young men who had previous experience with motor vehicle operation and maintenance was rather limited, and that although both sides obviously were able to fill the required slots, there was not a superabundance of technically proficient

---

1  Michael Hopkinson, *Green Against Green*, page 61.
2  Various telegrams and memoranda from late 1922 to early 1923, primarily between the Duke of Devonshire and the Governor General of the Irish Free State, T.M. Healy.
3  Presumably, whenever possible, the British would have kept the most serviceable equipment for themselves and transferred less desirable equipment to the Irish; the Rolls-Royce armoured cars evacuated to Belfast likely were the best of the lot available at the time.

*A Rolls-Royce 1920 Pattern armoured car of the National Army, Henry Street, Dublin, 5 July, 1922. The car is named "Custom House", and has a puppet labeled "Rory Boy" above the machinegun, representing one of the Republican leaders who was later executed. (NPA/NLI HOG 134, Courtesy of the National Library of Ireland)*

soldiers on hand. Even though the number of vehicles involved was quite small, qualified, competent drivers likely were in a special skill category. Indeed, there are accounts of poor performance by drivers,[4] and close inspection of period photographs shows an abnormally high incidence of fender damage on Rolls-Royce Whippets that probably is attributable to driver error.

It is generally accepted that by August 1923 the Free State had a total of 13 Rolls-Royce 1920 Pattern armoured cars[5] (christened "Whippets" by the Irish), seven Peerless armoured cars, and 111 Lancia armoured personnel carriers.[6] These figures tend to be accepted at face value and are repeated in most writings that address the subject of armoured vehicles during the early years of the Free State. The general impression also seems to be given that all of these vehicles were delivered to Irish Republican Army elements that were in favor of the treaty and were all available at the beginning of hostilities between the Provisional Government forces and the Republicans, giving them a qualitative advantage over the Republican elements opposed to the treaty, and that Republican forces were severely disadvantaged because they had to rely on capturing armoured vehicles from National Army forces, or had to construct their own improvised armoured cars. However, a somewhat closer and more reflective examination of various bits and pieces of information leads to some interesting findings. To begin with, not all of the vehicles were turned over by the British prior to the beginning of the internecine warfare between pro-Treaty and anti-Treaty elements of the IRA that began on 28 June, 1922. In fact, the chronology of the turnover of these vehicles

---

4  Karl Martin, *Irish Army Vehicles: Transport and Armour Since 1922*, page 16.

5  The figure of 13 Rolls-Royce armoured cars is commonly accepted as the number turned over to the Free State; however, a fourteenth, Ballinalee, was captured by the Republicans in July 1922, and used by them until it was destroyed rather than letting it fall into Free State hands again. Based on the chassis numbers, there is some speculation that one of the cars (AAR 10, Flying Fifty) may have been an earlier Admiralty Pattern, or possibly a transitional pattern, and not a 1920 Pattern; however, in an E-mail dated 8 September 2008, Mr. Bob Webster states that Pat Lynch, retired workshops foreman and son of Paddy Lynch, assured him that when maintaining vehicles in storage in Kilkenny Barracks in the early 1950s, Lynch remembers all 13 to be 1920 Pattern cars.

6  See footnote 11. pervious chapter, for a discussion of the numbers of Lancias in the Free State inventory.

*An unidentified Rolls-Royce Whippet on Sackville Street, during the fighting for The Block in June 1922. The turreted building on the corner was the Dublin United Tram Office (subsequently destroyed in the fighting), and to its left the Hibernian Bible society. The building with the clock on it is Boots, Dublin. The street between the Tram Office and Boots is Chapel Street. Note the horses pulling the fire apparatus to the left of the armoured car. This photograph was taken from Henry Street, looking north toward the east side of Sackville Street. (Broe Collection)*

*Rolls-Royce armoured car Slievenamon (later numbered A.R.R. 2) parked in front of Gilbey's Wine Merchants, 46-49 Sackville Street, Dublin, sometime during the fighting in Dublin in June/July 1922. A number of civilians, one of whom appears to be armed, have taken the opportunity to be photographed along with the car. (Broe Collection)*

to the Free State is not well documented and is far from clear. It appears possible that as early as February 1922 some of the Whippets were in National Army hands.[7] There is also one reference to the Republican capture of two armoured cars in February as well;[8] these two cars presumably would have ultimately been included in the National Army inventory following cessation of hostilities between the opposing Irish factions. The Rolls-Royce car generally accepted as being the first such car to be turned over by the British to the Provisional Government was the car that was sent from Portobello Barracks in Dublin to Limerick in March 1922, under the command of Staff Captain Bill Stapleton (whether the car was turned over in March or earlier is not clear). However, while stopping at Templemore Barracks, thought to be in the hands of pro-Treaty elements, the car was seized by Commandant J. Leahy who in fact had gone over to the Republican side, who arrested and disarmed the crew. The crew of the car consisted of two National Army officers and two Black and Tan officers seconded for training on handling the vehicle; presumably this was a somewhat uncomfortable arrangement for all of the parties directly involved. Despite the disrepute in which the Black and Tans were held in general, these two individuals were treated well by Leahy before sending them back to Dublin. Subsequently, a party of thirty men, including the very same Black and Tans who had been with the car when it was captured, set off for Templemore with three armoured cars under Commandant-General Dermot McManus in an attempt to recapture the car. Upon reaching Templemore, McManus, unable to commandeer the car, removed some critical

---

7 Coogan and Morrison, photograph 157 on page 148, shows Custom House present at the turnover of Portobello Barracks (now Cathal Brugha Barracks), Dublin. Although the caption states that the photo is from February 1922, Portobello Barracks were not formally handed over by the British until 17 May 1922.
8 Eoin Neeson, *The Civil War 1922-23*, page 91.

parts, disabling it. A discussion then ensued with Leahy, who refused to turn over the car, and McManus, who refused to turn over the parts that had been taken. McManus returned to Dublin with the parts, but shortly thereafter a staff officer at Beggar's Bush Barracks himself appropriated the parts and took them to Templemore, where the car was put back in running order and then driven to Dublin, where it was handed over to Rory O'Connor in the Four Courts. The car was christened Mutineer by the Republicans and used by them in the defense of the Four Courts.

By the beginning of the Civil War (28 June), at least four Whippets and seven Lancias were in National Army hands. In September and November two more Whippets and two Peerless armoured cars were added to the inventory, bringing the total to at least seven Whippets (including Mutineer that was recaptured from the Republicans and added to the inventory) and four Peerless cars (two Peerless cars are known to have been used in National Army seaborne landings in August 1922). Evidence of the presence of other cars being engaged in actions subsequent to the Four Courts/Dublin fighting escalates the numbers so that essentially by November only four Rolls-Royces and three Peerless cars cannot be accounted for specifically by reference to photographs or written references. The count for the Rolls-Royce cars was three in Republican hands (those captured at Clonmel in February, plus Mutineer captured in April), and four in National Army hands in Dublin at the beginning of hostilities at the Four Courts on 28 June. Scrutiny and analysis of photographs, as well as written accounts, lead to the conclusion that on the National Army side at least four Whippets (Custom House, The Big Fella, Slievenamon, and The Fighting 2nd), and at least seven Lancia armoured personnel carriers[9] were used to support the attack on the Four Courts, and later against Republican strongholds on the east side of O'Connell Street known as "The Block". On 12 July, Ballinalee was captured in County Sligo by the Republicans, bringing the total to eight. Danny Boy and The Manager were present in actions in July and August (at Limerick and Cork, respectively), thus accounting for ten Whippets. There is a reference to Moneygall being used in Dublin during the guerrilla phase of the war, possibly in September. Two Rolls-Royces were turned over on 1 November, thus accounting for a total of twelve cars; if Moneygall was not one of the cars turned over in November, the count for the Whippets reaches thirteen, but is still one short of the total of fourteen ultimately acquired, at one time or another, by the Free State. The case of the Peerless cars is somewhat more straightforward, although in a sense, less conclusive. As previously mentioned, two were known to have been involved in the Cork landings in August, and another two were handed over by the British on 22 September; just when the other three Peerless cars were handed over to the Free State has not been indicated, although by August of 1923 all seven were in the Free State inventory.

The armoured vehicles in National Army hands were parceled out to the various operational commands for use as the commanders saw fit, although at least initially, prior to the seaborne assaults conducted in late July and early August 1922, a number of the Rolls-Royces remained in Dublin, from where they were embarked upon ships as part of the seaborne assault groups. It appears that the Peerless cars[10] were retained at their base in Dublin, as they were too large, slow, and cumbersome to be used effectively in other parts of the country. The exception to this, however, was the use of two Peerless cars in the seaborne landings against Cork on 8 August, but even this caused problems because the seven-ton weight of the Peerless cars complicated their

---

9  *Coogan and Morrison, photograph 195 on pages 168-169 shows two Lancias shielding the artillery on Winetavern Street and Merchants Quay on 30 June; photograph 201 on pages 172-173 and photograph 202 on page 174 show an immobilized Lancia blocking one of the gates to the Four Courts. Photograph 219 on page 182 shows Lancia OI 9213, probably on 2 July; photograph 220 on page 183 shows Lancias OI 9213 and OI 9173 at the same location (Henry and O'Connell Streets). Photograph 226 on page 186 shows a Lancia whose number appears to be OI 9202, and a Whippet on 5 July on "The Block". All of these Lancias appear to be different cars; in addition, in Karl Martin's Irish Army Vehicles, a photograph on page 5 shows a Lancia cage car on Dame Street during the siege of the Four Courts. Photographs showing different clearly identifiable Rolls-Royce Whippets are The Big Fella on 26 June and Custom House on 5 July, both on page 9 of Karl Martin's book, and the Broe photograph of Slievenamon, date unknown. A number of other photos show Whippets during the fighting in Dublin, but because of distance, camera angle, or obscuring of detail, it cannot be ascertained if these were other views of The Big Fella and Custom House. Written accounts, however, make reference to The Fighting 2nd also as being present during the fighting; to this must be added Mutineer on the Republican side.*

10  *It is not clear if at this date there were two or four Peerless vehicles in National Army hands.*

*A Peerless armoured car belonging to the National Army forces, probably in Cork, 1922. Although the Fianna Fail insignia is clearly visible, the markings in the oval underneath the driver's cab are illegible. (NPA/NLI HOG 6, Courtesy of the National Library of Ireland)*

unloading at Cork. The Rolls-Royces, on the other hand, were extremely mobile and were ideal for counter-Republican operations. Once the armoured cars left Dublin for other operational areas, maintenance and support arrangements in the field likely were the responsibility of the area commander, which in practice probably was delegated down to the individual crews themselves. One could speculate that any field maintenance not within the capabilities of the vehicle crew may likely have been contracted out to local garages or mechanics. Similar arrangements presumably would have applied to the Lancias as well.

The earliest use of armoured cars by both sides was during the battle for the Four Courts building complex in Dublin on 28 June, 1921. Written accounts indicate that Republican forces that had occupied and fortified the buildings had one of the Whippets, named Mutineer, on the building's grounds, where it was used within the confines of the courtyard to fire upon National Army troops once they had gained entry into the complex. The Republicans, however, were severely disadvantaged not only in the number of armoured vehicles they had available to them (limited to the one armoured car), but also by the fact that Mutineer was confined to the grounds of the Four Courts, thus effectively losing the advantage of mobility.[11] During the attack on the Four Courts complex National Army forces parked at least one Lancia personnel carrier in front of the gates and disabled it in order to prevent Mutineer from sallying from the grounds to attack National Army artillery crews. Two other Lancias, which likely were used as prime movers for the 18-pdr artillery pieces, also were deployed alongside the artillery itself, on Winetavern Street across the Liffey, to shield the crews from Republican fire. The next few days saw Mutineer providing fire support from within the courtyard of the building against National Army forces that had gained a foothold within the building's west wing. The Republican forces in the Four Courts surrendered on 30 June, but other Republican forces throughout Dublin continued to resist. A National Army Whippet, The Fighting 2nd, drove Republican troops out of the Swan Pub on the south side of the River Liffey; the Swan was being used as HQ of the Republican 3rd Battalion. On 4 July, Republican positions in "The Block" on O'Connell Street were attacked by National Army forces supported by

---

11 *Although specific dimensions of the inner courtyard of the Four Courts are not available, one source indicates that the front façade along the River Liffey is 456 feet long, while another claims 433 feet. Allowing for the width of the wings on either side of the courtyard, this would probably leave no more than 375 feet of maneuver space in any direction for the car within the courtyard.*

at least two Rolls-Royce Whippets providing covering fire. By this date, Mutineer, captured by the National forces, was put back in service, re-christened Ex-Mutineer, and added to the National Army armoured car inventory. Two Lancias, numbers OI 9213 and OI 9173, were used to provide protection to an 18-pdr artillery piece situated on the corner of O'Connell and Henry streets in the fighting against the buildings occupied by the Republicans. Probably contemporaneously, to the immediate east of O'Connell Street a National Army armoured car came down Talbot Street, parked in the middle of the street facing Moran's Hotel at the juncture of Talbot and Gardiner Streets, and raked the hotel with gunfire. The successful attack marked the end of fighting in Dublin.

Following the cessation of fighting in Dublin, the National Army wasted little time in mounting operations against Republican forces in other parts of the country. On 5, or possibly 6 July, an armoured car was used to lead a group of government soldiers into Ballyknockan, at the south end of what is now the Poulaphouca Reservoir. On 6 July, armoured cars supported infantry in an attack against Republican forces near Blessington, about 15 miles from the center of Dublin; about 20 miles further south of Blessington, at Baltinglass, another National Army armoured car was used to spearhead the attack. A third column consisting of two armoured cars, two Lancias, an 18-pdr, and 22 trucks set out on 6 July, bound for Wexford. These columns illustrate the tactical skill and strategic vision of the National Army commanders in using armoured cars for convoy protection and providing mobile firepower for the attacking forces, as well as displaying an adeptness at creating combined arms teams of infantry, armour, and artillery.

Attacks incorporating armoured cars continued along the general axis aimed at seizing Waterford, which was the eastern anchor of the so-called "Limerick-Waterford Line" that ran from Limerick in the west, then eastwards to Tipperary, Clonmel, Carrick-on-Suir, and Waterford. On 16 July a sizeable National Army convoy consisting of 25 troop-carrying trucks and two armoured cars seized Thurles, some 40 miles northwest of Waterford, after which a smaller column with nine trucks carrying troops and the two armoured cars was detached to take control of Templemore Barracks, evacuated by the Republicans, about ten miles to the north. The National Army effort to capture Waterford itself had initially envisioned the use of three or four Whippets to lead an attack force against the city, but the option was discarded due to a number of factors that made it impractical to carry out (including the fact that the required number of Whippets was not available in the area). The only armoured vehicle known to have participated in action in Waterford was a National Army Lancia used to shield an 18 pdr. artillery piece attacking Ballybricken Prison on 21 July.

*This photograph likely is that of the Republican armoured car Mutineer that fought inside the Four Courts complex, was immobilized by Lewis gun fire that damaged its rear tires, and reportedly backed up to a door allowing its crew to escape. The Vickers gun has been removed from the turret, possibly by the crew when it abandoned the car. The armoured radiator doors as well as one of the bonnet covers are opened, and one of the headlights appears to have been shot out. The two individuals in the background are firemen; a fireman's helmet is visible on top of the turret. (Broe Collection)*

*A group of three Lancia armoured troop carriers on Henry and Sackville Streets. The two Lancias in the foreground are shielding an 18-pdr field artillery piece, whose shield is just barely visible between the cars. Also visible between the cars, on Sackville Street, is a third Lancia. The chalked inscription on the right-hand Lancia reads "We have no time for truces". (Broe Collection)*

29

Meanwhile, at the western end of the line, on 13 July Republican forces captured the National Army position of Munster Tavern in Limerick, but a counterattack led by armoured cars regained the site. On 15 July an unsuccessful attack involving armoured cars was launched against Republican positions at the Strand Barracks and King John's Castle in Limerick. On 22 July National Army forces entered Limerick, which had been abandoned by Republican forces the previous day. Among the National Army forces entering Limerick was the Whippet named Danny Boy.

Considerable use of armoured vehicles marked the fighting at Kilmallock, located some 20 miles south of Limerick, beginning on 23 July when National Army forces used a number of Lancia personnel carriers to move attacking troops into the area. Fighting in the area continued; on 30 July National Army forces launched an attack on the vital town of Bruree, about five miles west of Kilmallock, with the successful assault supported by an unspecified number of Whippet armoured cars. A Republican counterattack on 2 August employed a strong force that included three improvised armoured cars[12] in a coordinated attack launched from Patrickswell (about ten miles north of Bruree and five miles southwest of Limerick). The armoured cars achieved surprise; the first car attacked the National Army commandant's headquarters in the Railway Hotel, forcing the government forces to flee. The second car rammed the front door of the schoolhouse in which 25 National Army troops were lodged, and who promptly surrendered. There are varying accounts concerning the participation of the third Republican armoured car, the River Lee, which is reported to have developed engine trouble and remained far behind. Meanwhile, a National Army relief force was led by the Whippet armoured car Custom House in which the National Army troop commander, General Seamus Hogan, was riding. Events soon turned this into an armoured car against armoured car engagement, as Custom House began to be followed by the third Republican armoured car, the River Lee, which had dealt with its engine problems and was now running. The River Lee, however, halted at some point and remained concealed from the view of Custom House, but its presence was discovered by National Army troops who alerted Hogan, who turned and gave chase. Upon rounding a bend in the road, Custom House came upon not only River Lee, but the two other Republican armoured cars as well, all of which opened fire on Custom House. Although clearly outnumbered and outgunned, Hogan in Custom House nevertheless began to engage all three cars. In the event, the Vickers machine-gun on Custom House jammed, forcing Hogan to withdraw. On 3 August some 2,000 National Army troops, supported by an unspecified number of armoured cars (Danny Boy has been specifically mentioned, and Custom House likely was present as well) and artillery, began an advance on Kilmallock, joined the following day by 700 more troops and another armoured car. When National Army forces succeeded in entering Kilmallock, they found the town virtually abandoned by Republican forces that had moved southwest to the larger town of Charleville. Reportedly, Danny Boy was also present in the fighting at both Patrickswell and Bruree.

Almost concurrent with the government assault on Kilmallock, on 24 July a Whippet armoured car was among the equipment that was brought ashore in the National Army's first naval landing[13] carried out about a hundred miles further north at Westport, County Mayo. The Whippet was ferried to Westport from Dublin aboard the cross-channel ferry *Menevia* that had sailed around the north coast of Ireland down the western coast to Clew Bay. Republican forces in Westport promptly pulled out, and the government forces drove about ten miles inland to Castlebar.

On 2 and 8 August, government forces carried out two more seaborne landings, one in County Kerry and the other in County Cork, both of which included armoured cars as well as artillery in the landing force. On 2 August, the cross-channel steamer *Lady Wicklow*, having departed from Dublin (South Wall) on 31 July, arrived at Fenit in Tralee Bay, where the seaborne attackers defeated

---

12 One, the River Lee, was built in Cork on the chassis of a heavy coal truck fitted with armour plates and armed with two Lewis machine-guns. There are no details relating to either of the two other improvised armoured cars.

13 Considering the brief period of the conventional phase of the Civil War, the National Army made extensive use of naval landings to outflank Republican forces. The primary architect of these operations was Major General James Emmet Dalton, who had been born in the USA but who was raised in Ireland, and who at the time of the Civil War was only 24 years old. He had served as an officer in the British Army during World War I, distinguishing himself on the battlefield and receiving the Military Cross for heroism.

Republican elements who attempted to oppose the landing. The Ex-Mutineer, aboard the *Lady Wicklow*, assisted in suppressing Republican fire by using its Vickers machine-gun while still on board, prior to landing, targeting the upper gable end of the coast guard station. The landing force then continued on the six or seven miles to Tralee, securing the city that same evening. Ex-Mutineer was used to considerable effect in engaging the Republican forces at Sammy's Rock on the road to Tralee, as well as in Tralee itself. The 8 August landing at Cork harbour was even more ambitious, consisting of two steamers, the *Arvonia* and the *Lady Wicklow* (which had already returned from the landing at Fenit), ferrying a landing force of some 800 men supported by the largest contingent of armoured vehicles to be included in a landing of this sort, consisting of one Whippet and two Peerless armoured cars, as well as several Lancia armoured troop carriers. The *Arvonia* carried one Peerless and the Rolls-Royce named The Manager, as well as some Lancias. *Lady Wicklow* carried another Peerless. Disembarkation of the Peerless cars proved to be challenging; the cars had been loaded aboard the ships in Dublin with the assistance of a heavy Titan dockside crane, but the cranes available in Cork had a much more limited capacity. This necessitated waiting for the tide to ebb so that the decks would be more or less flush with the dock thus allowing the Peerless cars to be driven off the ships on heavy timber planks, while being assisted by the available crane to lessen the weight on the planks. Photographs show one of the Lancias being used as a prime mover to tow an 18-pdr field piece. Three landing parties, each supported by an armoured car, landed at dawn on 8 August. As this landing was being carried out in Cork, two other landings were being conducted simultaneously to the east and west of Cork, at Youghal (25 miles northeast of Cork) and at Union Hall (40 miles southwest of Cork) respectively. The force that disembarked at Youghal included two Lancia personnel carriers, while that at Union Hall included an undetermined number of vehicles. The River Lee appears to have been wandering about the area on 9 August, but was thwarted from doing any damage at one point by a barricade placed across the road by government troops. On 10 August one of the Whippets from the Cork

*A Lancia armoured lorry (troop carrier), Dublin, 1922. The car bears the name "Fernside" on its armoured radiator cover; the dark-coloured diamond on the radiator cover seems to have been applied as a recognition symbol by the National Army. The wire cage over the troop compartment is meant to protect against grenades being thrown into the vehicle. The configuration of the armour on this vehicle marks it as being built on a Lancia Iota chassis. (NPA/NLI IND H 219A, Courtesy of the National Library of Ireland)*

*A Lancia Triota armoured lorry on Dame Street in Dublin, 1922. The vehicle shows signs of having been damaged by fire, as evidenced by the condition of the rear tire and the discolouration on the armour plate above it. (NPA/NLI IND H 219B, Courtesy of the National Library of Ireland)*

landing force, advancing on Douglas to the west of Cork, gave chase to a truckload of Republican troops with which it had almost collided, in the process capturing a group of some 32 Republicans who had planned to ambush the car but whose plan had been compromised by the warning of a local woman to the National Army commander.

On 12 August, Ex-Mutineer, still in Kerry supporting the force that had landed at Fenit, drawn to the scene by the sound of gunfire, came to the assistance of a National Army infantry column that was ambushed a few miles from Listowel. Its appearance, and the covering fire provided by its Vickers gun, soon put the ambushing Republicans to flight, ending the engagement. Less than a week later, a National Army motorized column departed from Killarney, bound for Rathmore. An armoured car and an 18-pdr (presumably Ex-Mutineer and the Rose of Tralee) formed an integral part of the column. About halfway to Rathmore, the column split at Barraduff, with part of the column continuing towards Rathmore and the other part directed towards Headford. At Doum Bridge the second column was ambushed by a Republican force, but the sound of the fray soon brought both the armoured car and the field piece to the scene. The car brought fire to bear from its Vickers gun, while the 18-pdr likewise loosed a few shells. The government forces withdrew, leaving behind two lorries.

Kerry continued to be the thorn in the side for the government forces, and as late as 5 March, 1923, an armoured car figured in an engagement against Republican forces still active in the county. Government forces had conducted a sweep operation in the general area of Caherciveen, beginning at 7 am. By 10 am the Republicans were fighting a rear-guard action, managing to keep the fight going until an armoured car arrived at 7:30 pm, forcing the remaining Republican force to withdraw. The author assumes that the car in question was Ex-Mutineer.

There is little doubt that the National Army commanders were imaginative, innovative, and bold in the conception, planning and execution of the seaborne combined arms assaults against Republican positions, and that they appreciated the combat advantage that the armoured cars and personnel carriers afforded them in terms of both mobility and firepower against their Republican opponents, who often outnumbered them. Aside from the cars specifically identified by name in the preceding narrative (Danny Boy, Custom House, Ex-Mutineer, and The Manager), the

*Rolls-Royce: A Rolls-Royce 1920 Pattern armoured car apparently in the process of loading aboard a ship prior to one of the seaborne landings carried out by the Provisional Government in late July and early August 1922. The date of the photograph is unknown, but it appears that the location may be Dublin. (NPA/NPA HOG 24, Courtesy of the National Library of Ireland)*

records do not establish which armoured cars participated in which landing actions, but given the dates and the distances involved between the different actions (Limerick, Waterford, Kilmallock, Fenit, Cork, Youghal, and Union Hall), it seems likely that at least six of the Whippets available to the National Army forces, and two Peerless cars, were committed to operations against the Republicans. The question again arises as to how many Whippets and Peerless cars were actually in the National Army roster at the time. It is possible that in August as few as nine Whippets were on hand (fourteen minus Ballinalee, the two cars captured in Clonmel in February and presumably still in Republican hands, and the two Rolls-Royces not turned over by the British until November. It should be noted that only seven Rolls-Royces (Custom House, The Big Fella, Slievenamon, The Fighting 2nd, Danny Boy, The Manager, and Ex-Mutineer) can be accounted for by name during that timeframe, and that the two Peerless cars employed in the Cork landings were the only two available. (Two were reported turned over by the British in September, and the other three remain unaccounted for; thus, a maximum of five Peerless cars would have been on hand in August, although that is tenuous at best).

Viewed from a slightly different perspective, the National Army commanders had the equivalent of less than a company of armoured cars available for operations and were able to employ them over the length and breadth of most of Ireland over a relatively short time span (less than two months). (Very roughly, on a north-south axis from Sligo to Cork, about 160 miles, and a rough east-west axis from Dublin to Castlebar, about 125 miles, for an overall operational area of about 20,000 square miles). National Army commanders showed little hesitancy to commit the Rolls-Royces and Lancias to rather long road marches, and seem to have been able to engage enemy forces quickly as the occasion arose. Perhaps there needs to be more research done to appreciate just how effectively individual field commanders employed their armour (including the coordinated use of armoured cars and armoured troop carriers). One is tempted to say that the commanders achieved results despite the absence of any formal doctrine relating to the employment of the armoured assets, but in reality, it likely was precisely because there was no mandated "school solution" promulgated by higher echelons that the commanders could develop their own tactics as they went along. The National Army was still in the process of growing and forming and had little time to philosophize or formalize doctrine. There was no stifling of ingenuity or initiative; the National Army seems to have had more than its fair share of field commanders who, left to their own devices, proved to be extremely capable. On the opposing side, the Republicans likewise showed an appreciation of the utility of armoured cars and, within the limits imposed by the numbers and nature of the equipment at hand, also showed ingenuity and skill in their use of that type of vehicle.

## REPUBLICAN ARMOURED OPERATIONS

Although the Republicans had not been the direct recipient of any armoured vehicles from the British, they nevertheless managed to capture a number of vehicles from the National Army forces, as well as fabricating a small number of improvised armoured cars themselves. While reports of use of armoured cars (and to an even lesser extent, of Lancia personnel carriers) by the Republican side tend to be overshadowed by similar reporting of National Army use of armour, on balance, in terms of numbers of armoured cars the disparity with respect to the Free State inventory was not as great as might appear at first glance. As has been shown previously, by August 1922 the total number of armoured cars available to the National Army forces may have been as low as nine (seven Whippets

*A Whippet bearing no name on the turret, but bearing the barely visible identifying code R2 on the driving compartment side just ahead of the spare tire. Note the presence of the ditching board carried above the running board. Although the precise date and location are unknown, it is believed to be in Dublin during or shortly after the fighting for the Four Courts and The Block. (Broe Collection)*

and two Peerless), and not the higher total of thirteen Rolls-Royces and seven Peerless cars conventionally accepted as valid. It should also be noted that, except for the seaborne operation against Cork which saw two of the Peerless cars deployed in action against the Republicans, the Peerless cars (whether it was only two or possibly as many as five) were retained in Dublin and were of little value operationally. Against this, during the July-August timeframe, the Republicans probably could muster three Rolls-Royces (Ballinalee and the two cars captured in Clonmel) and three improvised armoured cars (River Lee and two others), for a total of six cars. Later, the Republicans would build another four or five[14] improvised armoured cars. Thus, the Republican inventory included a total of at least ten armoured cars of varying description, although not all of these were available at the same time. Further, whereas the National Army mounted offensive operations

---

14 *The improvised armoured cars were the Queen of the West and three other cars built in Mulrany in County Mayo in October-November 1922. A second car named River Lee may also have been built.*

against multiple locations, more or less at the same time, and often used its cars against Republican forces that lacked armoured assets, the Republicans were more likely to concentrate their cars, such as at Kilmallock (County Limerick) and later, in County Mayo, to achieve local superiority in numbers. This was often countered by National Army use of artillery against the Republican armour, which the Republicans were unable to match.

The first reported incident of capture of armour by Republican forces occurred in early February 1922 when the IRA 3rd Tipperary Brigade (an anti-Treaty unit) raided a barracks in Clonmel that had been evacuated by British troops and was under police guard. Among the booty seized by the raiders were two armoured cars (type unspecified) and two Lancia armoured personnel carriers.[15] Unless this report is completely erroneous, which would seem unlikely in view of the detailed list of the equipment captured, it raises the question as to what happened to the cars once they were in Republican hands. One has to assume that these cars in all probability were Rolls-Royces and not any of the improvised cars that the Republicans are credited with using later in the campaign (the British certainly would not have had any improvised cars in their inventory), but there are no accounts of Whippets, other than Mutineer, Ballinalee, and Slievenamon, all of which were captured later and elsewhere, having been used operationally by the Republicans. Two possibilities suggest themselves as explanations. The first is that for some inexplicable reason the cars never were used by the Republicans and fell into the hands of the National Army upon the capture of Clonmel in early August, when they then became part of the National Army inventory. This however is highly dubious, as the Republicans demonstrated their willingness and ability to use armoured cars in all theaters of operations. Even if one posits that the armoured cars were unserviceable when seized, one would have likewise to assume that one would be cannibalized to make the other serviceable, or that both would have been repaired to restore them to service. At any rate, there is no indication that the British ever intentionally damaged any of their equipment prior to turnover, so in all probability both vehicles were in running order. The more likely probability is that occasional vague references to actions in which Republican "armoured cars" (not further identified, and not caveated by the adjective "improvised") played a role may refer to these two vehicles, which were later abandoned by the Republicans at the end of the conventional phase of the fighting, or were at some point captured by National Army forces, although the capture was not specifically chronicled. There are at least two examples which support this possibility. As early as 26 March an anti-Treaty officer from Cork reports having gone with his men to the Republican-sponsored Army Convention "with full equipment and an armoured car."[16] The possibility that this was one of the Clonmel cars should be considered. Later during the fighting, on 9 August an anti-treaty armoured car is reported to have capsized while making a tight turn, its occupants fleeing but carrying their machine-gun.[17] One knowledgeable author[18] has suggested that this likely was a Lancia rather than an armoured car, theorizing that the center of gravity on the Lancia would make it more likely than a Whippet to overturn. While that observation certainly is reasonable and logical, other factors such as road surface, slope, vehicle speed, tightness of the turn, etc., could make it likely that a Whippet would overturn as well. Thus, the possibility that one of the Rolls-Royces was the vehicle involved cannot be dismissed out of hand, especially in view of the action taking place in Clonmel where the cars were seized in the first place. Given the fact that a number of Rolls-Royces that ultimately were listed in the Free State inventory cannot be accounted for by name (The Baby, Moneygall, Flying Fifty, Kilmichael, Knockanana, and High

---

15  Eoin Neeson, *The Civil War 1922-23*, page 91. The complete list of equipment included *"more than 300 rifles, 200,000 rounds of ammunition, two armoured cars, two armoured Lancia cars, ten ordinary Lancia cars and Crossley tenders and two other cars as well as seven machine-guns and hundreds of boxes of bombs."* Also, according to Hopkinson, page 74, the British Cabinet were told that the capture of arms at the barracks had put the rebels in a relatively better position than the forces of the Provisional Government. In all likelihood the barracks in question were Kickham Barracks, built by the British between 1780 and 1805, and taken over by the 3rd Tipperary Brigade on 9 February, 1922.

16  Hopkinson, page 67.

17  Neeson, page 176, and Younger, page 402.

18  Paul V. Walsh, *The Role of Armoured Fighting Vehicles in the Irish Civil War, 1922-1923*, page 12.

*An improvised Republican protected vehicle captured at Listowel, date and circumstances unknown. Despite the poor quality of this photograph, it is possible to appreciate the rational lines of the vehicle which appears to be made of wood with angle-iron reinforcements along the top edges of the body. Of interest are the tandem tires on the front as well as rear axles, and the spare tires on the front as well as on the side of the vehicle. There do not appear to be any loopholes or firing ports in the sides. (Source undetermined)*

*The only known photograph of any of the improvised Republican armoured cars is this one of the Queen of the West, here shown with a group of Free State soldiers on Shop Street, Westport, County Mayo. Locally, the car was more often referred to by its nickname Fág a' bealIach, an Irish term meaning "leave the way". The car was captured from the Republicans following the battle of Clifden on 29 October, 1922. (Mayo County Library)*

Chief) in chronicles of the fighting during July and August, it is possible that two of these were the two cars reported captured in Clonmel in February. Moneygall and Kilmichael are both towns in the so-called Munster Republic, where much of the fighting between the opposing sides occurred, and although admittedly it is a stretch to imagine, the cars bearing those names may have been the cars involved.

The earliest use of armour by the Republicans was, as we have seen, that of the Mutineer that had been captured from National forces in May 1922, and was used operationally only briefly during the siege of the Four Courts in Dublin (28 June to 30 June). During the fighting it sustained damage to its tires, and its Vickers machine-gun was put out of action, but a Lewis gun was substituted for it and it continued to fight within the confines of the building complex. However, with the fall of the Four Courts, Mutineer was recaptured, quickly renamed Ex-Mutineer, and was then pressed once again into National Army service, participating against the Republicans in the remainder of the fighting in Dublin (until 4 July).

On 13 July, about ninety miles northwest of Dublin, Republican forces captured a National Army Whippet named Ballinalee at Drumkeen, near Ballinamard, County Fermanagh. Ballinalee was renamed Lough Gill by the Republicans and wrought havoc with National Army forces in County Sligo between July and its ultimate destruction in September. Generally, its possession provided the Republicans in the area a psychological advantage; it roamed far and wide, and caused apprehension and concern in small garrisons in the area. On 21 July it took part in a raid on a mail train near Ballymote. It participated in attacks on Tobercurry and Ballina on 10 and 12 September;

by 12 September, another armoured car (unfortunately, the name is not mentioned in accounts) had been provided to MacEion's National Army force in the area and engaged in a shootout with Lough Gill in Ballina. The National Army driver was killed in the exchange of gunfire, and Lough Gill made its escape. On 18 September Lough Gill was active at Cliffony.[19] It was not until 20 September that Lough Gill finally was brought to bay by MacEion's unidentified armoured car at Liscally Bridge, near Grange, about nine or ten miles northwest of Sligo. The Lough Gill was cornered on a dead-end road, and its engine reportedly wrecked by fire from a National Army armoured car.[20] The crew of the Lough Gill (all of whom subsequently were killed under questionable circumstances) removed the Vickers machine-gun, and fled.

While the National Army attack on Kilmallock was beginning on 23 July, at Ballycullane Cross (about a mile north of Kilmallock), Republican elements of the 5th Cork Brigade, supported by an improvised armoured car from the 1st Cork Brigade (possibly the River Lee), successfully attacked a National Army column. The River Lee was a coal truck of gargantuan proportions that had been fitted with armour plating in Cork; it was armed with two Lewis machine-guns. The following day Republican forces at Thomastown, south of Kilmallock, supported by an armoured car (not further identified) fought a lengthy battle with National Army forces, but eventually surrendered. Whether or not the armoured cars referenced in these two engagements were the same cars (a possibility, given the fact that the 23 July attack by the Republicans was successful, and the distance between Ballycullane Cross and Thomastown is negligible) or two different cars is not known; similarly, the fate or disposition of the car or cars is not known.

As previously recounted, three improvised Republican armoured cars, including River Lee, made their appearance on 2 August at Bruree. The Republicans achieved surprise by concentrating the three cars in a coordinated attack; these improvised cars counted a total of ten machine-guns (most likely Lewis light machine-guns) among them, an impressive amount of firepower by any standards. There are no details for the other two cars engaged in this action. River Lee continued to be active along the Limerick-Waterford line. On 11 August it participated in action at Rochestown (between Waterford and Wexford), where it may have engaged in a running gun battle with the National Army Whippet The Manager. Whether or not the gun battle actually occurred, on 11 August River Lee was captured, driven from Rochestown south to Cork and then to Fermoy and ultimately to Cappoquin, where reportedly it was abandoned, but possibly not disabled. On 2 September the River Lee reportedly participated in a Republican attack on Macroom. This raises the question as to whether the National Army forces that left it in Cappoquin a few weeks earlier in August would have let it once again fall into Republican hands, or if yet another improvised car was built and christened River Lee in memory of the earlier car, and then faded into obscurity.

Following cessation of the conventional phase of the Civil War, the Republicans reverted largely to guerrilla warfare. This did not, however, preclude them from continuing to build improvised armoured cars. In October and November, the Republicans established a munitions factory in Mulranny in County Mayo, still controlled by Republican forces. Among other items manufactured by the factory were four improvised armoured cars. The armour plating for these vehicles came from a variety of sources: steel plates from a local barracks, as well as a boiler from a local hotel,[21] were used to construct three of the cars, while steel shutters taken during a raid on Clifden were used in building a fourth car. One of the first three cars was named Queen of the West, and was the car that participated in the Republican attack on Clifden on 29 October, 1922.

There is only one known photograph of any of the improvised Republican vehicles (the Queen of the West, built in County Mayo). One can only speculate on generalities concerning these cars.

19 *The 20 September, 1922 edition of The Irish Times refers to the car by its original name, Ballinalee.*
20 *Hopkinson, page 215. There is no mention by Hopkinson or other sources as to the identity of the Free State armoured car involved in this action.*
21 *The Mulranny Hotel, today known as the Park Inn Hotel. Efforts to obtain more information from the current (2008) management of Park Inn concerning the requisition of the boilers from the old Mulranny Hotel have proven negative. According to an account on page 69 of Bernard Share's In Time of Civil War: The conflict on the Irish railways 1922-23, in late October 1922 it took the Republicans, who had occupied the hotel, over a week to remove the fresh-water boiler from the hotel.*

Although the preference may have been to use a commercial truck chassis (River Lee, as seen, used a heavy coal truck as its basis[22]), the Republicans would have used whatever was at hand that suited the purpose. The most complete description of any of the improvised Republican vehicles, insofar as it goes, is that of the River Lee, which one chronicler has described as "…a very mountain of an armoured car with a huge domed roof and an enormous span. Two Lewis guns and two Thompsons bristled from its sides."[23] Armour plating on all of the improvised cars, such as it was, almost certainly was some form of mild steel and would have been bolted to a steel framework, or added as "appliqué armour" to the existing truck body's sides. How, or to what extent, the cabs and engine compartments were armoured is a matter of conjecture. It is possible that as early as 2 and 3 July the Republicans had begun to gather materials for the construction of their improvised armoured cars; on 2 July a group of Irregulars gained admittance to the Cork, Bandon & South Coast railway workshops and appropriated a small piece of plate iron. They returned on 3 July and commandeered additional plate and round iron, remaining on the premises all that day and into the early morning hours of the following day, keeping eleven men occupied with cutting and drilling the metal.[24] Although not conclusive, this suggests the possibility that these plates were used in the manufacture of one or more of the improvised cars, including River Lee, known to have been built in Cork. It is highly unlikely that any of the cars mounted a turret, although the reference to a domed roof on River Lee indicates that at least some of the Republican cars had enclosed tops to protect the occupants against grenades; any weapons probably would have been fired through loopholes or over the top of the armoured compartments (if they were open-topped). In the 2 August Republican attack on Bruree involving the three armoured cars, the cars are described as containing troops armed with rifles, machine-guns and rifle grenades. This suggests that some of the Republican improvised cars were more in the nature of what today would be termed armoured infantry fighting vehicles rather than an armoured car with a small crew. Certainly, descriptions of the River Lee as being a huge vehicle "bristling" with guns would tend to point in that direction. Each car was likely a "one-off" example, as witnessed by the disparate materials used in the construction of the Mulranny vehicles. The Queen of the West appears to have been based on a Crossley tender or Crossley 25/30 touring car chassis and utilized the boiler from the Mulranny Hotel, set up in a horizontal position on the chassis. The boiler, although not bulletproof, was bullet resistant and the designer, one Thomas Moran, is said to have relied on the cylindrical shape of the body to divert bullets; tests confirmed this to be reasonably satisfactory. Because of the use of the hotel boiler, the car bore somewhat of a resemblance to the three improvised cars using locomotive boilers mounted on Daimler trucks that were built in Dublin during the time of the Easter Rising in 1916. Whatever the case may have been, the Republican engineers displayed ingenuity and creativity in producing vehicles which they realised, as did their National Army opponents, were important combat multipliers.

A very poor quality photograph also exists showing an improvised vehicle described as an "armoured car captured from the irregulars at Listowel". The vehicle, however, is not an armoured car in the classic sense, as protection appears to consist of substantial wood planking rather than armor plate, with angle iron reinforcing the juncture of the vertical and horizontal surfaces. The front and rear of the vehicle are well sloped, and the top may be enclosed. Even though not an armored car in the true sense, the vehicle nevertheless reflects the ingenuity and resourcefulness of the resource-starved Republicans to provide protection and mobility for their forces. In a generic

---

22 *In an attempt to ferret out any possible information pertaining to the River Lee based on its presumed connection with the Cork coal supply industry, on 31 May, 2008, the author called a number of coal companies located in Cork, only one of which resulted in some relevant information. In a conversation with Mrs. Deirdre Condon of Southside Coal (Cork), she suggested that in 1922 any large lorries would almost certainly have been owned by British interests, as investment in a vehicle of that type would have been financially impossible for most Irish businessmen. Based on that assumption, as a matter of conjecture, it would seem likely that the lorry in question was an English model. Possible contenders in the heavyweight category would be the Thornycroft Model Q or Model W, both with engines rated at 40 HP and a wheelbase of 14'6", capable of loads of 5000 or 6096 kg respectively. This, however, is only conjecture and should be regarded as such.*

23 *Eoin Neeson, The Civil War 1922-23, page 206, likely quoted from the 4 August issue of The Irish Times.*

24 *Bernard Share, In Time of Civil War: The conflict on the Irish railways 1922-23, page 35.*

sense, this bizarre vehicle predates the World War II British vehicles known as Armadillos, which used stout wooden planking mounted on commercial truck chassis as their "armour."

The final and undoubtedly the most famous armoured car to be captured and used briefly by the Republicans was Slievenamon, which was the car that was escorting General Michael Collins' convoy when he was ambushed and killed in August 1922 at Beal na mBlath in West Cork[25]. On 2 December one of the crew of Slievenamon defected to the Republicans, driving the car from its base at Bandon, southwest of Cork. On 5 December the car led an attack by Republican troops against a National Army position in Ballyvourney some ten miles northwest of Macroom. The successful attack netted the capture of another National Army armoured car (not further identified by name) among other booty, but Slievenamon's tires had been severely damaged during the exchange of gunfire. With some difficulty, it managed to make it approximately ten miles southwest to Gougane Barra where it was hidden in a barn or under some straw (accounts differ). Based on a tip-off, it was found and recovered by National Army troops who, because of the damage it had sustained, were obliged to tow it back to Macroom, first by horse and then by truck. What became of the other captured armoured car, or which car it was, was not made clear.

One extremely interesting improvised armoured car appears to have been built by the Republicans following cessation of hostilities between the National Army and the Republicans in 1923. Although many details of the story are vague or missing, a Rolls-Royce Silver Ghost belonging to the Clark family, proprietors of the Clark Tobacco Company in Cork, came into the hands of a surviving Republican faction and was converted into a sort of armoured car used in various forays against British forces still remaining Ireland under the Treaty Port provisions of the Anglo-Irish Treaty. The vehicle is said to have been modified by fitting thick steel plate to the rear passenger compartment, to which were bolted twin Lewis machine-guns, and the bodywork was strengthened with armour plating as well. Because over a period of time the car was used almost entirely during the hours of darkness in a series of raids against British military forces, it earned the nickname "Moon Car". One raid in particular was described in a 21 March, 1924, newspaper article; the car attacked a group of British soldiers in Queenstown (now Cobh), reportedly wounding twelve and killing one. For good measure, as the car was driving from the scene, it fired a machine-gun volley at the British destroyer Scythe in the adjacent waters. The car was described as a "yellow Rolls-Royce of the touring type equipped with two Lewis machine-guns." The car seems to have ceased its depredations following the uproar created by that raid. It was not until 1981 that an enterprising local historian, one Liam O'Callaghan, intrigued by the story, managed ultimately to find the remains of the car that had been burnt and buried at an isolated farm in Dunamore, County Cork.

In addition to the armoured cars, both captured and improvised, that were employed by the Republicans, a small number of Lancia armoured troop carriers also were used. As previously noted, among the equipment seized by the Republicans at Clonmel in February were two armoured Lancias. One engagement in which the Republicans were specifically recorded as having used a Lancia was at Golden, north of Tipperary, on 29 July (during which the driver, attempting to flee while under fire, rammed the railing of a bridge and stalled the engine)[26]. Given the large number of Lancias available throughout Ireland and the presumption that, at least in the larger cities and towns, Lancias were to be found in the RIC establishment, it is probably safe to assume that more than just a few fell into Republican hands, but not even a rough estimate of the number is available.

---

*25 Calton Younger, Ireland's Civil War, page 430, incorrectly makes reference to Dublin Liz as an armoured car that had originally been a part of the Collins column, later to be replaced by Slievenamon. Dublin Liz was in fact a Lancia armoured troop carrier, not an armoured car.*

*26 Hopkinson, page 168, refers specifically to a Lancia, while Neeson, on page 162, refers to the vehicle involved in the incident as an "armoured car".*

# Organization of Irish Armoured Units

## CAVALRY ORGANIZATION:

The historical antecedents of the Irish Cavalry Corps date back to as early as 1915 when Dublin Brigade volunteers organized cyclist companies in each of their battalions; similar units were also organized in other parts of the country. Although their operational life was very brief following the abortive 1916 Easter Rising, the cyclists, known as the Fingal Volunteers, were used in the classic cavalry roles of reconnaissance and raiding, and represent at least an embryonic development of cavalry tactics and organization in Ireland. During the Civil War itself, a rather sizeable group of bicycle mounted troops (150 bicycles, or about a full company) took part in the successful 24 July, 1922, seaborne landing at Westport by National Army forces. These mounted "mechanized" units were the prototype for the Cyclist Squadrons that were raised in World War II and which constituted a significant part of the Cavalry organization during The Emergency. The reliance on mechanical transport, rather than the traditional hoof-borne variety of cavalry mobility, is both noteworthy and curious, especially in a country such as Ireland that has such a rich equine tradition. However, both in 1916 as well as after the establishment of Ireland as an independent state with its own army, it is perhaps easy to understand that not adopting horses was dictated by both practical and financial realities. In 1916, few if any Irish volunteers would have owned a horse, while bicycles were common; following establishment of the Free State in 1922, and even into the World War II Emergency period, the austere Army budget made bicycles, whose initial cost was low and whose maintenance costs were minimal, a much more attractive option than horses, which were expensive to purchase, feed, care for, and house. Consequently, by accident or by design, Ireland can claim to be the first country in the world to have a totally "mechanized" cavalry corps since its inception.

*A bicycle squadron parading in Dublin. Although the bicycles were fitted with brackets to hold the Enfield rifles, for parade purposes the troopers are marching with rifles in the slung position. (62 Reserve Cavalry Squadron)*

As a point of interest, from 1931 until The Emergency, the Irish Army did have a horse-mounted unit for ceremonial purposes. However, the unit did not belong to the Cavalry Corps, but instead, belonged to the Artillery Corps which had horse-drawn field artillery batteries. The unit bore the Gaelic title of An Marc Sluagh, but were popularly known as The Blue Hussars, in reference to their colourful sapphire blue ceremonial uniforms. Although disbanded at the outset of World War II, the unit was revived in 1945, only to be definitively disbanded in 1949, to be replaced by a motorcycle escort. This escort, still known as the Blue Hussars (they ride on motorcycles painted gloss blue), was originally from the Cavalry Corps' 4 Motor Squadron, but in 1955 the duties were taken over by the 2nd Cavalry Squadron which continues to perform this function. The Escort Detachment has been equipped with a variety of motorcycles. Until 1990 it was equipped with Yamaha XS500 machines, and between 1990 and 1999 was equipped with Kawasaki GT550 motorcycles. In 1999, the Kawasakis were replaced by Honda Deauville 650cc motorcycles.

Following the Anglo-Irish Treaty of December 1921 departing British forces began to hand over a limited number of Rolls-Royce and Peerless armoured cars, as well as Lancia armoured troop carriers. Their use and operations, by both opposing sides in the Civil War, have been covered earlier in this book. Organizationally, however, during the early stages of the Civil War National Army armoured assets were parceled out to individual area commanders and were not retained under centralized control. The armoured cars were, in fact, often referred to as the "Free Lances". It was not long, however, before the National Army began to assume a more structured organization, and in August 1922, Captain Joseph Hyland was appointed as Officer in Command of the Armoured Car Corps, although the Corps itself, with its headquarters located at Portobello Barracks in Dublin, was not made official until about a month later, on 14 September. Captain Hyland

*The Blue Hussars ceremonial motorcycle detachment of the 2nd Cavalry Squadron. The motorcycles are Honda Deauville 650cc machines. (Sean O'Sullivan)*

*A restored Landsverk L 180 at the Curragh in May 2005. The vehicle is painted in the "Battleship Grey" used after 1946. The L 180 cars, delivered in 1938, marked a significant improvement to the army's combat vehicle inventory. (Terry Ward)*

*Paddy Lynch standing to the left of A.R.R. 2, Sliabh na mBan (Slievenamon), admiring the armoured car that he rescued from the scrap yard. The armoured radiator doors are open, as is the engine compartment. Front visors and rear door likewise are opened. Date of photograph unknown. (Sean O'Sullivan)*

> Sergeant Paddy Lynch was a legendary figure in the Cavalry Workshops in the 1920s through 1972. He joined the National Army in 1922, and his first assignment was assembling Triumph motorcycles that had been handed over in crates by the British. He became a dispatch rider for a time, and then transferred to armoured cars in September 1922, and was NCOIC of A.R.R. 14. In 1924, as a sergeant, he was instrumental in setting up the Cavalry Workshops; achieving the rank of Sqn Sgt (Company Sergeant), retiring in November 1947. From 1950 to 1972 he was a civilian foreman at the Workshops. His son, Pat Lynch Jr., also served in the Workshops from 1947 to 1990. Working under the direction of Commandant Lawless and Captain Mayne, Lynch was instrumental in the production of the Leyland armoured cars at the Cavalry Workshops. At the Workshops not only was he a competent foreman and skilled mechanic, but he was somewhat of a magician, having been able to save A.R.R. 2 (Slievenamon) from being sold or scrapped, simply by declaring the car itself as "scrap," while in fact the car was in full working order and being polished weekly by a workshop apprentice. Lynch unquestionably is the person responsible for having saved A.R.R. 2 as a priceless historical artefact.

*Equipment being loaded through the rear door of a Mk VI. The cavalry personnel all sport the distinctive Glengarry headdress and are suitably attired for the cold weather. The Ford Mk VI was issued to each of the seven Motor Squadrons at one time or another. (Matt McNamara).*

was faced with the task of asserting his authority over the individual field commanders who considered the armoured cars to be theirs to control. By January 1923 Hyland had begun to establish his authority over the cars, and the armoured cars in the field were officially assigned to companies, with nine armoured car companies[1] parceled out to the regional commands. The companies consisted of a variable number of cars (often only one car) depending on local requirements; each car was regarded as an independent unit and had a sergeant as the car commander, and three other crew members. Each of the regional commands had a captain from the Armoured Car Corps commanding the companies operating within the command, as well as acting as the link between the companies and the Armoured Car Corps headquarters in Dublin. Training was rudimentary, in the form of Training Memos issued by the Corps headquarters, implemented by crew training supervised by the individual car commander. Collective training was nonexistent due to the dispersal of the cars throughout the various commands as well as to the operational tempo at the time. Maintenance and repair, however, were officially made the responsibility of the Transport Corps.

In 1924 the headquarters of the Armoured Car Corps was moved from Dublin to the Curragh, and concurrent with the move the corps was reorganized. The number of companies was reduced from nine to four, with the new companies being located in the Curragh (1st Company, Curragh Command), Dublin (2nd Company, Eastern Command), Cork (3rd Company, Southern Command), and Athlone (4th Company, Western Command). Each of the companies consisted of eight vehicles, with varying mixes of Rolls-Royce and Peerless cars, and Lancia armoured troop carriers. At the same time, the Armoured Car Corps workshops were established at what was then known as Tintown, but which is now referred to somewhat less colourfully as the Combined Vehicles Base Workshops (CVBW) in the Curragh, and responsibility for maintenance and repair

---

1  The designation of "Company" with reference to the organization is a colossal misnomer, as most "companies" consisted of either a single armoured car, or possibly of two. In 1923, the total number of armoured cars in the Free State inventory was twenty (thirteen Rolls-Royces and seven Peerless).

> Commandant (later Colonel) J.V. Lawless was a hallmark figure connected with the design and development of home-grown armoured cars in Ireland. He was the innovator of the Leyland armoured car, Ireland's first attempt at producing its own armoured vehicle. He proposed, designed, and oversaw construction of the Leylands between 1931 and 1934, and in 1940 (along with Captain Aubrey W. Mayne) was responsible for design of the Ford Mk V (and its follow-on Mk VI) armoured car. Interestingly, both the original concept for the Leyland and the Ford Mk V relied on components of the old Peerless armoured cars (the body and the turrets, respectively). In 1941 Lawless (now a Colonel) and Mayne (now also promoted to Commandant) teamed up again to design the Dodge Mk VII and Mk VIII heavy armoured cars. Lawless also is credited with the design of a much more mundane piece of equipment, a two-wheeled handcart designed for carrying heavy equipment such as Vickers guns and mortars. These handcarts were popularly known as "prams" and, despite their usefulness, were the subject of humorous and often ribald comments.

was transferred from the Transport Corps to the Armoured Car Corps itself. In 1925 all of Ireland's armoured assets were consolidated by moving the 2nd, 3rd, and 4th companies to the Curragh, joining 1st Armoured Car Company there. At that time, the total Irish armoured vehicle inventory consisted of 13 Rolls-Royce and 7 Peerless armoured cars, and 64 Lancia armoured troop carriers.

During the mid-1920s the situation in Ireland mirrored the general trend in Europe toward austere military budgets limiting purchases of major items of equipment, as a result of which the Armoured Car Corps languished. It was not until 1928 when Major A.T. Lawlor took over command of the Corps that he imparted an impetus for the creation of a more capable mobile arm for the Army. He began by taking over McDermott Barracks, at the time unoccupied, in the Curragh, as well as instituting an intensive training program; a Corps school was also established at the

*A cyclist squadron on parade; visible on the second bicycle on the left is the position of the .303 Enfield rifle as mounted on the bicycle frame. (MA, Hanley Collection, G116)*

> Major A.T Lawlor was Officer Commanding the Armoured Car Corps from June 1928 to 1931 and became first Director Armoured Car Corps in November 1931, serving in that post until March 1934, when the Armoured Car Corps was redesignated as the Cavalry Corps. He served as Director of Cavalry Corps from 1934 until June 1935, and then again from 1943 to 1952 . A dynamic figure, he was largely responsible for improving the capabilities of the Armoured Car Corps, ultimately instituting policies that would carry over to the Cavalry Corps. The first tank purchased for the Irish Army was bought during his tenure commanding the Armoured Car Corps. Later, in 1936, along with Commandant Lawless, he traveled to Sweden and was responsible for procurement of the Landsverk L 180 armoured cars.

time. It was during Lawlor's tenure that the first tracked vehicle, a lone Vickers Mark D tank, was purchased in 1929.

In 1931, true to form for all military organizations, the Corps was reorganized and consisted of a Corps Director, a depot, school, workshops, a tank cadre, and the 1st Armoured Car Squadron. 1st Armoured Car Squadron was equipped with the 13 Rolls-Royce armoured cars and four Lancia armoured troop carriers. The 2nd Armoured Car Squadron was also formed as a cadre unit, equipped with the lone Vickers Medium D tank, the seven Peerless cars, and nine Lancia armoured troop carriers. These first two squadrons established the basic organization for Irish armoured squadrons, in terms of numbers of vehicles, namely, seventeen vehicles. Given the disparate armoured vehicle inventory of the Irish Cavalry Corps well into the 1960s, the composition of armoured squadrons has always been quite heterogeneous. A November 1932 sanction basically called for an emergency measure to put 13 Lancias in commission as armoured vehicles for one final year. This sanction was conditional on review inside 12 months. The Q.M.G. proposed that the following vehicles be retained in commission: 13 Rolls-Royce, 4 Lancias as armoured cars to complete the 17 armoured cars in a squadron, 9 Lancias as supply tenders, 4 Peerless armoured cars, and 1 tank.

By this time, it seems that unit and echelon designations began to reflect those traditionally associated with cavalry units, i.e. the company and platoon designations were dropped in favor of squadrons and troops. There appears to have been some study and debate around that time as to what direction the Corps should take with respect to its organization and equipment, specifically, whether the Corps should be based on wheeled, tracked, or horse-mounted units. At the time, probably in consideration of the traditional use of horses by cavalry units, as well as due to the great numbers of horses and horsemen in Ireland, it was proposed that a horse squadron, to be designated the 1st Horse Squadron, should be raised from the personnel and horses available at the Equitation School, and that the squadron participate in the 1933 maneuvers. There is no confirmation that the squadron was ever raised, however.[2] Instead, 1933 saw the establishment of a new type of unit, the cyclist squadron, with the formation of the 1st Cyclist Squadron, based at McKee Barracks, Dublin.

Significant organizational changes occurred in 1934, resulting in a totally new establishment consisting of both Regular units and Volunteer Force units. Along with the reorganization, the title of the Corps was changed from Armoured Car Corps to The Cavalry Corps (An Cor Marcra in Irish) in March 1934. The new organization (Regular forces) consisted of the Office of Director of Cavalry, 1st Armoured Car Squadron, 2nd Armoured Car Squadron (Cadre), 1st Cyclist Squadron, 1st Horse Squadron, 2nd Horse Squadron,[3] and the Cavalry School, depot, and workshops. The

---

2  *The Army Equitation School records do not reflect any horse squadrons ever being associated with the School, per E-mail dated 7 October, 2008, from Lt. Sharon Crean to the author.*

3  *Despite their designations, the horse squadrons in actuality were cyclist squadrons. The reason for or logic behind assigning different designations (horse and cyclist) for the same type of unit is unclear. The designation of Horse Squadron apparently confused some in the Irish military itself, as reportedly on one occasion, as 2nd Squadron was moving to Athlone on exercises, the unit at which they were to be billeted had arranged for stables, straw and fodder for the horses they expected to have to accommodate, only to find that upon their arrival the troopers rode bicycles rather than horses.*

Cavalry Corps adopted a number of easily recognizable symbols at this time, including a new corps badge as well as a distinctive headgear known as the Glengarry. The Glengarry is similar to the British pattern "Caubeen", which is also patterned after a traditional Irish peasant cap, and has a ½ inch black ribbon around its edge to secure it, ending in two trailing collar tails worn to collar length. The Corps also adopted red, green and black as the Corps colours.

Between 1936 and 1938 the Cavalry's vehicle inventory was significantly upgraded, at least by Irish standards, with the addition of two Swedish Landsverk L 60 light tanks and eight Landsverk L 180 armoured cars. These vehicles represented an increase of almost fifty percent in the armoured car/tank fleet, and represented a marked increase both in capabilities and firepower (all of the Swedish vehicles had a common turret that mounted a 20mm Madsen anti-tank gun), although the two L 60 light tanks, along with the older Vickers Mark D, provided precious little in the way of a viable tank force. The tanks, in fact, comprised the 1st Tank Squadron and were used largely to train Irish infantry units in anti-tank tactics.

*A restored Ford Mk VI armoured car. Irish-built Ford armoured cars were the mainstay of the armoured vehicle fleet during the 1940s, outnumbering all other makes in the inventory combined. (Paul Murphy)*

*A lineup of various armoured vehicles at Curragh Camp, date unknown. Although the image quality lacks clarity, at least five Rolls-Royce cars can be identified, as well as a few Ford Mk IV and several Mk V cars. (Peter Leslie)*

# WORLD WAR II ORGANIZATION:

In 1939, on the eve of The Emergency, the Army was reorganized to cope with the developing political and military situation in Europe. The brigade organization that was adopted required reconnaissance assets; these were provided by the formation of new cavalry units designated Motor Squadrons integral to each brigade. Each motor squadron initially consisted of a headquarters and four troops equipped with Ford light trucks, mounting various types of armament, including .303 Bren guns and .55 inch Boys anti-tank rifles; these vehicles were referred to colloquially as "Bug Chasers". In 1940 one of the troops of 1 Motor Squadron was replaced by a troop equipped with four armoured cars (two new production Ford Mk V cars and two Landsverk L 180 cars transferred from 1st Armoured Car Squadron). By 1941 a total of seven Motor Squadrons had been formed, numbered 1 through 7, reflecting the number of their parent brigade; each had a troop of armoured cars, and although the type of armoured car issued varied from squadron to squadron, most were equipped with the Ford Mk VI cars. The motor squadrons, location of original establishment, subordination, and principal stations were as follows:

1 Motor Squadron (McKee Barracks): 1 Brigade/1 Division (Clonmel, Saltersbridge House)
2 Motor Squadron (Cathal Brugha): 2 Brigade/2 Division (Ballmacoll House, Dunboyne)
3 Motor Squadron (Fermoy): 3 Brigade/1 Division (Fermoy)
4 Motor Squadron (Custume Barracks): 4 Brigade/2 Division (Boyle, Co. Rosscommon)
5 Motor Squadron (Curragh): 5 Brigade (Kilkenny, CTC)
6 Motor Squadron (Dublin): 6 Brigade/2 Division (Clondalkin-The Monastery)
7 Motor Squadron (Limerick): 7 Brigade/1 Division (Mount Trenchard, Foynes, Co. Limerick)

Between the end of 1939 and December 1942, the position of Director of Cavalry was abolished, to be reestablished in January 1943. In the intervening period, the duties and functions previously carried out by the Director were assigned to the Officer Commanding, Cavalry Depot. In the spring of 1942 Corps headquarters moved from McDermott Barracks to Plunkett Barracks, Curragh Camp.

In 1941, ten years after the establishment of the 1st Armoured Car Squadron, the 2nd and 3rd Armoured Car Squadrons were formed. Equipment issue varied among the squadrons: 1st Armoured Squadron at varying times had Rolls-Royce, Leyland, Landsverk L 180, Dodge, and some Ford cars in its roster; 2nd Armoured Squadron had a mix of Rolls-Royces and three different marks of Ford cars; 3rd Armoured Squadron was equipped with the Ford MK VI cars.

1st Armoured Car Squadron (Curragh)
  2nd Armoured Car Squadron (Templemore):
  1 Division
  3rd Armoured Car Squadron
  (Rineanna/Shannon): 1 Division

The year 1941 also saw creation of another Cavalry unit, designated the Carrier Squadron, equipped with 26 tracked Universal Carriers (quite often referred to as "Bren-gun carriers" because of the armament they normally carried). The Carrier Squadron was disbanded in 1944, the carriers being turned over to infantry units, and its personnel transferred to the newly formed 4th Armoured Car Squadron which was equipped with seventeen British Beaverette light armoured cars.

One failed experiment during The Emergency was organizing the Cavalry Corps units (1st, 2nd, and 3rd Armoured Car Squadrons, and the Carrier Squadron) as a regiment under the Officer

Commanding, Cavalry Depot in 1942. The unit was designated the 1st Cavalry Regiment, but was disbanded following the 1942 exercises.

The Emergency period also witnessed the expansion of the cyclist squadrons. In 1933 the first Volunteer Cyclist Squadrons were established, and as the name implies, consisted of volunteer personnel, with a small cadre of regulars. Between 1933 and 1939 a total of nineteen Volunteer Cyclist Squadrons were formed, whose members were avid cyclists and who became highly proficient soldiers as well. With the advent of The Emergency, fourteen cyclist squadrons were formed, replacing the Volunteer squadrons, but naturally enough retaining many of the original volunteer personnel. Historically, 1 Cyclist Squadron claims to have been formed in 1933; Squadrons 2 through 8 were formed in 1940, and Squadrons 9 through 14 were formed in 1941. The squadron commander rode on a motorcycle, while the rest of the squadron pedalled along on bicycles. The bicycles themselves were supplied by both Raleigh and BSA (Birmingham Small Arms), and were imported from England, although some may have been assembled by the Raleigh Cycle Company in Ireland. They were painted a light green, and essentially were civilian models that had been modified to carry a rifle in a semi-vertical position; the butt of the rifle rested in a bracket on the rear frame, and the upper portion of the rifle was secured by a clip near the handlebar. Normal squadron establishment was a headquarters and three troops totaling 120 personnel (5 officers, 5 NCOs, 13 corporals, and 97 troopers). The cyclist squadrons were divisional level assets. The cyclists were used largely in a coast-watching role, for which they were ideally suited. The bicycles provided an effective method of transportation, especially in view of the scarcity of gasoline. The cyclist squadrons were somewhat derisively referred to by the infantry as the "Pedalling Panzers" or "The Piddling Panzers", although the cyclists referred to themselves proudly as "The Bikes". The

*A Universal Carrier on parade in September 2002. A squadron equipped with Universal Carriers furnished by Britain was formed in 1941, and although the squadron was disbanded in early 1943, some carriers remained in the inventory until the early 1960s. (Sean O'Sullivan)*

*A VTT M3 photographed at the Curragh in April 2008. The M3s were for a time part of the establishment of the Motor Squadrons. (Sean O'Sullivan)*

*Beaverette ZD 3402 as it appeared while in Irish service. The Beaverette was based on a Standard Motor Company saloon chassis. It was underpowered, overweight, and had very poor handling characteristics due to those factors. (Sean O'Sullivan)*

cyclist squadrons, location and year of original establishment, subordinations, and principal stations were as follows:

1 Cyclist Squadron (Curragh, 1939): Southern Command; 1 Division (Mallow, Bantry, Foynes, Limerick)
2 Cyclist Squadron (Fermoy, 1940): Southern Command; 1 Division (Bantry, Foynes)
3 Cyclist Squadron (Cathal Brugha, 1940): Eastern Command; 2 Division (Dundalk Military Barracks)
4 Cyclist Squadron (Cathal Brugha, 1940): Eastern Command: 2 Division (Dundalk Military Barracks)
5 Cyclist Squadron (Dundalk, 1940): Eastern Command: 2 Division (Dundalk, Blackcastle House, Navan)
6 Cyclist Squadron (Wellington Barracks, 1940): Eastern Command; 2 Division (Wexford, Ballsbridge, Cavan, Castlebar)
7 Cyclist Squadron (Cork, 1940): Southern Command; 1 Division (Cappoquin, Co. Waterford)
8 Cyclist Squadron (Cork, 1940): Southern Command; 1 Division (Middleton, Whitegate, Cobh)
9 Cyclist Squadron (Curragh, 1941): Curragh Command (CTC, Wexford, Portlaoise)
10 Cyclist Squadron (Curragh, 1941): Curragh Command (CTC, Wexford, Portlaoise)
11 Cyclist Squadron (Athlone, 1941): 2 Division (Castlebar, Athlone)
12 Cyclist Squadron (Athlone, 1941): Western Command (Hazelwood House, Sligo, Castlebar)
13 Cyclist Squadron (Cork, 1941): 1 Division (Tarbert, Co. Kerry, Kilrush, Co. Clare, Mallow, Cobh, Ballylongford)
14 Cyclist Squadron (Cork, 1941): 1 Division (Kinsale, Co. Cork)

*A restored Unimog, lacking its armament. The interior of the vehicle is painted white, as is common on most armoured vehicles. The Unimogs were a stop-gap measure to provide a modest light armour capability while awaiting the arrival of the more capable Panhard VTT M3 armoured personnel carriers. They served in various units from 1971 to 1987. (Sean O'Sullivan)*

At the end of the war, the Cavalry establishment consisted of four armoured car squadrons, seven motor squadrons, and fourteen cyclist squadrons, plus the Depot, School, and Workshops, but by 1946 it was reduced to only one armoured car squadron, three motor squadrons (1, 2, and 4 Motor Squadrons, ultimately to become 1st, 2nd, and 4th Cavalry Squadrons), and the Depot, School, and Workshops. In January and February 1945, at least seven cyclist squadrons were disbanded (5,7,9,11, 12, 13, and 14).

## 1st Armoured Car Squadron

The 1st Armoured Car Squadron began life as the 1st Armoured Car Company in 1923, and was renamed as a Squadron on 12 September, 1931; it was equipped with the 13 Rolls-Royce armoured cars. The organization, size and equipment issue of the squadron subsequently varied according to circumstances. In May 1940 the squadron ceased to exist as such, as its four troops

*An AML 90 leading a small convoy through town. The AML 90 began service in the Irish Army in the early 1970s, and are still in service in 2009. (Bob Cantwell)*

were assigned to various Motor Squadrons (A troop to 2 Motor Squadron, B Troop to 1 Motor Squadron, C Troop to 3 Motor Squadron, and D Troop to 4 Motor Squadron). On 23 October, 1940, the squadron was reformed, its equipment consisting of nine Rolls-Royces, four Leylands, and four Ford Mk V armoured cars. In 1942 the Dodge "heavy" armoured cars were assigned to 1st Armoured Car Squadron, and remained in service with the same squadron until their definitive retirement in 1962; the Landsverk cars similarly were assigned to the 1st Armoured Car Squadron for most of their service life, except for a period when they were assigned to a few of the Motor Squadrons. For some period during the 1950s and 1960s, four Beaverettes were assigned to the squadron. In 1972 the Leylands were transferred to 5 Motor Squadron, and the Landsverks to 3 and 11 Motor Squadrons. In 1998, prior to its disestablishment and amalgamation as part of the 1st Armoured Cavalry Squadron, it was equipped with four AML 90 and six AML 60 armoured cars, as well as three Panhard VTT M3 APCs.

## 2ND ARMOURED CAR SQUADRON

2nd Armoured Car Squadron was formed in 1940 in response to The Emergency, and was subordinate to 1 Division (Cork). In late 1940, with only fourteen cars, it was still not up to full

*AML 20 NZH 9 of the 4th Cavalry Squadron. The AML 20 vehicles started life as the AML 60 CS armoured cars with a 60mm mortar as main armament, subsequently converted to the AML 127 configuration armed with a 12.7mm heavy machine-gun, and the further upgraded with the 20mm cannon as well as being Dieselized. (Terry Ward)*

49

*The entire squadron of eight Comets lined up for an inspection, date unknown. The gun barrels are all aligned, and all have canvas covers over the muzzles. Along with the four older Churchills, the Comets constituted the 1st Tank Squadron. (Matt McNamara)*

establishment of seventeen cars; its equipment consisted of four Rolls-Royce cars, one GSR Morris Mk IV, seven GSR Ford Mk IV, and two Ford Mk V cars. It appears that in 1941 or 1942, equipment may have consisted of thirteen Rolls-Royce cars and four Ford Mk V cars; equipment issue within the armoured car squadrons fluctuated according to availability of specific types of vehicles. The squadron was disestablished following The Emergency. During the Irish UN deployment to the Congo in 1962 the name was revived and assigned to the 2nd Armoured Car Squadron, equipped with Ford Mk VI cars, formed specifically for service in the Congo. The squadron was disbanded in April 1963 when its personnel returned to Ireland.

### 3rd Armoured Car Squadron

3rd Armoured Car Squadron was formed in 1942 in the Curragh. Various sources indicate differing equipment issue, varying from ten Mk V and seven Mk VI Ford armoured cars, to a full complement of seventeen brand-new Carlow-built Ford Mk VI armoured cars. In either case, the squadron seems to have been equipped exclusively with Ford cars from the outset. It was stationed at Rineanna (now Shannon Airport). As with the 2nd Armoured Car Squadron, the 3rd was disestablished following the war. A 3rd Armoured Car Squadron was briefly reestablished in April 1963, organized specifically for UN duty in the Congo and equipped with Ferret Mk II armoured cars. It was disbanded in October or November 1963.

### 4th Armoured Car Squadron

This armoured squadron was authorised on 17 February 1943 and formed on 22 April, 1943, and was equipped with seventeen Beaverette armoured cars (designated Mk IX cars). It replaced the Carrier Squadron, whose personnel were transferred to 4 Armoured Squadron while the Universal Carriers were allotted to infantry battalions. The squadron was disbanded on 1 January, 1945, and the Beaverettes were distributed to 1st Armoured Squadron and three of the Motor Squadrons.

*Scorpions, assigned to 1st Armoured Cavalry Squadron, on Dame Street, Dublin, 16 April 2006. The relatively light weight, low ground pressure and track design of the Scorpion combine to cause little or no damage to paved roads, unlike larger tracked vehicles which tend to cause stress and damage to road surfaces. Typically, all corner angles of the vehicles are painted in black. (Sean O'Sullivan)*

## Carrier Squadron

The Carrier Squadron was formed in late 1940, and consisted of five troops, each equipped with five Universal Carriers; in addition, one carrier served as a headquarters vehicle. Each troop was organized with a headquarters vehicle and two sections with two carriers each. Each carrier was equipped with a .303 Bren gun (hence the alternate and frequently used name of "Bren gun carrier" or "Bren carrier" in reference to the vehicle), and each troop also had one .55 in. Boys anti-tank rifle. Shortly after formation of the squadron, its A and B Troops were assigned to airfield defence duties at Rineanna (now Shannon Airport), and the remaining three troops were based in the area of Dunboyne. Although tactical doctrine called for the use of the carriers as transport vehicles rather than as fighting vehicles, during the 1941 and 1942 exercises the carriers were used in an attacking role, simulating hostile tanks, a role in which they proved very effective. In the spring of 1942 the three troops left Dunboyne to rejoin the two troops in the Rineanna area and were stationed at Dromoland Castle and Hurlers Cross until January 1943, when they returned to the Curragh, soon to be followed by A and B Troops. The move was a prelude to disbandment of the squadron in late January, when the carriers were handed over to infantry battalions.

## 1 Motor Squadron

1 Motor Squadron was formed in the summer of 1939 at McKee Barracks, Dublin, and was the first motor squadron to be formed. It consisted of four reconnaissance troops, each with five scout cars and fifteen motorcycles. In 1940 one of the reconnaissance troops was replaced by an armoured troop with two Landsverk L 180 armoured cars and two Ford Mk V cars. From 1939 to 1940 the squadron operated between Griffith Barracks, Dublin, and Castleblaney. Later in 1940 it moved to the Curragh for a short period before moving to Mount Juliet Estate, Kilkenny. In June 1940, one troop from the squadron was detached to form the nucleus of the newly formed 4 Motor Squadron, and by December 1940 the squadron was back in the Curragh. Another troop of 1 Motor Squadron remaining in the Curragh was detached in 1941 to form 5 Motor Squadron. In the meantime, the remainder of the squadron moved to Clonmel, moving again in November

*A trio of AML 90s at the Glen of Imaal in September 2006. All are fitted with electronic fire control and range-finding gear. The AML 90s are issued to Permanent Defence Force as well as Reserve Cavalry Squadrons. With the advent of the RG 32M light tactical vehicle, most AML 90s likely will be transferred to the Reserve Cavalry Squadrons. (Bob Cantwell)*

*The Blue Hussars parading in the Curragh on the occasion of the 80th anniversary of the Cavalry Corps, September 2002. (Sean O'Sullivan)*

1941 to Ormonde Castle. In 1942 it moved to Salterbridge House, followed by a move back to Clonmel. Following the Emergency, it moved south to Ballincollig. The unit's wanderings continued when in 1948 it displaced to the airfield at Fermoy. At some time between 1946 and 1959, the squadron was equipped with six Ford Mk VI cars, four Beaverettes, and eight Universal Carriers. In 1960, personnel from 1 Motor Squadron were selected to accompany the 32nd Battalion on its deployment with ONUC in the Congo, subsequently serving with the 35th and 36th Battalions there. During the extended period of deployment in the Congo, more than 350 officers, NCOs, and troopers from 1 Motor Squadron served with the UN forces there. Between August 1969 and 1978 the squadron was assigned to security duties along the border with Northern Ireland, with elements located at Columb Barracks (Mullingar), Athlone, Finner Camp, Letterkenny, Cootehill, and Monaghan at various times. During the 1960s and 1970s, equipment included Unimog scout cars, VTT M3 APCs, AML-60 and AML-90 armoured cars. In July 1983 the squadron was redesignated as a Cavalry Squadron, and in September 1999 the squadron moved from its location at Fermoy to Collins Barracks, Cork.

## 2 Motor Squadron

2 Motor Squadron was officially established on 13 June, 1940, at Cathal Brugha Barracks, Dublin, although the unit was actually in existence since the summer of 1939. Its predecessor was 2 Horse Squadron (actually equipped with bicycles rather than horses) that was disbanded in May 1939 and, along with personnel of 11 Cyclist Squadron, formed 2 Motor Squadron. In 1939 the unit (not yet designated as 2 Motor Squadron) was stationed at Mullingar and was equipped with light Ford trucks known as "Bug Chasers". The squadron became part of 2 Brigade and was stationed at Collins Barracks, Dublin. In May 1940 two troops of 2 Motor Squadron were detached and formed the basis of 3 Motor Squadron in Fermoy, later to be based in Clonmel. In September 1940 2 Squadron moved to Cabra Castle, Kingscourt, County Cavan, as part of the Army's overall defensive strategy. At about this time a troop of Landsverk armoured cars from 1 Armoured Car Squadron were assigned to 2 Motor Squadron, in addition to the four reconnaissance troops, each with five light Ford "Bug Chasers" armed with machine-guns, and ten BSA M20 motorcycles. In 1941 the unit was moved back to Dublin, where it was stationed at The Monastery, Clondalkin, and later at Ballsbridge. During the war years, 2 Motor Squadron was the forward reconnaissance element of 2 Division, which had a northern defence line across the Boyne River. The squadron's area of responsibility ran from Dundalk to Ballybay. In the event of a cross-border attack from Northern Ireland, the unit's mission was to delay and harass attacking forces as long as possible. In the event of a breakthrough, the unit would operate independently behind the lines, much in the

fashion of the "Flying Columns" of the War of Independence some twenty years earlier. In 1945 the unit moved to Griffith Barracks for the first time. In 1955, 2 Motor Squadron was tasked with providing the Presidential Escort of Honor, hitherto the responsibility of 4 Motor Squadron. For a period prior to 1959, the squadron was equipped with six Ford Mk VI cars, four Beaverettes, and eight Universal Carriers. In the 1960s and 1970s the squadron was relocated to Cathal Brugha Barracks in Dublin. In the 1960s, 2 Motor Squadron personnel served in ONUC in the former Belgian Congo. This was followed by a UN deployment to Cyprus, as part of UNFICYP, and continued with other UN deployments to Somalia, Rwanda, UNIFIL (Lebanon), Western Sahara, Bosnia, Kosovo, East Timor, and Eritrea. During the 1960s and 1970s the unit was based at Cathal Brugha Barracks, Dublin, and was equipped at various times with Unimog scout cars, VTT M3 APCs, Panhard AML 60s, AML H-90s and AML H-20s. The unit's A Troop moved to Cavan for a time, then to Castleblayney and Dundalk, where it remained actively involved in border operations from 1972 to 1984. In 1975 the squadron again moved to Griffith Barracks, Dublin. In 1983 the title of the unit was changed from 2 Motor Squadron to 2nd Cavalry Squadron, and on 15 September, 1988, the Squadron moved from Griffith Barracks back to Cathal Brugha Barracks. 2nd Cavalry Squadron remains quartered at Cathal Brugha Barracks. 2nd Cavalry Squadron continues to perform the Escort of Honor duties for the President of Ireland.

### 3 MOTOR SQUADRON

In 1940, as the Irish Army was expanding in response to The Emergency, 3 Motor Squadron was formed from elements of the existing 2 Motor Squadron, then based at McKee Barracks. On 19 May, 1940, as part of the reorganization of the Cavalry Corps, two troops of 2 Motor Squadron were dispatched to Collins Barracks, Cork. By 13 June, these two reconnaissance troops were joined by an armoured troop from 1st Armoured Car Squadron and the new unit, now based at Kilworth Camp, was designated 3 Motor Squadron of 1 Division. During The Emergency, 3 Motor Squadron consisted of a HQ Troop, one armoured troop with Ford Mk VI armoured cars, and three motor troops with soft-skinned vehicles and motorcycles. Like most other squadrons, 3 Squadron made a number of moves. In late June 1940 the squadron moved to Tralee for a period, and in July two troops were sent to Sarsfield Barracks in Limerick while the remainder moved to Ballincollig. In November there was a brief move to Bantry (to guard against a supposed submarine landing there), and in January 1941 the squadron displaced to Fermoy airfield. In May 1941 A Troop was detached in order to establish 7 Motor Squadron. In addition to training, the summers of 1941 through 1945 were spent in the peat bogs, cutting turf. In October 1945 the unit moved to Kickham Barracks, Clonmel. With the end of The Emergency, in January 1946 the decision was taken to stand down the squadron, with the majority of its personnel posted to 1 Motor Squadron in Clonmel. The squadron was reactivated on 2 October, 1959, as an FCA unit, with headquarters located at Kickham Barracks. Equipment issue seems to have been limited to Ford armoured cars, light trucks, Beaverettes, Landrovers, and motorcycles. By the late 1960s, the squadron had no vehicles at all, and was a squadron in name only, and training reverted to infantry rather than cavalry training. However, in early 1969, the first Orienteering competition in Ireland was held by 3 Motor Squadron in Clonmel. The competition included map navigation, running, and stamina. In 1979, five Unimog scout cars arrived in the unit, allowing a modicum of cavalry training to be reinstated. In 1982 the squadron was redesignated as 3rd Cavalry Squadron, and the Unimogs were replaced by two Panhard AML 60 armoured cars. In 1985 a new training center was established at Fitzgerald Camp, Fermoy, County Cork, which enabled 3rd Cavalry Squadron to train along with its sister unit, 1st Cavalry Squadron. During the nineties, emphasis was placed on cavalry skills, with officers and NCOs attending cavalry courses at the Cavalry School in the Curragh. In October 2005 3rd Cavalry Squadron was stood down and was replaced by 31 Reserve Cavalry Squadron, comprising elements of both the former 3rd Cavalry Squadron and 13 Infantry Battalion.

## 4 Motor Squadron

On 13 June, 1940, 4 Motor Squadron was activated at Custume Barracks, Athlone. The squadron was formed with a combination of Regular, Reserve, Emergency and Volunteer troops. The squadron was issued with Rolls-Royce and Landsverk armoured cars, as well as Ford "Bug Chasers". In August 1940 two of the Rolls-Royces were recalled to the Cavalry Depot and the Ford Mk V armoured car was introduced. (the Landsverk cars were withdrawn on 16 February, 1942, and replaced by Fords). In 1940 the unit was considered to be sufficiently trained to carry out patrols in the border area in County Cavan. The squadron occupied various locations, among them Newbliss, Kilnahara House, Ashfield Lodge, and Dartry Castle. In August 1940 the squadron was moved to Mullingar for rest and refitting, and in December 1940 the squadron occupied Edgeworthstown House, where they remained until May 1941, patrolling the areas of Drumshanbo, Mohill, Ballinamore, and Doogary Crossroads. In May, the squadron, minus a small element left behind at Edgesworthtown House, moved to Rynn Castle near Mohill. From May to August the squadron carried out numerous exercises in the areas of Cavan, Leitrim, and Sligo. On 28 August, 1941, the squadron occupied Boyle Barracks, County Rosscommon and remained there until 31 July, 1942, when it was withdrawn to Mullingar to take part in the 1942 maneuvers. On 5 October, 1942, the squadron returned to Boyle Barracks. During the summer months of May, June, and July of 1943 through 1945, squadron personnel were engaged in turf cutting in the bogs, as well as carrying out normal training in individual, troop, and squadron tasks. Exercises were also carried out with local LDF and Regular units. In 1945 4 Motor Squadron departed Western Command and Boyle Military Barracks, and moved to Plunkett Barracks, the Curragh, where it remained until June 1972. For some period between 1946 and 1959, squadron vehicles included six Ford Mk VI armoured cars, four Beaverettes, and eight Universal Carriers, and in the 1960s and 1970s equipment was upgraded to include the Panhard AML 60 and AML 90 armoured cars, and the VTT M3 APC as well as Unimog scout cars. In 1969 a reinforced troop was moved on short notice to Cavan and carried out patrols in the area of Butlersbridge, Aghalane Bridge, and Scotstown. On 1 June, 1972, one troop from 4 Motor Squadron moved to Connolly Barracks, Longford, preceding the rest of the squadron, which moved there on 25 June. The squadron then took up patrol duties around Ballinamore, Ballyconnell, Mohill, Doogary Cross, and Aghalane Bridge, as they had some 32 years previously. In 1983 the unit was renamed as 4th Cavalry Squadron.

## 5 Motor Squadron

As suggested by its designation, 5 Motor Squadron was subordinate to the Curragh Command's 5 Brigade and was based at Flood Hall/Thomastown. During The Emergency, equipment consisted of four armoured cars, 16 scout vehicles, and 39 motorcycles. In 1959, following the Army reorganization, 5 Motor Squadron was formed as the FCA Cavalry unit of 5 Brigade at Castlebar, County Mayo. Personnel came from Balla, Belcarra, Straide, Ballintubber, Mayo, Abbey, and Ara. The FCA squadron's original equipment issue consisted of Ford Mk VI armoured cars, Beaverettes, Landrovers, and motorcycles. Initial training camp was conducted at the Curragh in July, 1960 under the auspices of the Cavalry School. In the late sixties the Fords and Beaverettes were replaced with Leylands. The Leylands went to 5th Cavalry Squadron in Castlebar, because "the unit is located farthest from the Cavalry Workshops and OC Workshops considers it easier to keep the Leylands maintained than the Landsverks." The Leylands were supplemented by five Unimog personnel carriers in 1980. With the retirement of the Leylands and Unimogs in 1987, 5th FCA Cavalry Squadron was progressively re-equipped with the Panhard AML series vehicles, including the H-60, H-20, and H-90 variants. Upon its disbandment in October 2005, 5th FCA Cavalry Squadron became the nucleus of 54 Reserve Cavalry Squadron, based in Longford.

## 6 Motor Squadron

Organized in Dublin in 1941, 6 Motor Squadron was subordinate to 6 Brigade, and had its main station at The Monastery, Clondalkin. Its equipment was that of the standard motor squadron organization, the principal vehicles being four armoured cars (probably Ford Mk VIs). The squadron was disbanded shortly after the war, probably in 1946.

## 7 MOTOR SQUADRON

In 1941, A Troop of 3 Motor Squadron formed the basis of 7 Motor Squadron. The new squadron, subordinate to 1 Division's 7 Brigade, was stationed at Foynes, where it was tasked with guarding the transatlantic flying-boat base at Foynes on the River Shannon. Foynes had gained notoriety and stature as the site of the terminus of the first transatlantic commercial passenger flight from the US to Europe when on 9 July, 1939, Pan American's luxury flying boat, the "Yankee Clipper", landed there. During the war, Foynes was an important aviation and shipping point; indeed, in 1942 Eleanor Roosevelt, the wife of US President Franklin D. Roosevelt, arrived at Foynes under the alias "Mrs. Smith". The need for a Motor Squadron to protect this important locality was evident. The squadron was eliminated as part of the 1959 Army reorganization.

## 11 CAVALRY SQUADRON (FCA)

On 14 May, 1942, the 41st Cyclist Squadron was formed under Captain J.N Farrell. The squadron was to be part of the Corps in the North Dublin area, commanded by Col. J. Lawless. Training began in McKee Barracks. The 41st Cyclist Squadron was the genesis of the 11th Cyclist Regiment, Local Defence Force (LDF). Shortly after the 42nd and 43rd Cyclist Squadrons were formed. The next squadron, the 44th, was an Irish-speaking unit. The formation of a headquarters brought the regiment to full strength. After the war, the 11th Cyclist Regiment became reorganized and redesignated as the 11th Motor Squadron F.C.A., and the squadrons renamed Able, Baker, Charlie, and Dog. The last "cyclist camp" was held at Renmore in 1947, and in 1948 the unit began to be mechanized. In 1954, the regiment received eight Ford Mk VI armoured cars; other equipment included Beaverettes, "Bug Chasers," and BSA motorcycles. At the end of the 1950s, the FCA was integrated into the regular brigade structure. The regiment was reduced to squadron strength in 1959. In the 1960s, UN commitments stripped the squadron of its armour, and in 1970, members of the 11th were called on to assist the Army in security duties along the border with Northern Ireland, at Cootehill, Castleblaney, and Dundalk. In 1972 five Landsverk armoured cars were assigned to the unit and served until 1985, when they were retired from service. The Landsverks ultimately were replaced by Panhard AML 60s. In 1983 the 11th Squadron, renamed as a cavalry squadron, moved from McKee Barracks to Griffith Barracks and "twinned" with the 2nd Cavalry Squadron. On 15 September, 1988, the squadron moved to Cathal Brugha Barracks, and in October 2005 the 11th Squadron was "stood down," at least on paper, and was redesignated as 62 Reserve Cavalry Squadron.

*A Mowag CRV with ramp lowered, Glen of Imaal. A number of variants of the Piranha are now in service with the Irish Army. The Piranha is fitted with brackets that can carry two jerrycans on each side of the top of the ramp door, although most photographs show these brackets empty. (Roy Kinsella)*

# POST WORLD WAR II AND CURRENT ORGANIZATION

In 1946, the part-time Local Defence Force was reorganized and changed its name to the FCA (*An Forsa Cosanta Áitùil*), which was nothing more than the Irish translation of the original title. On 1 October, 1959, the FCA was integrated with the Permanent Defence Force (PDF), with FCA units serving alongside their PDF counterparts under an Army reorganization scheme. On 26 September, 1979, the FCA was formally separated (or "de-integrated") from the PDF and re-established as a separate reserve force, and the number of brigades was reduced from six to four. In July 1983 the FCA motor squadrons were redesignated as Reserve Cavalry Squadrons. In 1996, a military board was established to look at the possibilities of restructuring the FCA and re-integrating the organization into the PDF. By 2002, based on the findings of various boards, the recommendation was made to establish a Reserve containing integrated and non-integrated elements. On 1 October, 2005, a new organization came into effect, consisting of a non-integrated reserve organization that mirrors that of the PDF structure. The resulting organization consists of three Permanent Defence Force brigades (1st Southern, 2nd Eastern, and 4th Western) and three Reserve Infantry Brigades (3rd, 5th, and 6th). Each PDF brigade has an active Cavalry Squadron, and each RDF brigade has a counterpart Reserve Cavalry Squadron.

The current (2009) Permanent Defence Force cavalry organization consists of four cavalry squadrons (1st, 2nd, and 4th), plus the 1st Armoured Cavalry Squadron. The 1st, 2nd, and 4th Squadrons are light cavalry units equipped with the Panhard AML 90 and AML 20 armoured cars; one squadron is attached to each of the army's three infantry brigades as light armoured support. The 1st Cavalry Squadron is based at Collins Barracks, Cork, the 2nd at Cathal Brugha Barracks, Rathmines (Dublin), and the 4th at Custume Barracks, Athlone. Cavalry squadrons are organized with three reconnaissance troops, one support troop, and one administrative troop. The 1st Armoured Cavalry Squadron, an independent unit based at Curragh Camp, was formed in 1998 from the amalgamation of the 1st Armoured Squadron and the 1st Tank Squadron. It is equipped with the FV 101 Scorpion tracked combat reconnaissance vehicle and the Mowag III Piranha MRV. There are also three Reserve Cavalry Squadrons: 31 Reserve Cavalry Squadron (Kickham Barracks, Clonmel), 54 Reserve Cavalry Squadron (Custume Barracks, Athlone, collocated with the 4th Cavalry Squadron), and 62 Reserve Cavalry Squadron (Cathal Brugha Barracks, Dublin, collocated with the 2nd Cavalry Squadron).

The typical Cavalry Squadron is organized with a Headquarters element, an Administrative Troop, a Support Troop, and three Reconnaissance Troops. Establishment for the recce troops calls for four vehicles per troop (twelve vehicles per squadron). Until the LTAV replaces them, the AML 20 and AML 90 cars are standard troop equipment. The total number of reconnaissance troops in the Army establishment is 18 (9 PDF and 9 Reserve). In order to fully equip all 18 troops, a total of 72 vehicles are necessary, whereas in fact, slightly less than half that number of AML 20 and AML 90 cars are on hand (16 AML 20 and 19 AML 90). As a result, although the PDF squadrons may be at or near establishment, the RC squadrons, although organizationally similar to the PDF squadrons, have extremely limited equipment assets. With the advent of the LTAV programmed to be issued to the PDF squadrons, in theory all of the AML cars eventually could be transferred to the Reserve Cavalry Squadrons.

The roles and missions of the Irish Cavalry Corps are those historically associated with cavalry elements in all armies, i.e. reconnaissance, intelligence gathering, security, and economy of force operations. In addition, the Cavalry may be assigned to secure bridges and crossing points, provide flank protection, provide anti-tank and fire support, and to provide convoy protection. Duties peculiar to the Irish environment include conducting border operations along the border with Northern Ireland in support of the Gardai; escort duties (transfer of cash to banking institutions, safeguarding movements of explosives, and patrolling government installations).

## 1st Tank Squadron

The 1st Tank Squadron was officially established on 1 October, 1959, absorbing the assets of the Tank Cadre that had been formed in January 1949 following the purchase of four Churchill tanks from Britain. The 1st Tank Squadron was equipped with four Churchill and eight Comet tanks and represented the most formidably equipped unit in the Irish Army at the time, and in terms of firepower and vehicle weight was the most powerful unit ever to be established in the Irish Army. In 1973, due to the obsolescence of the Comets, the 1st Tank Squadron was amalgamated with the Cavalry School and was redesignated as the Tank Cadre. In 1980, the 1st Tank Squadron was reestablished at Plunkett Barracks, the Curragh, with the arrival of the Scorpion light tanks. From 1983 to 1998 or 1999, the five Timoney Mk VI armoured personnel carriers were also assigned to the squadron. The squadron was disestablished in 1998. When the new Defence Forces organization came into being in November 1998, the troops and equipment of 1st Tank Squadron together with the troops and equipment of the former 1st Armoured Car Squadron formed the newly established 1st Armoured Cavalry Squadron.

## 1st Armoured Cavalry Squadron

This unit was formally established on 1 November, 1998, as part of the Defence Forces reorganization. The unit absorbed personnel from the 1st Armoured Car Squadron, which was the oldest cavalry unit in the Defence Forces, dating back to 1923 (originally formed as the 1st Armoured Car Company, then renamed the 1st Armoured Car Squadron in 1931), and from the 1st Tank Squadron, which was one of the newest units in the Cavalry Corps (originally established in 1959, disbanded, then reestablished in 1980). The Squadron is comprised of one admin troop and three tank troops; each tank troop is equipped with four Scorpion CVR(T) light tanks. As of 2008, the Mowag MRV vehicles have also been incorporated into the squadron. 1st Armoured Cavalry Squadron is a highly mobile, flexible operational unit subordinate to the Defence Forces Training Centre in the Curragh.

## 1st Cavalry Squadron

The 1st Cavalry Squadron was officially stood up in July 1983, succeeding 1 Motor Squadron that had been formed in 1939. It was stationed at Fermoy until September 1999, when it moved to Collins Barracks, Cork. The squadron is subordinate to 1 Southern Brigade and is twinned with 31 Reserve Cavalry Squadron. It is equipped with Panhard AML 90 and AML 20 armoured cars.

## 2nd Cavalry Squadron

The 2nd Cavalry Squadron, which was stood up in July 1983, is the successor to 2 Motor Squadron that had been established in June 1940. The squadron is subordinate to 2 Eastern Brigade and is twinned with the 62 Reserve Cavalry Squadron. It is stationed at Cathal Brugha Barracks, Dublin, and is equipped with Panhard AML 90 and AML 20 armoured cars. The 2nd Cavalry Squadron has the distinction of providing the Presidential Escort for the President of Ireland. The Escort detachment is equipped with Honda Deauville motorcycles (as of 2009).

## 4th Cavalry Squadron

The 4th Cavalry Squadron was stood up in July 1983, succeeding 4 Motor Squadron that had been established in June 1940. The squadron is subordinate to 4 Western Brigade and is twinned with the 54 Reserve Cavalry Squadron. As with the 1st and 4th Squadrons, it is equipped with AML 90 and AML 20 armoured cars. The squadron was stationed at Connolly Barracks, Longford until 30 January, 2009, when the barracks was closed as a result of the decision to close bases along the border with Northern Ireland. The squadron relocated to Custume Barracks in Athlone.

## 31 Reserve Cavalry Squadron

31 Reserve Cavalry Squadron traces its lineage to 3rd Cavalry Squadron, and its predecessor, 3 Motor Squadron. In October 2005, 31 Reserve Cavalry Squadron was established from elements of 3rd Cavalry Squadron and 13 Infantry Battalion, which had been disestablished. The squadron is headquartered at Kickham Barracks, Clonmel, and has its D Troop located at Collins Barracks, Cork. Equipment includes the AML H-90.

## 54 Reserve Cavalry Squadron

54 Reserve Cavalry Squadron is the former 5th Cavalry Squadron, which in turn was the successor to 5 Motor Squadron. 54 Reserve Cavalry Squadron was established in October 2005, and was located at Connolly Barracks, Longford until January 2009, when it relocated to Custume Barracks, Athlone. It continues to be equipped with the Panhard AML AML 90.

## 62 Reserve Cavalry Squadron

62 Reserve Cavalry Squadron is the successor to 11 Cavalry Squadron. In October 2005 the 11th Cavalry Squadron F.C.A. was stood down, and the new 62 Reserve Cavalry Squadron assumed its place. As of 2009, 62 Reserve Cavalry Squadron is the only reserve cavalry squadron that has drivers trained and qualified to drive the Mowag III H personnel carriers.

## Non-Cavalry Armour Assignments

The Irish Army has maintained infantry battalions as traditional "straight leg" units, and although they train with armoured personnel carriers, they do not fit the definition of mechanized infantry units. Although some battalions were equipped with a company of the Panhard VTT M3 armoured personnel carriers in the past, the vastly more expensive, capable, and complex Mowag III H Piranhas are kept under centralized control and are located at the Curragh, where they are stored under cover and where vehicle maintenance is performed. Infantry personnel are transported for Mowag training to the Curragh from other parts of Ireland; presumably this is more cost-effective than actually assigning the Mowags to individual units, but what effect it has on unit readiness and training proficiency is open to question.

Although likely not complete, the following reflects some of the non-Cavalry units that are known to have had armoured personnel carriers assigned to them:

## 3rd Infantry Battalion (The Bloods)

Three companies of this battalion (formerly the 30th battalion) are based at James Stephens Barracks in Kilkenny. One company of the battalion was equipped with 16 AML VTT M3 APCs in 1996. The battalion stationed at Kilkenny is an anomaly in terms of location and subordination, as Kilkenny is located in the 1st (Southern) Brigade, while the brigade HQ Co is located in the 2nd (Eastern) Brigade area.

## 27th Infantry Battalion

In about 1989, this battalion was equipped with the upgraded (dieselized) Panhard VTT M3 armoured personnel carriers; seven of the APCs were issued to the battalion.

## 28th Infantry Battalion

Like the 27th Battalion, this battalion also was equipped with the upgraded Panhard VTT M3 armoured personnel carriers; seven of the APCs were apparently issued to the battalion.

## 29th Infantry Battalion

Prior to its deactivation in 1988, this battalion, which was specifically raised to serve on the border with Northern Ireland, was equipped with five Timoney Mk IV APCs.

# Armour in Support of Irish Peacekeeping Contingents Abroad

Since Ireland gained its independence in 1922 it has sought to maintain a neutral status and has avoided military alliances, or joining in any kind of security pacts. It has, however, provided military observers, personnel, and units to a number of peacekeeping and humanitarian missions throughout the world since its first deployment of fifty Irish soldiers to the United Nations Observer Group in Lebanon (UNOGIL) on 28 June, 1958.

The first peacekeeping mission to which an armed Irish contingent was committed was to the Operation des Nations Unies Congo (ONUC), from 1960 to 1964. Since then, except for the period from May 1974 to May 1978, the Irish Defence Forces have continuously provided an armed contingent to the UN. These contingents were normally an infantry battalion of about 600 personnel or an infantry group of over 400 personnel. These contingents often were accompanied by an armoured support element. These infantry battalions are not part of the normal Irish Army establishment and are organized specifically for each peacekeeping mission. They have been consecutively numbered, beginning with 32 Infantry Battalion that deployed to the Congo in 1960, and normally serve a six-month tour of duty on station. By early 2009 the battalion number deployed to Chad reached 99, to be replaced by 100 Battalion in late June or early July 2009. These infantry battalions have been supported by deployed cavalry elements in the past, but beginning with the UNMEE deployment to Eritrea increasingly have been equipped with Mowag III Piranha APCs and variants.

## ONUC – Congo

On 30 June, 1960, the Belgian Congo (now The Democratic Republic of the Congo, but from 1971 to 1997 known as the Republic of Zaire) gained its independence. In August, the Congolese province of Katanga, under the leadership of Moise Kapenda Tshombe, declared its secession and independence from the Congo. Fighting erupted, and the Congolese Prime Minister, Patrice Lumumba, requested intervention by United Nations forces, which was provided in the form of ONUC. On 27 June 1960, the 689-man 32 Infantry Battalion departed Dublin bound for the Congo, and by August two battalions were deployed to the theater (33 battalion, with 706 men, joined 32 battalion; together, the two battalions formed the 9th Irish Brigade). On 9 November, 1960 nine Irish peacekeepers were killed in an ambush at Niemba. As a result, on 1 December, 1960, the Director of Cavalry submitted a proposal to the Chief of Staff for an armoured car group to support the 648-man 34th Battalion which had replaced 32 and 33 battalions in January in the Congo, ultimately leading to Ireland's first deployment of armoured vehicles outside its own borders. The proposal called for three armoured car troops, each with two Landsverk L 180 cars and two Landrovers. However, although the Landsverk was the most capable armoured car in the Irish inventory at the time, it was decided against sending the Landsverks because only a limited number of personnel (those assigned to 1st Armoured Car Squadron, which at the time was down to about a quarter of its authorized establishment) were proficient in its use and maintenance. This led to the assignment of the Ford Mk VI armoured cars to equip the ad hoc group. Although less capable than the Landsverks, they were however in relatively plentiful supply. The first eight Fords were hastily assembled at Plunkett Barracks in early December 1960, where they were thoroughly checked

*A UN-supplied SISU XA-180 armoured personnel carrier on loan to the Irish contingent in Lebanon in the 1989-1990 timeframe. The SISUs as supplied to the Irish contingent were fitted with the 12.7mm Russian NSV heavy machinegun, license-built in Poland. For safety reasons, the NSV was replaced by the .50 caliber (12.7mm) Browning HB M2 heavy machinegun on the Irish operated vehicles. (Bob Cantwell)*

the contingent returned to Ireland. With the resumption of conflict along the Israel/Lebanon border in June and July 2006, Irish troops returned to Lebanon on 31 Oct, 2006; the contingent consisted of a mechanized infantry company group with Mowag Piranhas operating alongside a Finnish engineering company, as part of joint Finnish-Irish Battalion.

## UNOSOM II - Somalia

From August 1993 to January 1995 Ireland provided a troop contingent to the Second United Nations Operation in Somalia (UNOSOM II). The 1st Transport Company arrived in Somalia in August 1993 with 40 vehicles. The main task of the Irish contingent, which was based at Camp Shannon in Baidoa, was ferrying supplies from the port of Mogadishu to the UN brigade based some 175 miles distant in the Baidoa region. The convoy runs were a weekly affair, and initially convoy protection was entrusted to two ACMAT VLRA TPK420 S3 "gunship" trucks armed with the Browning .50 caliber heavy machine-gun, but as tensions in the region increased, Ireland's two SISU XA-180 APCs based in the Curragh were sent to Baidoa to provide enhanced convoy protection. The two SISUs were withdrawn in September 1994 when the 2nd Transport Company, which had replaced the 1st Transport Company, returned to Ireland.

*A Mowag Piranha with the Irish KFOR contingent in Kosovo. Although a coating of mud appears to have obscured the camouflage scheme over most of the hull, curiously the small Irish flag and white KFOR markings remain fairly visible. (Roy Kinsella)*

# KFOR - Kosovo

In August 1999 Ireland provided an initial contribution consisting of a transport company to the NATO-led multinational peace support operation designated as the Kosovo Force (KFOR). In October 2004 the composition of the Irish contingent changed significantly when 8 Irish Transport Company was replaced by an infantry company designated 27 Infantry Group. The company is a mounted company, equipped with Mowag armoured personnel carriers and operates as part of Multinational Task Force (Center). The company is split between two locations, namely Camp Clarke located at Lipjan, 15 km south of Pristina, and Camp Karhu, which is a former Finnish position in the Serb village of Donja Gusterica.

# UNMEE - Eritrea

In December 2001, an Irish contingent was deployed to the UN Mission in Ethiopia and Eritrea (UNMEE). UNMEE consisted of approximately 3,600 troops from 45 countries. The Irish contingent, based in Asmara, numbered some 200 troops, and included six Mowag Piranha APCs. Part of the mission of the Irish contingent was to provide security for convoys and protection for key personnel in the operational area. The Mowags provided both mobility and protection for these missions. The contingent was withdrawn on 18 June, 2003.

# UNMIL - Liberia

Ireland provided a troop contingent to the UN Mission in Liberia (UNMIL) from November 2003 to 31 May 2007. UNMIL had some 14,000 troops from 34 different countries. The Irish contingent, beginning with 90 Infantry Battalion, was based at Camp Clara, Monrovia, and ranged in size from about 330 to 450 troops. The infantry battalions that served in UNMIL were 90 through 95 Infantry Battalions; 22 Mowag APCs were deployed to Liberia to support the infantry battalions. The contingent also included a cavalry troop with AML 90 and AML 20 armoured cars, which together with a Swedish mechanized infantry company made up the Irish-Swedish Quick

*An Irish Mowag in white U.N. livery outside the Irish workshops at Camp Clara, Monrovia in 2004. The black discolouration caused by the exhaust is in stark contrast to the white livery; on vehicles painted in camouflage colours, that area of the hull is normally painted black, thus attenuating the discolouration. (Mats Hjorter)*

*An AML 90 at Camp Clara, Monrovia, in late 2004. The car bears prominent UN markings on its front glacis, and bears a U.N. UNMIL registration plate. The original green livery shows through the white U.N. paint in several places. (Mats Hjorter)*

*A Mowag returned from Liberia, in open storage at Curragh Camp, 27 May, 2009. (Ralph Riccio)*

Reaction Force (QRF) battalion, based at Camp Clara from summer 2004 to summer 2006. The QRF conducted reconnaissance patrols and was ready to move into action on 30-minute notice. In November 2004, in reaction to serious rioting that broke out in Monrovia, the QRF was deployed and played a significant role in quelling the violence.

# EUFOR - Chad/Central African Republic)

*A Mowag stuck in the mud in Chad in September 2008. Despite its excellent mobility characteristics, there is always the risk that nature will triumph over technology. Note the wheel and tire carried on the front glacis. (Roy Kinsella)*

Beginning on 21 February, 2008, Ireland deployed a peacekeeping contingent of some 440 troops, including personnel of the Irish Ranger Wing and 97 Infantry Battalion, to Chad as part of Operation EUFOR Tchad/RCA (or EUFOR Chad/CAR). The EU operation consisted of some 3,700 troops from fourteen nations and was headed by an Irish officer, LTG Pat Nash. The operation was designed to assist and provide protection to refugees fleeing from the crisis in Darfur. The majority of the Irish contingent is stationed at Goz Beida, at Camp Ciara. In April, 18 Mowag Piranhas were deployed to Chad to provide mobility and to enhance protection for the dismountable troops of 97 Infantry Battalion. Of the 18 Mowags, 14 are the standard infantry carrier, three are the CRV variant, and one is an ambulance. On 8 October, 2008, 98 Infantry Battalion replaced 97 Infantry battalion, and in late January 2009, 99 Infantry Battalion in turn relieved 98 Infantry Battalion. On 15 March, 2009, the UN took control of the peacekeeping mission from the EU. The size of the force had risen to 5,000, with the Irish contingent remaining at 440 troops.

# Armoured Vehicles in Irish Service 1922-2010

## ROLLS-ROYCE 1920 PATTERN ARMOURED CAR

Between 1922 and 1925 the Rolls-Royce Whippets were parceled out to as many as nine companies, as the Armoured Corps underwent several reorganizations. In 1925, the Rolls-Royce cars, now identified by individual numbers rather than by name,[1] returned to the Curragh where they served with the 1st Armoured Car Squadron until 1937-38, at which time they were replaced by the eight newly-acquired Swedish Landsverk L 180 armoured cars. Their retirement did not last long, however, as in 1939, with the arrival of The Emergency (as World War II was referred to in Ireland at the time), the cars were returned to active service. Most (nine) were once again assigned to the 1st Armoured Squadron and four were assigned to the 2nd Armoured Squadron until 1945, when they again were removed from service. Some of the Rolls-Royces briefly served in at least one of the Motor Squadrons until replaced by newer cars as they became available. In 1942, the Irish Rolls-Royces were upgraded to a standard similar to that of the British 1924 pattern Rolls-Royces, with the installation of a commander's cupola and a ball mounting for the machine-gun, both of which were designed and made in Ireland. The first conversion was done at the Cavalry Workshops, and the remainder at Thompson and Son, in Carlow. In an attempt to prolong the operational life of the Rolls-Royce cars, in 1942 six second-hand Rolls-Royce civilian motorcars were purchased for cannibalization. Previous to this, in 1941, replacement of tires had begun to be a problem, so eight of the cars were fitted with wheels from Morris-Commercial 2-ton trucks; unfortunately, these wheels were damaged because of compatibility problems between the Morris wheels and the Rolls-Royce wheel studs and nuts. By late 1944 stocks of tires for the five cars that retained the

*Rolls-Royce: A Rolls-Royce 1920 Pattern armoured car, date and location unknown. It was common practice to carry as many spare tires as possible as punctures and tire failures were common. (NPA/NLI IND H 260, Courtesy of the National Library of Ireland)*

[1] The numbers and names were: ARR 1 *Danny Boy* (later *Tom Keogh*); ARR 2 *Slievenamon*; ARR 3 *The Fighting 2nd*; ARR 4 *The Baby*; ARR 5 *The Manager*; ARR 6 *Custom House*; ARR 7 *Moneygall*; ARR 8 *The Big Fella*; ARR 9 *Ex-Mutineer*; ARR 10 *Flying Fifty*; ARR 11 *Kilmichael*; ARR 12 *Knockanana*; ARR 14 *High Chief*.

*Maj. Gen. Tom Ennis with other officers in front of two Rolls-Royce armoured cars, "The Big Fella" and "The Fighting 2nd", in late 1922. The background colour on which the names are painted is darker than the colour of the rest of the cars, suggesting that the names were masked off and the cars repainted in a lighter colour, over which white Fianna Fail insignia were applied. (NPA/NLI HOG 113, Courtesy of the National Library of Ireland)*

original wheels were exhausted, and it was determined that it would be cost-prohibitive to allocate any further money to rectifying the wheel and tire problem, effectively condemning the fleet to non-operational status. In April 1954, 12 of the 13 cars, stripped of their armoured bodies, were finally sold.[2] Peter Leslie adds that at least some of the chassis were converted for use as hearses. Sliabh na mBan,[3] known in Hiberno-English as Slievenamon, today restored and preserved at the Curragh, was the car escorting General Michael Collins, Commander-in-Chief of the National Army Forces, when his column was ambushed and killed by Irregular forces at Beal-na-mBlath on 22 August, 1922. Slievenamon survived through a bit of chicanery on the part of the legendary Sergeant Paddy Lynch, who was the foreman at the Cavalry Workshops, who listed the vehicle as "scrap", whereas in reality it was in full working order. It is only one of three Rolls-Royce armoured cars still in existence; Slievenamon is used on ceremonial occasions. A similarly restored model is on display at The Tank Museum in Bovington, Dorset, England. Interestingly, the Bovington example served in Dublin in 1921 with the No. 5 Armoured Car Company, Royal Tank Corps, and returned to England after 1922. The third survivor (ARR1, Danny Boy/Tom Keogh) is one of the Irish Whippets that was sold off in 1954 and has been restored by a collector in England.

---

2  Although twelve cars reportedly were sold off in 1954, this number is somewhat suspect as in addition to ARR 2, Slievenamon, which was retained by the Cavalry Corps as a historic relic, one at least appears to have survived until the early 1970s as a target at the Glen of Imaal range in the Wicklow Mountains. According to information provided by Terry Ward on 25 July, 2008, during the early 1970s he personally viewed the fairly complete and intact remains of one of the Rolls-Royce cars, stating that "The car was still recognizable and was in reasonable condition. All the armour was in place. The distinctive front louvers in the front protecting the radiators were still there, the turret was complete and the mud guards were in place. The wheels were gone but the leaf springs and axles were still in place. The distinctive flat bed (mud guards) behind the turret was still intact. The engine block was still there but the cylinder head was gone exposing the six cylinders. The armour covering the engine was there but I cannot remember the side panels. I don't think they were there because I could see the engine. I believe it could have been restored at that point."

3  Sliabh na mBan is the name of a mountain located in County Tipperary. The translation from Gaelic is Mountain of the Women. According to Karl Martin, the name may refer to a popular ballad from the 1900s called Slievenamon, or the name may have been suggested by someone from that area who was connected with the vehicle. In an account of the attack on Clonmel, reference is made to Sliabh na mBan as a "breast-like mountain" (Neeson, page 174).

*A Rolls-Royce car, probably in the late 1940s. The turret bears modifications to the mounting for the Vickers machinegun and also has an observation cupola. The modifications were conceived and designed by the Cavalry Workshops, although much of the fabrication was done by Thompson's of Carlow. The officer on the left is wearing the traditional Cavalry Corps Glengarr y cap. (MA)*

## ROLLS-ROYCE 1920 PATTERN SPECIFICATIONS:

| | |
|---|---|
| Manufacturer: | Rolls Royce |
| Dates of service (Irish Defence Forces) | 1921-1954 |
| Number in Irish service: | 14 (one captured by Republican forces and destroyed) |
| Crew: | 3 |
| Empty weight: | 7974 lbs (3617 kg) |
| Combat weight: | 10,237 lbs (4643 kg) |
| Armament: | One Vickers .303 in. machine-gun; one Hotchkiss .303 in. machine-gun |
| Ammunition capacity: | 1,000 rounds (Vickers); 300 rounds (Hotchkiss) |
| Engine: | Rolls Royce 6-cylinder in-line gasoline, 7,428cc |
| Horsepower: | 80 HP |
| Transmission: | 4-speed manual |
| Fuel capacity: | 18 Imperial gallons (21.6 US gallons; 82 litres) |
| Maximum speed: | 55 mph (89 km/h) road; 37.5 mph (60 km/h) cross-country |
| Operating radius (road): | 192 miles (309 km) |
| Armour: | 6.5-9mm |
| Length: | 200.5 inches (5093mm) |
| Width: | 86 inches (2184mm) |
| Height: | 92 inches (2330mm) |
| Tire size: | 895 x 150 (Palmer Cord) |
| Wheelbase: | 143.5 inches (3645mm) |
| Track: | 56.5 inches (1435mm) front, 66.5 inches (1689mm) rear |
| Ground clearance: | 10 inches (254mm) |
| Trench crossing: | 72 inches (1829mm) with ditching boards |

*The driving compartment of a Rolls Royce 1920 Pattern car as seen from the open access doors. The white interior is typical for armoured vehicles. (Ralph Riccio*

**Bottom, left:** Detail of the Vickers armament and shield on A.R.R. 2, Sliabh na mBan, Curragh Camp, May 2009. (Roy Kinsella

**Bottom right:** Rolls-Royce engine of A.R.R.2, 27 May, 2009. The attention lavished on this historic vehicle is evident from the photograph. (Roy Kinsella))

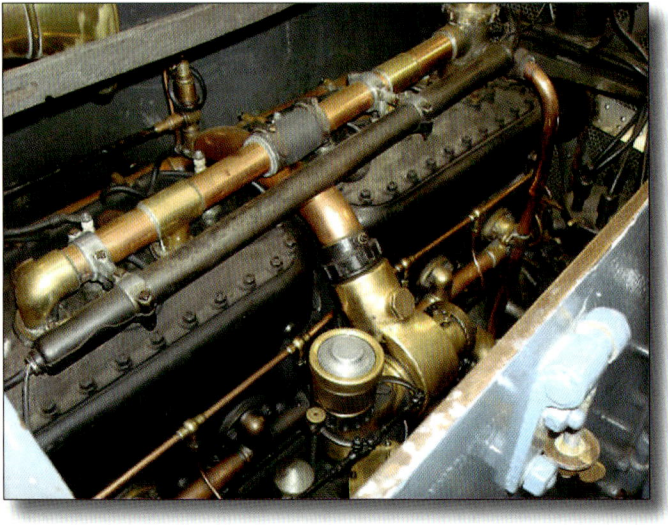

*Rolls-Royce 1920 Pattern. 1/35 scale.*

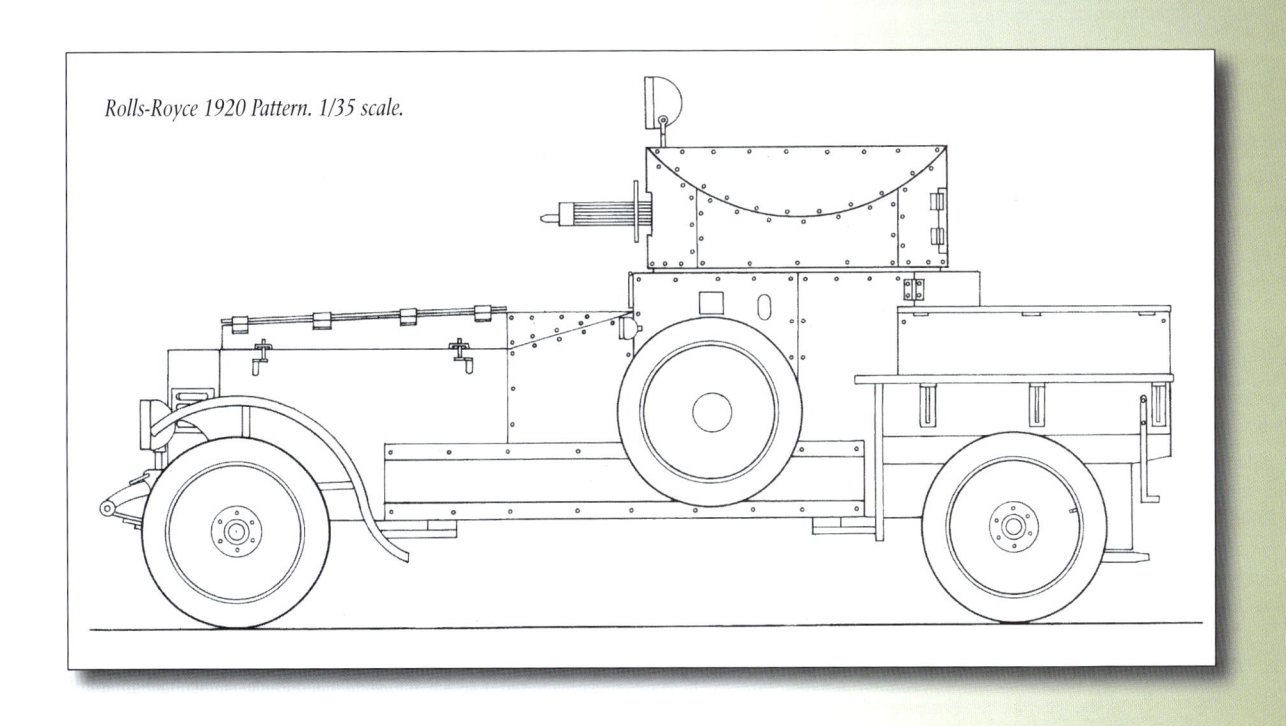

*The restored A.R.R. 2 Sliabh na mBan (Slievenamon) on display at Curragh Camp in 2006. The grey livery is appropriate for the period from about 1946 through about 1956. (Bob Cantwell)*

*Peerless armoured car A.P. 1 in the late 1920s. Although the front and rear wheel styles on this car are different, Peerless cars also could be encountered with both sets of wheels of the same pattern as the rear wheels on this car. (MA IAC, Kodak neg. 1)*

# PEERLESS ARMOURED CAR (1919 PATTERN)

Seven Peerless armoured cars were included in the turnover of equipment by the British in 1922. Although the car was reliable, it was also slow, heavy, unstable, and suffered from poor cross-country performance. It was not popular in Irish service, and because of its shortcomings was largely restricted to use in urban areas. The Peerless cars were retired from service in 1932, but their armour and turrets were retained for possible future use, and in fact, a few years later an attempt was made by the Cavalry Workshops to mount major body components onto a Leyland commercial truck chassis. The attempt met with mixed results, and major modifications had to be made to ultimately produce the Leyland armoured cars. The turrets, however, were able to be used with little or no modification on the 1940 Ford Mark V armoured cars designed and built in Ireland.

*The Peerless reproduction of A.P. 1, fabricated by the Irish Army's Combined Vehicle Base Workshops, shown on parade on 2 July, 2009, during its first public showing. The plate on the bottom front of the glacis reads Peerless. Following the Peerless are a Universal Carrier and an AML 60. (Terry Ward)*

## Peerless Specifications:

| | |
|---|---|
| Manufacturer: | Peerless Truck and Motor Company (chassis) |
| Dates of service (Irish Defence Forces): | 1922-1932 |
| Number in Irish service: | 7 |
| Crew: | 4 |
| Empty weight: | 12,992 lbs (5893 kg) |
| Combat weight: | 15,456 lbs (7011 kg) |
| Armament: | Two Hotchkiss .303 in. machine-guns (in two separate turrets) |
| Ammunition capacity: | 2,200 rounds |
| Engine: | Peerless 4-cylinder gasoline |
| Horsepower: | 40 |
| Transmission: | Chain drive |
| Fuel capacity: | NA |
| Maximum speed (road): | 18 mph (29 km/h) |
| Operating radius (road): | 90 miles (145 km) |
| Armour: | 3-8mm |
| Length: | 242 inches (6147mm) |
| Width: | 88 inches (2230mm) |
| Height: | 100 inches (2540mm) |
| Tire size: | NA |
| Wheelbase: | NA |
| Track: | NA |
| Ground clearance: | NA |
| Trench crossing: | No capability |

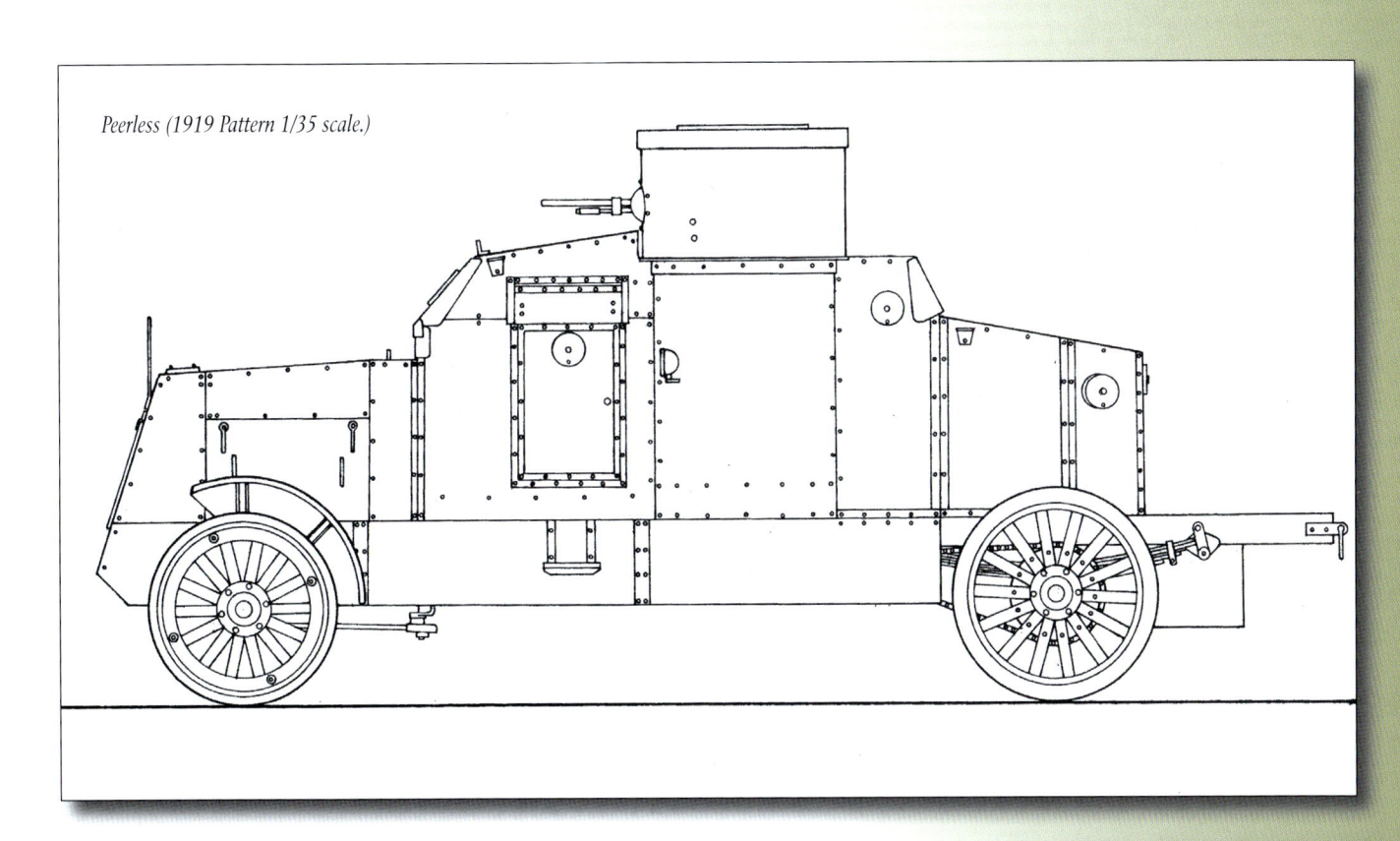

*Peerless (1919 Pattern 1/35 scale.)*

# LANCIA ARMOURED TROOP CARRIERS

Between April 1922 and August 1923, British forces in Ireland reportedly turned over a total of 111 Lancias (although this total is open to question) with armoured bodies to the Free State Army. Subsequent to their turnover to the Free State, 64 of the Lancias were retrofitted with closed tops by the Inchicore works, thus increasing the degree of protection afforded the occupants. In addition to adding the closed top, the vehicle was fitted with firing ports for Lewis guns on the front as well as on both sides of the vehicle – none were ever fitted with turrets due to lack of technical expertise at the Inchicore workshop. A period photograph shows one of these enclosed vehicles emblazoned with the name "Hooded Terror"; some sources make reference to all of the enclosed version being referred to generically as "Hooded Terrors".

During the 1922-1923 Civil War a total of seven Lancias were assigned to the Railway Protection, Repair and Maintenance Corps (RPR&MC) to assist in patrolling the railway right-of-way. Two of the Lancias were extensively rebuilt; the rebuild consisted of replacing the standard armoured body with a larger square-shaped body and the addition of a large flat–topped cylindrical turret, as well as fitting special wheels that enabled the car to be driven on the railway tracks themselves. Their overall square appearance is highly reminiscent of the previously-described square-bodied Daimlers improvised by the British in 1916. Another five Lancias were modified by adding a raised roof with firing ports on the sides and front of the raised portion, as well as having the railroad wheels fitted; the railway Lancias had their axles widened to fit the 5 ft 3 inch Irish railway gauge. The conversions were carried out at the GW&SR's Inchicore shops in April 1923. The railway Lancias were reported to be able to reach speeds of 45 miles per hour forward and twenty miles per hour in reverse. AL (Armoured Lancia) 47 was assigned to Dundalk, and AL 51 appears to have been assigned to Dublin. One of the railway Lancias, the "Grey Ghost", was ambushed on 15 October 1922 by Republican forces, was captured, stripped of its weapons and set on fire, partially burning it. There are conflicting reports as to what subsequently happened; one version is that both attackers and defenders adjourned to a convenient public house and drank to each other's health, while another says that the Irregulars marched the government soldiers to a private home, paid the housewife £2 for their refreshments, and then allowed them to go.[4] In June 1923,

4  Bernard Share, *In Time of Civil War*, page 67.

*A Lancia armoured troop carrier built on the Iota chassis at Beggar's Bush Barracks in Dublin in 1922. It was fairly common practice to name the Lancia cars; this one bears the nickname "Handy Andy". The swiveling horseshoe mount towards the rear of the troop compartment was for a Lewis gun. The individual standing in the front of the vehicle wearing goggles above his cap visor and dressed in what appears to be civilian garb presumably is the driver. (MA ARM1 no. 17)*

*A closed-top Lancia nicknamed "Hooded Terror". This name was often used to describe closed-top Lancias in general. The closed tops were added to the Lancias after they had been taken over by the National Army; Lancias in British service all had open tops, although some were fitted with protective wire mesh cages. (Peter Leslie)*

*One of the Lancias converted for railway use. The top was enclosed, and a series of armoured flaps below the roof acted as firing ports. The Lancias modified for railway use bore small two-digit numbers, in this case 47, enclosed in circles painted on the lower edge of the driver's compartment, on both sides of the vehicle. (MA/92)*

*One of the turreted Lancia railway cars, Number 51, pictured at Salins in April 1923. The substantial up-armouring compared to that of the normal Lancia armoured troop carriers is evident, as are the special flanged wheels fitted for railway use. The car was also fitted with a high speed reverse gear. (Peter Leslie)*

*A Lancia armoured lorry being converted at the Inchicore Works for assignment to the Railway Protection, Repair, and Maintenance Corps. This is one of possibly two such vehicles mounting a turret, capable of traveling on rails, and was used for protection of the railway lines in 1923. (NPA/NLI HOG 101, Courtesy of the National Library of Ireland)*

upon disbanding the RPR&MC, all of the railway Lancias, with the exception of AL 51, were sent to the Inchicore works where their railway wheels were removed, and normal wheels were fitted. Presumably, standard axles were also retrofitted. They were subsequently sent to Gormanstown Camp in December 1923. It should be noted that the armoured Lancias formed only a part of the RPR&MC's armoured inventory. In addition to the Lancias that were modified for railway use, more substantial protection was represented by nine armoured trains based at seven separate locations[5] throughout Ireland.

All of the Lancias were retired from Irish Army service and disposed of by November 1937, although of the at least 70 that remained in Northern Ireland after the creation of the Free State in 1922, many continued to serve with the Royal Ulster Constabulary until the 1960s. One Lancia Triota, with spurious British Army markings (the Lancias, it will be recalled, were issued to the Royal Irish Constabulary, not to the British Army), was restored privately in the UK but has been acquired by the Italian Army's Motor Museum near Rome, where it is presently located.

5   The train numbers, location, and composition were as follows: No. 1 at Clonmel (one armoured locomotive, one partially armoured boxcar, and two flatcars); No. 2 at Thurles (one armoured locomotive, two fully armoured cars, one boxcar, and one flatcar); No. 3 at Limerick (one armoured locomotive, two fully armoured cars, and two flatcars); No. 4 at Cork (one armoured locomotive, two fully armoured cars, one partially armoured boxcar, and two flatcars); No. 5 at Cork (one armoured locomotive, one fully armoured wagon and one flatcar); No. 6 at Cork (one armoured locomotive, one fully armoured car, and one flatcar); No. 7 at Dublin (one armoured locomotive and two fully armoured cars); No. 8 at Dundalk (one partially armoured locomotive and two fully armoured cars); No. 9 at Mullingar (one armoured locomotive, two fully armoured cars, and an additional separate armoured locomotive).

## Lancia Triota Specifications:

| | |
|---|---|
| Manufacturer: | Lancia 1920-1921 truck chassis; armoured body built in Ireland (possibly Belfast and Inchicore, Dublin) |
| Dates of service (Irish Defence Forces): | 1921-1932 (?) |
| Number in Irish service: | Uncertain; estimates vary from 64 to 111 |
| Crew: | 3 (plus up to 9 troops in rear troop compartment) |
| Combat weight: | 9237 lbs (4190 kg) |
| Armament: | One .303 in. Lewis light machine-gun; additional Lewis guns may have been carried on occasion |
| Ammunition capacity: | NA |
| Engine: | Lancia Tipo 64 4-cylinder side-valve gasoline, 4940cc<br>Horsepower: 70 BHP @ 2200 rpm |
| Transmission: | Manual; 4-speed (?) |
| Fuel capacity: | 22 Imperial gallons (100 litres; 26.4 US gallons) |
| Maximum speed (road): | 37 mph (60 km/h) |
| Operating radius (road): | 249 miles (400 km) |
| Armour: | 6mm |
| Length: | 206 inches (5232mm)* |
| Width: | 102 inches (2590mm)* |
| Height: | 84 inches (2134mm) |
| Tire size: | 895 x 135 (twin rear) |
| Wheelbase: | 132 inches (3350mm) |
| Track: | 55 inches (1400mm) (possibly 56 inches/1430mm) |
| Ground clearance: | NA |
| Trench crossing: | No capability |

\* Dimensions for Triota Mod. 1920-21 truck chassis

*Interior of the troop compartment of a Lancia Triota armoured troop carrier. The center-mounted benches oblige the occupants to sit back to back, allowing them easy access to the firing ports. (Pignato)*

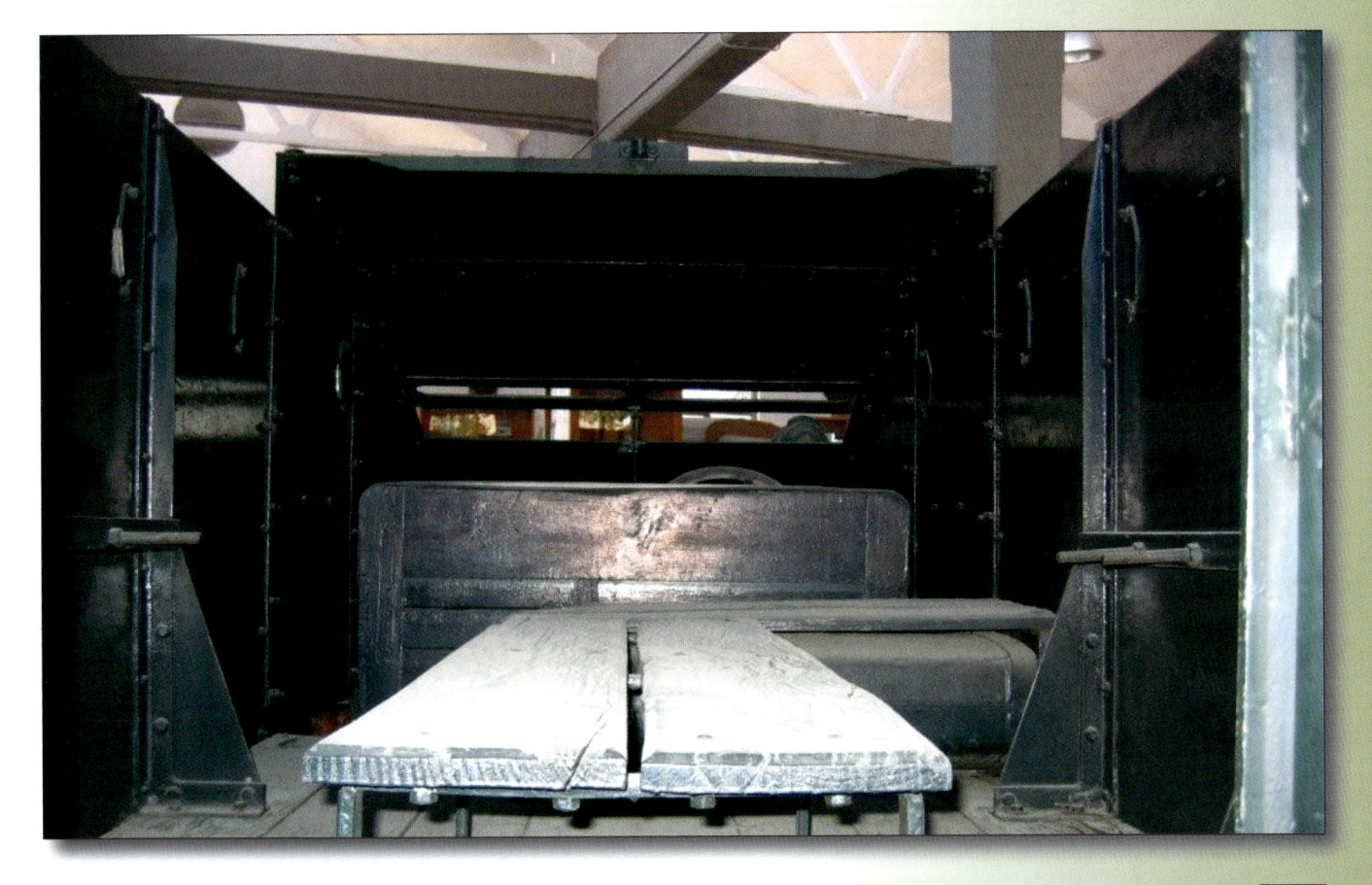

*Lancia Jota. 1/35 scale.*

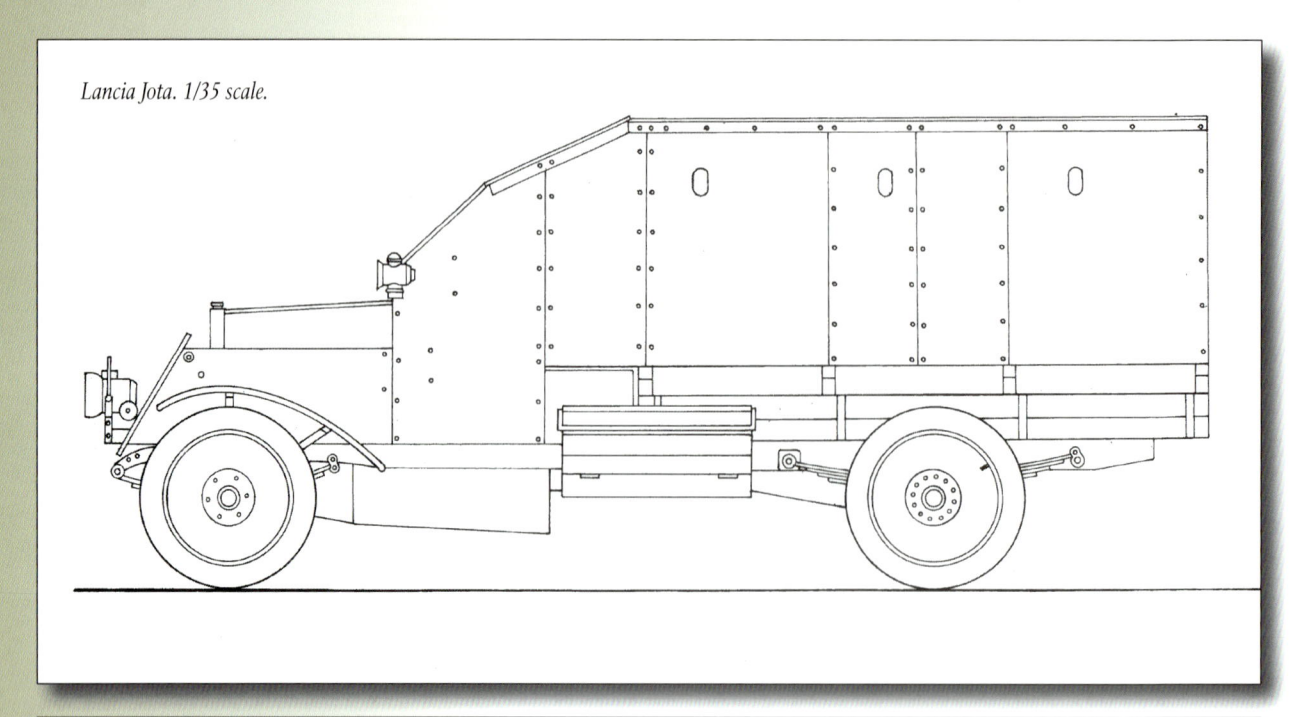

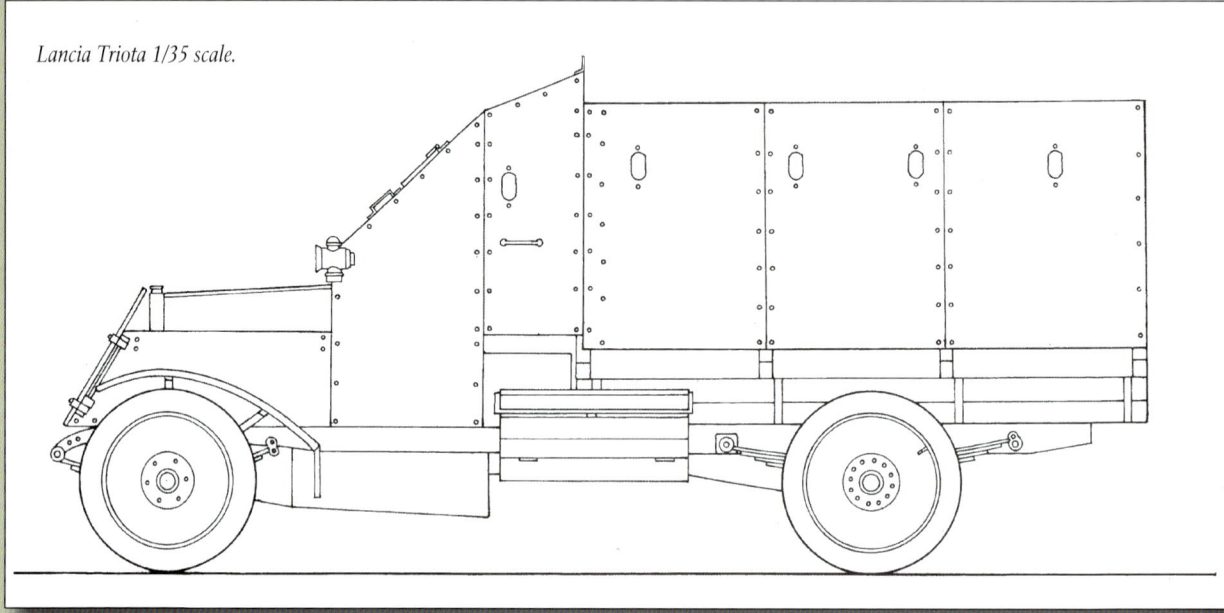

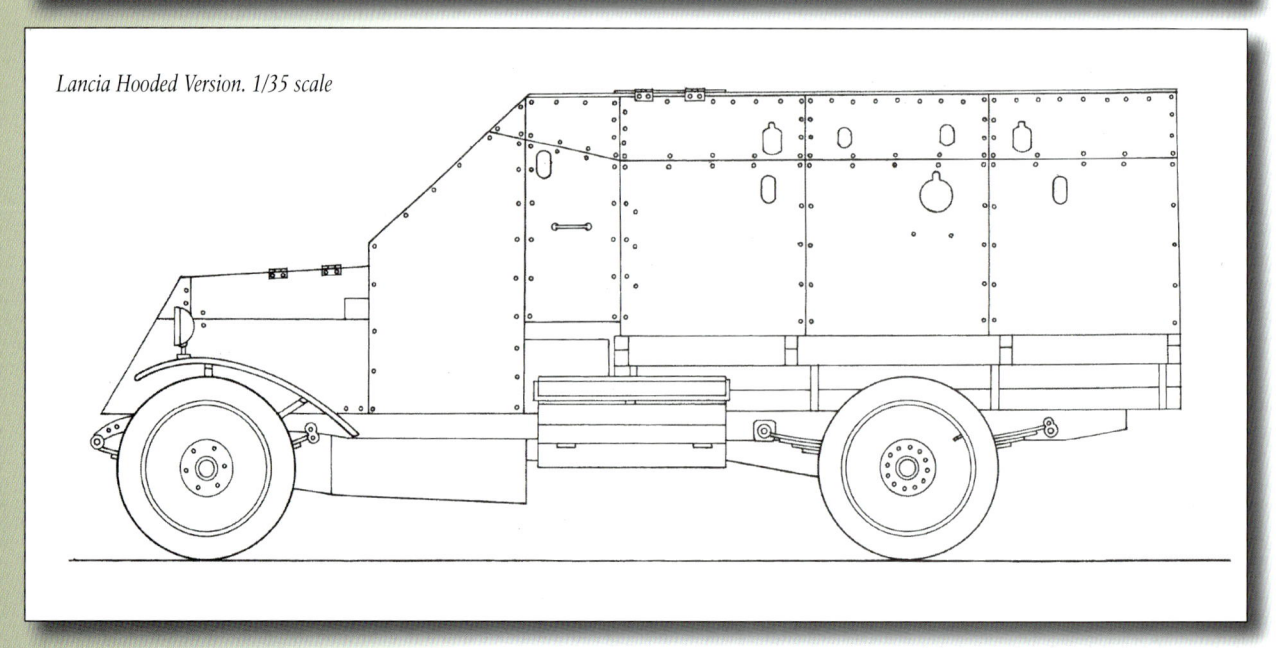

*Lancia Triota 1/35 scale.*

*Lancia Hooded Version. 1/35 scale*

# FIAT ARMOURED CARS

One source[6] indicates that among the vehicles turned over by the departing British to the Provisional Government were ten "Armoured Fiats." These were not armoured cars, but rather were heavy touring cars that were armoured and used to protect Lord French, (Lord Lieutenant of Ireland and Supreme Commander of the British Army in Ireland from May 1918 to April 1921) and other VIPs when traveling. On 19 December, 1919, Lord French's convoy was ambushed by members of the IRA in Ashtown, just to the north of Phoenix Park in Dublin. Lord French escaped with his life. A New York Times newspaper account of the ambush stated that French was traveling in a "Viceregal armoured car" that had "armoured sides".[7] This may have been one of the Fiats. Although specific details and photographs are lacking, these cars were not suited for use as combat vehicles, given their intended purpose as VIP vehicles. their use was extremely limited because they were too heavy and unreliable.[8]

# PARTIALLY ARMOURED VEHICLES

There is some fragmentary photographic evidence hinting that in addition to the armoured vehicles described above, some vehicles were only partially armoured or were fitted with improvised armour. One photograph shows a Crossley tender in British service in Ireland that has had armour plates fitted to provide some protection to the driver; the vehicle has also been fitted with a Lewis gun mounted in the bed behind the driver. Given the considerable number of Crossley tenders handed over by the British (454 according to Karl Martin), it is almost a certainty that a number of them were similarly modified and utilized in Irish service, but specific reference to this type of vehicle in Irish service is lacking.

# LEYLAND ARMOURED CAR

The Leyland armoured car was the brain child of Comdt J.V. Lawless, who in 1931 proposed that the hulls of the obsolete Peerless armoured cars be mounted on a contemporary 6 x 4 truck chassis. The choice fell upon the Leyland Terrier T.E.2, which was a robust chassis designed to British War Office specification. It was not until March 1934 that a Terrier chassis, factory-modified to Irish specification, was delivered to the Army. What originally was envisioned as a rather simple process of mounting a Peerless body on a new truck chassis turned out to be considerably more involved and complicated than expected. The front hull had to be redesigned, while the rest of the body, including the rounded fighting compartment sides and the short rear compartment, were unchanged. The work was carried out in the Cavalry Workshops by Sgt. Paddy Lynch, supervised by Comdt. Lawless and Capt. Mayne. The first version of the Leyland, configured with the twin Peerless turrets, was ready for testing on 10 September, 1934, and was presented to a board of officers for evaluation on 12 February, 1935. The board recommended that the twin turret configuration be replaced by a single turret of more modern design. A further three Leyland Terrier chassis were bought in 1935, and in February 1936 the Department of Defence proposed that the Leyland cars should be equipped with the same turret used on the Swedish Landsverk L 60 tanks that had recently been added to the Irish armour inventory. The 20mm Danish Madsen cannon of the Landsverk turret was a quantum improvement over the .303 in. Hotchkiss machine-guns in the Peerless turrets, not only in firepower but in reliability as well. A .303 in. Madsen coaxial

---

6  Karl Martin, *Irish Army Vehicles*, page 4.
7  *New York Times*, 19 December 1919.
8  The only direct reference the author has been able to uncover to the existence or use of the Fiat armoured car was in a description of cargo carried by the SS Lady Wicklow from Dublin to Limerick between 15 and 17 August, 1922.

*Leyland 1938 1/35 scale.*

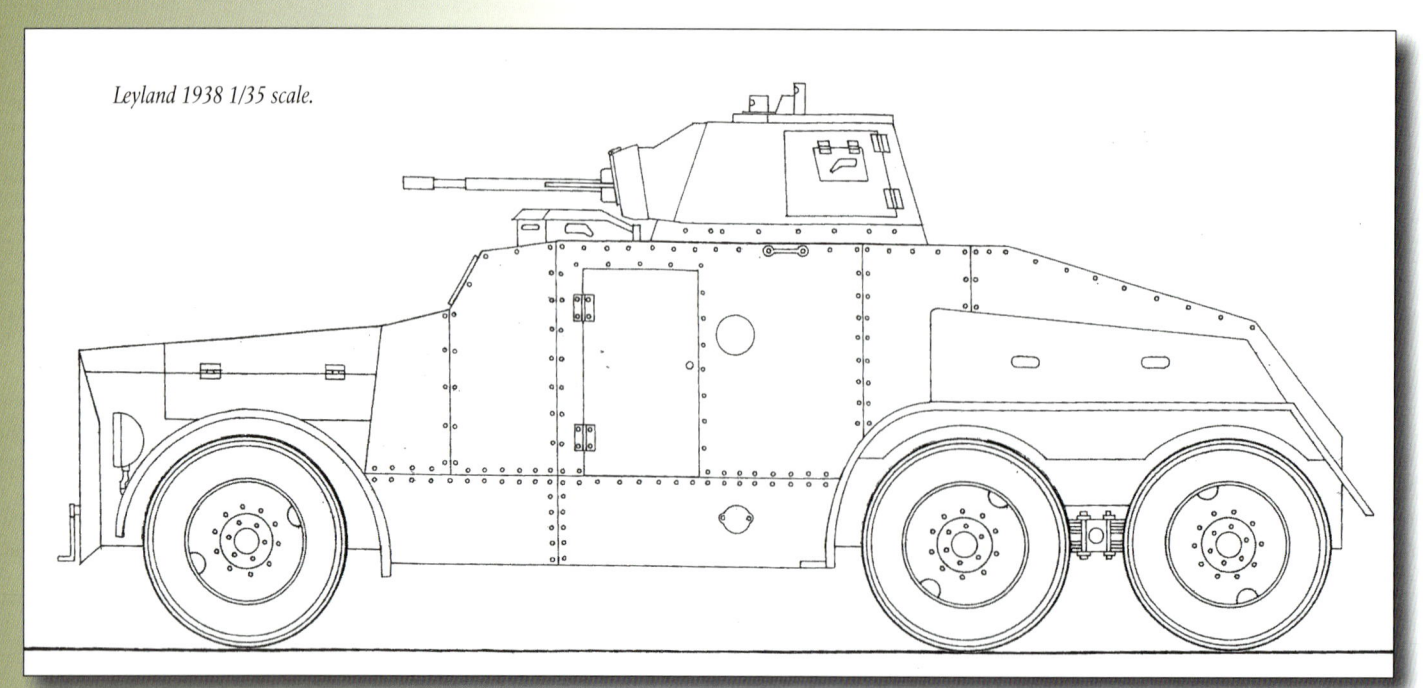

*Leyland ZC 776 in October 1972. Its original .303 Madsen machineguns have been replaced by two .30 caliber Browning machineguns. This vehicle is now located at the National Transport Museum in Howth. (Sean O'Sullivan*

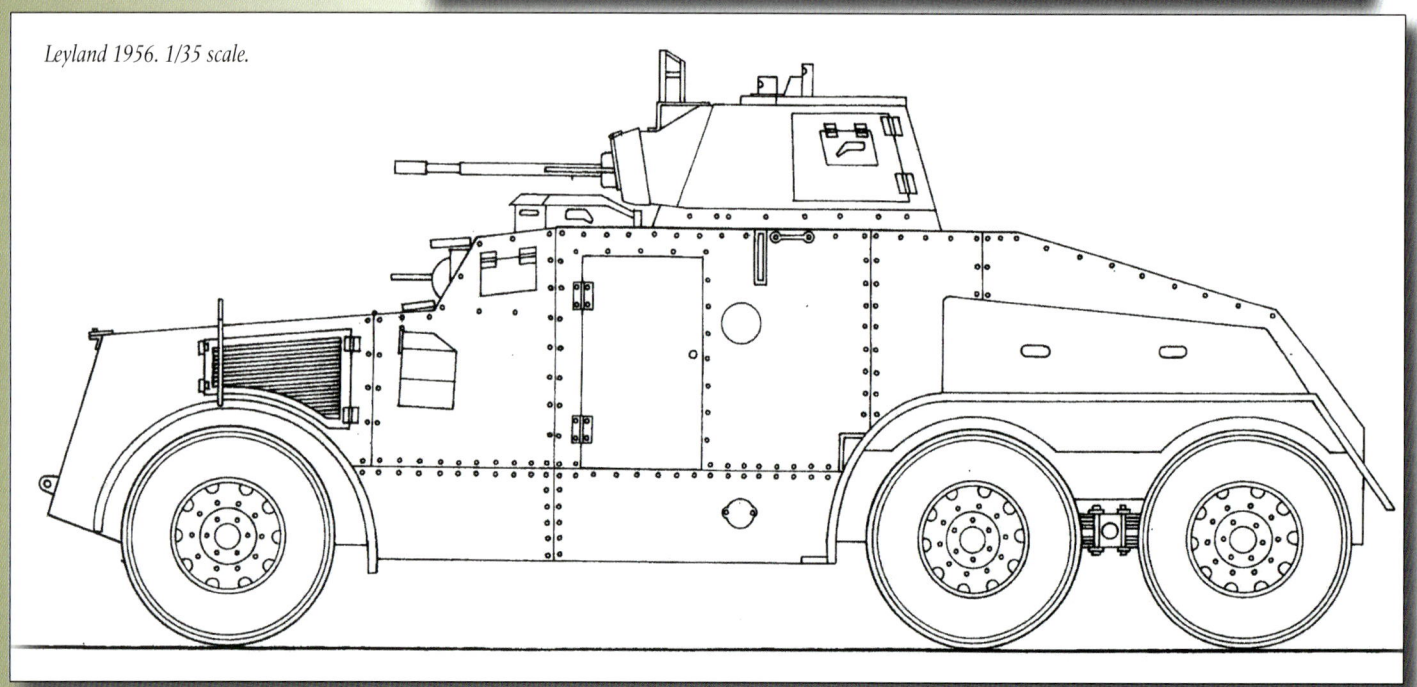

*Leyland 1956. 1/35 scale.*

machine-gun was also fitted. A considerable amount of strengthening and modification was necessary to adapt the vehicles to mount the new Landsverk turret. Comparison of photographs of the Peerless cars with those of the early version of the Leyland show noticeable differences in the hull configuration, the most apparent differences being a slab-sided hull rather than the rounded hull of the Peerless, and a much elongated rear compartment, partially due to the 6 x 4 configuration, and partly due to the fact that the Peerless hull did not extend the full length of the Peerless chassis, even though the Peerless chassis was nearly as long as that of the Terrier. Construction of the first modified car commenced in July 1937; the second car was completed in May 1938, and all four were in service by July 1939. They were assigned to the 1st Armoured Squadron and remained in service with that squadron until May 1940, when it was disbanded to provide armoured cars to the newly formed Motor Squadrons. In 1942 they were returned to the Curragh, and along with the Landsverk L 180s and the Dodge armoured cars, formed a heavy armoured car squadron (1st Armoured Squadron). In 1957 the Leylands were upgraded by installing the same Ford V-8 engine used to upgrade the L 180 cars during the same timeframe, as well as reconfiguring the front of the vehicle in a fashion closely resembling that of the L 180 Landsverk armoured cars then in Irish service. Other changes made at the time included replacing the turret-mounted Madsen machine-gun with a .30 caliber Browning machine-gun, fitting another .30 caliber Browning next to the driver, adding a driver's door, and modifying the turret hatch. One Leyland (ZC 775) was scrapped in the 1960s, and the other three Leylands were withdrawn from front-line service in 1972, but remained in Irish service with 5 Motor Squadron until the 1980s. They were definitively withdrawn from service in 1987. Two of the Leylands still survive in museums - the first (ZC 774) has been restored at the Tank Museum in Bovington, England, and the second (ZC 776) is in the Transport Museum in Howth, Ireland.

*Static photograph of ZC 773 on display at a gathering in the Curragh in 2006. Comparison with photographs of the Landsverk L 180 show the unmistakable influence that the Swedish vehicle had on the design of the Leyland. (Bob Cantwell)*

## LEYLAND SPECIFICATIONS:

| | |
|---|---|
| Manufacturer: | Leyland Terrier 6 x 4 chassis; armoured body fabricated in Ireland (in Cavalry workshops) |
| Dates of service (Irish Defence Forces): | 1938 to the 1980s |
| Number in Irish service: | 4 |
| Crew: | 4 |
| Combat weight: | 19,600 lbs (8890 kg) |
| Armament: | 20mm Madsen L.60 anti-tank gun and two .303 in. Madsen machine-guns |
| Ammunition capacity: | 240 rounds 20mm; 3500 rounds .303 inch |
| Engine: | Original Leyland Terrier 6-cylinder gasoline replaced by Ford Type 317 V-8 gasoline (5198cc) in 1957 (Horsepower: 62 (Leyland); 155 (Ford) |
| Transmission: | NA |
| Fuel capacity: | 26.4 Imperial gallons (31.7 US gallons; 120 litres) |
| Maximum speed (road): | 45 mph (72 km/h) |
| Operating radius (road): | 150 miles (242 km) |
| Armour: | 7-8mm hull; 15mm turret front |
| Length: | 251 inches (6375mm) |
| Width: | 87 inches (2210mm) |
| Height: | 96 inches (2438mm) |
| Tire size: | 750 x 20 |
| Wheelbase: | 119 inches (3015mm) |
| Track: | 68 inches (1730mm) |
| Ground clearance: | 9 inches (225mm) |
| Trench crossing: | No capability |

*Leyland ZC 773 restored and maintained by the Cavalry Corps in the Curragh. It mounts dummy armament. (Sean O'Sullivan)*

# LANDSVERK L 180 ARMOURED CAR

As related previously the Irish, apparently ever mindful of budget limitations but at the same time aware of the increasing age of the Rolls-Royce fleet, had decided to try their hand at developing their own armoured car, and did in fact develop the Leyland in a very small number of copies (only four vehicles). However, it soon became apparent that the four Leylands had cost more in terms of money, time, and Cavalry Workshop resources than originally had been envisaged, and that there still was a requirement for additional armoured cars. Consequently, it was decided to explore the possibility of purchasing new armoured cars from abroad. Although there would have been a natural tendency for the Army to look to Britain as a source of new vehicles, their recent experience with Swedish Landsverk products (the L60 tanks and turrets for the Leyland cars) prompted them to send a delegation consisting of Comdt. Lawless and Major Lawlor to Copenhagen in December 1936 to examine the Landsverk L 180 armoured car. The L 180 was based on a Swedish Scania-Vabis 6 x 4 truck chassis, and its main armament consisted of the same 20mm Danish Madsen anti-tank gun mounted on the L 60 tank. The turret and armament fit of the L 180 were the same as those of the L 60 and the Irish-produced Leyland cars. Tires were of bullet-proof resilient rubber, but later in Irish service were replaced by pneumatic tires. The L 180 had a dual-drive layout enabling rapid withdrawals to be made without exposing the flanks of the vehicle to enemy fire while making a turn to reverse direction. A rear-firing machine-gun was also operated by the second driver. The dual-drive layout was not new to the Irish (it was a standard feature of the Peerless cars). The officers were favorably impressed, resulting in an order in March 1937 for two of the Landsverk armoured cars. Cost of the order was £12,000, plus £900 for supply and installation of two Gambrel radio sets. These two cars were delivered in early 1938; in the meantime, a further six cars were ordered in October 1937 and were delivered in early 1939. Despite the realization that there was a pressing need for a further tranche of similar cars, a contract for an additional five cars and much-needed spare parts was not signed with Landsverk until late June 1939. Unfortunately for the Irish Army, although a deposit of £22,005 had been paid and a year later the cars were in Sweden, ready for delivery, the worsening international political situation

*A Landsverk L 180 in two-tone camouflage scheme, with its Madsen machinegun mounted on the turret mounting for AA defence. The L 180's crew of five included a radio operator who doubled as a rear driver; the car was equipped with a dual-drive feature that allowed it to reverse direction without turning the car around. (MA IAC C-154/PTO5)*

*A pair of Landsverk L 180 cars passing in review in front of the Taoiseach (Prime Minister), Eamon de Valera, in Dublin in 1942. Their paint scheme is the dark grey-green over light grey. Note that the gun barrels are lowered in deference to the Prime Minister. (MA/N/352)*

*An overhead view of ZC 5838 during the course of a parade, circa 1942. The front of ZC 5837 is visible behind the lead car. (MA, Cavalry Collection)*

effectively precluded final payment by Ireland and delivery by the Swedes, who had strong German connections. The five cars were eventually transferred to the Royal Swedish Army in 1942, and the deposit, plus interest, was refunded. The eight Landsverk cars that had been delivered were assigned to the 1st Armoured Squadron in the Curragh, where they served until 1972, at which time they were transferred to the 11th Motor Squadron. In 1957, the L 180s were upgraded and modernized by replacing the original Büssing-Nag engine with a Ford V-8,[9] as well as replacing the original 20mm Madsen gun with a 20mm Hispano-Suiza cannon and the Madsen machine-guns with .30 caliber Browning machine-guns. Despite being a newer weapon, the Hispano-Suiza cannon did not work out very satisfactorily. Its standard rate of fire of 600 rpm had to be reduced to 150 rpm to work in the Landsverk; this modification, however, caused a high incidence of jamming. Overall, however, the L 180 performed extremely well throughout its career in Irish service, serving with reserve units (3 and 11 FCA Motor Squadrons) until the mid 1980s. The first to be delivered (ZC 757) is preserved at the Curragh Camp, and ZC 758 was presented to the Dutch Army in November 1982. In 1998, ZC 5837 was transferred to the Swedish Army in exchange for a Scania SKPF m/42 APC. ZC 5838 has been preserved, and is located at the Irish Transport Museum in Howth, and one (possibly ZC 5842) was purchased by a private collector in Ardfert, Ireland in 2002 as a rusting hulk, who partially restored it, and then sold it to a Dutch collector in February 2005. The Dutch owner is in the process of restoring it as an M38 Pantserwagen (the Dutch version of the L180). This represents a remarkable survival rate (over 60%) for these vehicles.

*Landsverk ZC 5837 complete with pioneer tools. The open driver's vision port on the left-hand side of the vehicle reflects the left-hand driver's position, atypical for Ireland; vehicles in Irish service normally are fitted with right-hand drive in conformity with Irish vehicle codes and practice. (Sean O'Sullivan)*

*A Landsverk on exercise in the Glen of Imaal. The commander is wearing the distinctive Glengarry used by the Irish Cavalry Corps. (Matt McNamara)*

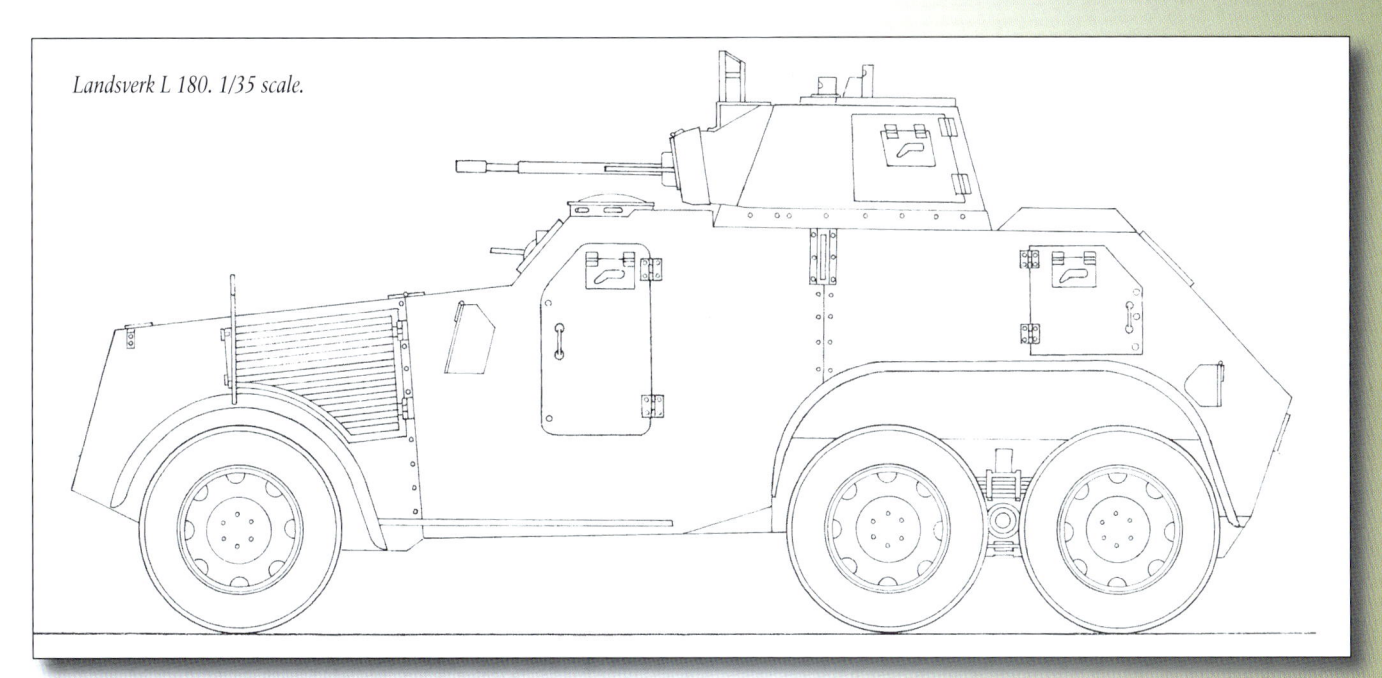

---

9 The Ford 317 V-8 was marketed as a Lincoln engine in the US. It was Ford's earliest overhead valve V8 engine, introduced by Lincoln in 1952, and was known as the Y-block engine.

*Landsverk L 180. 1/35 scale.*

## Landsverk L 180 Specifications:

| | |
|---|---|
| Manufacturer: | AB Kockums Landsverk, Landskrona, Sweden |
| Dates of service (Irish Defence Forces) | 1937 to 1982 |
| Number in Irish service: | 8 |
| Crew: | 5 (commander, 2 drivers, 2 gunners) |
| Combat weight: | 17,694 lbs (8026 kg) |
| Armament: | Originally fitted with one 20mm Madsen L.60 anti-tank gun and two 303 in. Madsen machine-guns; 20mm Madsen replaced by 20mm Hispano-Suiza HS.404 cannon in 1974 |
| Ammunition capacity: | 300 rounds 20mm; 2800 rounds .303 |
| Engine: | Original Büssing-Nag 7900cc V-8 replaced by Ford V-8 5195cc gasoline engine in 1956/1957 |
| Horsepower: | 160 (Büssing-Nag); 155 (Ford) |
| Transmission: | 5-speed manual |
| Fuel capacity: | 29.4 Imperial gallons (120 litres; 31.7 US gallons) |
| Maximum speed (road): | 36 mph (60km/h) |
| Operating radius (road): | 186 miles (300 km) |
| Armour: | 5mm hull; 9mm turret; 15mm turret mantlet |
| Length: | 231 inches (5860mm) |
| Width: | 88 inches (2240mm) |
| Height: | 90 inches (2285mm) |
| Tire size: | Dunlop 7.50 x 20 |
| Wheelbase: | 160 inches (4065mm) overall: 119 inches (3015mm) front axle to second axle, plus 41inches (1050mm) second axle to third axle |
| Track: | 68 inches (1730mm) front |
| Ground clearance: | 10.5 inches (268mm) |
| Trench crossing: | No capability |

*A 1983 photograph of a Landsverk L 180 upgraded with a 20m Hispano=Suiza cannon and a .30 caliber Browning machinegun, replacing the original Madsen weapons. Five of the eight L 180s were upgraded with the new weapons in about 1974. Although the Hispano cannon was a more modern weapon than the 20mm Madsen, the guns on the Irish vehicles originally had been mounted on Irish Air Corps jet trainers and did not perform satisfactorily when modified for use in the armoured cars. (By kind permission of Karl Martin)*

*Left side view of the restored L 180 at the Curragh in May 2005. Its imposing bulk is evident compared to the AML 60 parked beside it. (Terry Ward)*

*L 180 ZC 5839 in September 2002, during a parade for the 80th anniversary of the Cavalry Corps. It is in olive drab livery that began to be used in the 1960s. (Curragh History Group)*

*A Landsverk L 180 in rather pitiful condition at Curragh Camp, date unknown, but probably around 2000. This car (ZC 5842) is likely the car that was bought by a private collector in Ireland in 2002, was partially restored, then sold to a Dutch collector who as of 2009 was restoring it to a Dutch M38 Pantserwagen configuration. (Sean O'Sullivan)*

# GSR MORRIS AND GSR FORD MK IV ARMOURED CARS

The Mk IV armoured car had its origins as a supplementary vehicle designed for airport protection and security duties. Due to insufficient Cavalry Corps armoured resources, in June 1940, less than a month after the German Army crossed into France, impetus was given to a plan to develop improvised armoured cars using second-hand truck chassis. Possibly inspired by memories of the earliest improvised armoured vehicles built in Ireland by the British in 1916 to deal with the Easter Rising, the use of locomotive boiler barrels large enough for a driver and two-man machine-gun crew was considered. Although it was determined that seven boilers were available at the Great Southern Railway (GSR) Works at Inchicore (the railways in Ireland had been consolidated in 1925, and the GWS&R had become the GSR), the GSR was also able to provide case hardened mild steel, ultimately used in the construction of the first Mk IV car. A letter written by Major Lawless

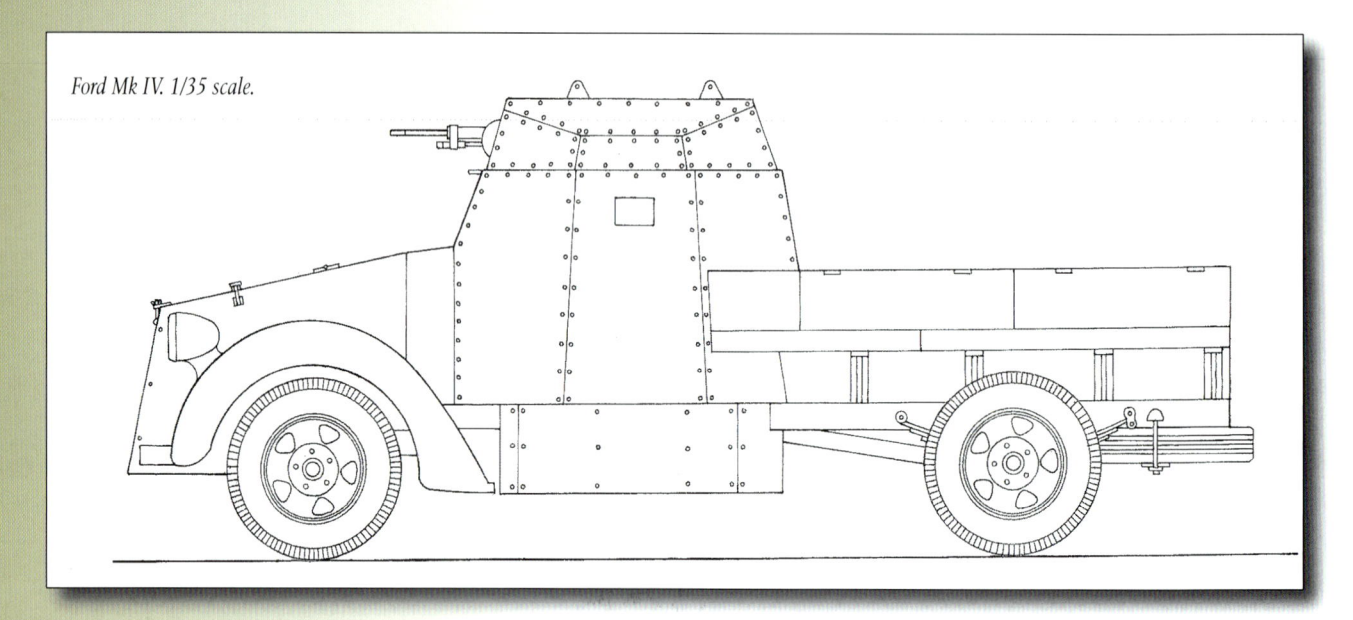

*Ford Mk IV. 1/35 scale.*

indicated that fifteen firms had been visited in search of suitable trucks, but only a few had second-hand vehicles that met the required parameters, and that the firm of Poole of Westland Row was the only firm that was able to supply the requisite quantity of vehicles.[10] The design of the vehicle was based on the overall layout of the Rolls-Royce armoured cars then in service in Ireland; rather than being built with a circular body, however, the body was designed as a tapering octagonal pyramid. The vehicle selected to serve as the basis for the prototype car was a second-hand 1934 Morris-Commercial SWB two-ton truck with dual rear wheels. It was stripped of its body and cab, and work on the armoured body began. The case hardened steel, however, could not be welded and had to be drilled with holes so that the plates could be welded to a steel frame. Although no plans or photographs exist of the vehicle, reportedly it appeared to be somewhat of a hybrid of the Rolls-Royce armoured car and the Landsverk L 180 car, with the front of the car resembling the Landsverk and the rear resembling that of the Rolls. Its armoured crew and engine compartments were of riveted construction. The car had no turret, the machine-gun being fired through loopholes. The GSR Morris Mk IV turned out to be underpowered and too heavy for its chassis, but was judged nevertheless to be a successful experiment, paving the way for the subsequent GSR Ford Mk IV armoured car. The Morris Mk IV survived until 1946, when it was disposed of.

The experience gained from the prototype Morris-Commercial Mk IV led to the realization that it would be preferable to build the remaining seven of the eight Mk IVs that were sanctioned on new rather than on used chassis. The choice fell upon the Ford 2-3 ton 4 x 2 chassis with a 134 inch wheelbase. Accordingly, seven Ford chassis, minus cab and body, were ordered. The engine was a

---

10 *Letter dated 7/6/40 from Major Lawless to Secretary (not further identified).*

Ford V-8 developing 85 horsepower. As on the Morris Mk IV, the bodies for the Fords were built by GSR, and included a turret, built by GSR, armed with a .303 in. Hotchkiss machine-gun taken from the Peerless cars. Entrance to the car was through a door in the back of the armoured compartment; the compartment itself was abbreviated and occupied only the front portion of the vehicle. The rear of the vehicle had a flatbed, and long wooden tool chests were mounted on each side of the bed, much the same as the layout of the Rolls-Royce cars. The first Ford Mk IV was completed on 11 September, 1940. Subsequent to inspection and initial testing, a number of modifications were made, including improved arrangements for the driver's and gunner's vision. Tests on the first Ford car also revealed that poor weight distribution resulted in inadequate road holding capabilities; this was remedied by adding a cast iron block[11] to the rear of the vehicle to improve road holding. Although the addition of more than 1000 pounds to the vehicle may have improved road holding, one would suspect that overall handling and performance would have been degraded by the additional weight that taxed both engine and transmission. Ford also modified both the front and rear suspension in an effort to improve road holding. The Mk IVs were delivered in September and October 1940; shortly thereafter the machine-gun, originally fitted with a small gun shield, was installed in a ball mounting. The cars were assigned to the 2nd Armoured Squadron, serving at Collinstown, Baldonnel, and Templemore. In 1954 the cars, stripped of their plating, were sold.

Although the original Morris prototype was disposed of in 1946, the Ford Mk IVs remained in service until 1954, being disposed of in May of that year. The Mk IV designation was assigned to this first model Irish designed and built armoured car, as Mark numbers I, II, and III had been assigned to previous cars in the Irish inventory (to the Rolls-Royce, Leyland, and Landsverk L 180 cars, respectively).

## Ford Mk IV Specifications:

| Manufacturer: | Ford (chassis); Great Southern Railway Company (armoured body) |
|---|---|
| Dates of service (Irish Defence Forces) | 1940-1954 |
| Number in Irish service: | 7 |
| Crew: | 3 |
| Combat weight: | 8062 lbs (3657 kg) |
| Armament: | One Hotchkiss .303 in. machine-gun |
| Ammunition capacity: | NA |
| Engine: | Ford V-8 gasoline, 3621cc |
| Horsepower: | 85 |
| Transmission: | 4-speed manual |
| Fuel capacity: | 15.8 Imperial gallons (19 US gallons; 72 litres) |
| Maximum speed (road): | 35 mph (56 km/h) |
| Operating radius (road): | 120 miles (193 km) |
| Armour: | 3/8 inch |
| Length: | 214 inches (5436mm) |
| Width: | 79 inches (2007mm) |
| Height: | 88 inches (2235mm) |
| Tire size: | 7.00 x 20, 8-ply |
| Wheelbase: | 134 inches (3404mm) |
| Track: | 57 inches (1448mm) front; 65 inches (1651mm) rear |
| Ground clearance: | NA |
| Trench crossing: | No capability |

---

11 *Sources differ as to the weight of the block; Martin cites 10 CWT (1120 lbs), while McCarthy cites 9 CWT (1008 lbs).*

*The Ford Mk IV armoured car (ZD 1525) built by GSR. The angular turret is somewhat similar to that on the Rolls-Royce 1920 Pattern armoured car, which served as the basic pattern for the Mk IV cars. However, rather than replicating the circular body and turret of the Rolls-Royce, likely because fabricating flat plate was easier than curving the plate, the Mk IV was built with a tapering octagonal body and angled turret. The front radiator louver style, used on all of the subsequent Irish Ford armoured cars, was similar to that of Leyland and Landsverk cars, although the Fords used fewer louvers. (MA)*

# FORD MK V ARMOURED CAR

Close on the heels of the GSR Mk IV machines, a new design for a domestically designed and produced armoured car was approved. The vehicle was designed by Commandant J.V. Lawless and Captain Aubrey W. Mayne. Lawless had gained experience with the design of the Leyland car, and had also drawn inspiration from the Rolls-Royce cars used by the Irish Army. The Ford Mk V was significantly different to the earlier Ford Mk IV machine. Mild steel plate was used in construction, enabling the body to be welded rather than riveted as on the contemporary Mk IV cars, resulting in significant cost savings; the Mk V cars cost £320 each, whereas the earlier Mk IV cost almost double, at £580 each. Although the prototype Mk V was built on a 134 inch Ford 4 x 2 chassis, the chassis for the remaining thirteen cars were shortened to 122 inches, enabling weight to be better distributed than on the Mk IVs, with resultant improvement in road holding and handling characteristics. As noted previously, the Peerless turrets originally were considered for mounting on the Leyland cars, but selection of the Landsverk turret for the Leyland resulted in retention by the Cavalry Workshops of the Peerless turrets, which remained available for use. The fourteen turrets thus enabled fourteen Mk Vs to be built. The straight-sided flat-topped turret of the Mark V easily distinguished it from the later Mk VI cars with the Landsverk-type turret. Although the .303 in. Hotchkiss machine-guns originally fitted in the Peerless turrets were obsolete, they remained as the armament of the Mk V cars. Construction of the Mk Vs was contracted to Thomas Thompson and Son, Carlow. The Mk Vs were delivered in 1940 and 1941 and were distributed between the 1st and 2nd Armoured Car Squadrons and the 1st through 4th Motor Squadrons. They were disposed of along with the Mk IV machines in May 1954.

## Ford Mk V Specifications:

| | |
|---|---|
| Manufacturer: | Ford chassis; Thomas Thompson and Son, Carlow fabricated the body |
| Dates of service (Irish Defence Forces): | 1940- 1954 |
| Number in Irish service: | 14 |
| Crew: | 3 (commander, gunner, driver) |
| Combat weight: | 12,432 lbs (5639 kg) (empty weight; estimated) |
| Armament: | .303 in Hotchkiss machine-gun |
| Ammunition capacity: | NA |
| Engine: | Ford V-8 flathead, gasoline, 3621cc (221 cubic inches) |
| Horsepower: | 85 |
| Transmission: | 4-speed manual |
| Fuel capacity: | 15.8 Imperial gallons (19 US gallons; 72 litres) |
| Maximum speed (road): | 45 mph (72 km/h) |
| Operating radius (road): | 150 miles (241 km) |
| Armour: | .5 inch (12.7mm) mild steel |
| Length: | 176 inches (4470mm) |
| Width: | 79 inches (2007mm) |
| Height: | 99 inches (2515mm) |
| Tire size: | 7.00 x 20, 8-ply |
| Wheelbase: | 122 inches (3099mm) |
| Track: | 57 inches (1448mm) front, 65 inches (1651mm) rear |
| Ground clearance: | NA |
| Trench crossing: | No capability |

*A Ford Mk V in the field during an exercise. The distinctive feature of the Mk V cars was the cylindrical Peerless turret. The seven Peerless cars that had been decommissioned, each mounting twin turrets, were able to supply enough turrets to equip the fourteen Mk V cars. (MA)*

*Ford Mk V. 1/35 scale.*

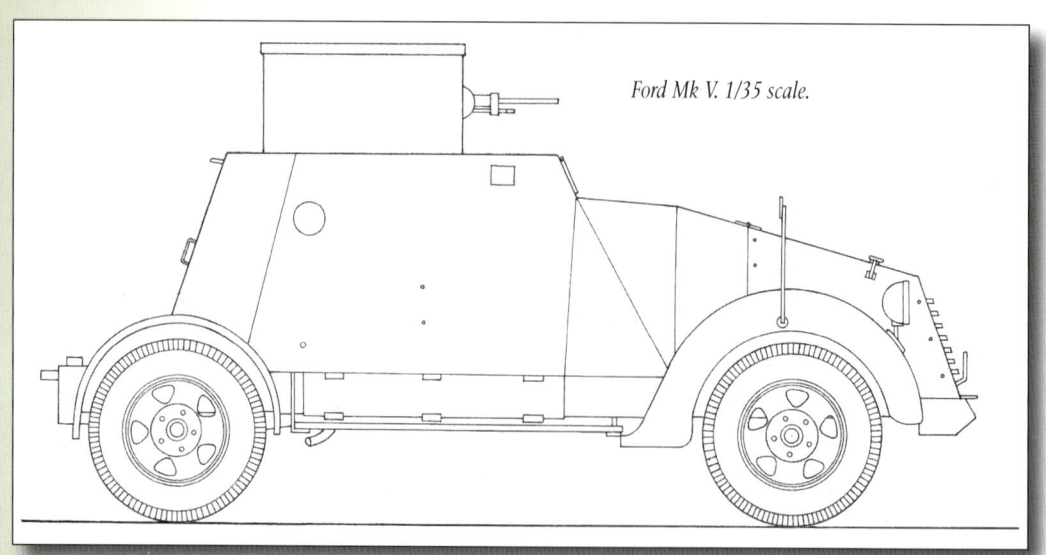

*Four Mk Vs on the assembly line at Thompson's in Carlow. The foremost car already is equipped with pioneer tools and appears to lack only its armament. The second car is nearly complete, while the third and fourth vehicles are chassis only, with no armoured bodies yet applied. (Thompson)*

# FORD MK VI ARMOURED CAR

The Ford Mk V armoured car being deemed a satisfactory design, in January 1941 it was decided to build a further series of 21 cars incorporating several improvements. These cars were needed to bring the 2nd Armoured Squadron up to authorized strength, as well as to allow formation of the 3rd Armoured Squadron. The major difference between the Mk V and Mk VI was fitting a new turret modeled after the Landsverk turret, as the Peerless turrets had all been used on the Mk V cars. The new turret was built by Thomas Thompson and Son of Carlow, and was armed with the reliable .303 in Vickers machine-gun. The Mk VI used the same 122 inch shortened chassis as the earlier Mk V. A second batch of seven Mk VIs was built by the end of 1941, but as new Ford chassis were unavailable, the Army withdrew seven Ford trucks from the Supply and Transport Corps for modification by the Ford factory in Cork. As with the Mk V, the armoured bodies were built and fitted by Thompson. The Ford V-8 engines had a reputation for toughness and reliability. In the words of one squadron commander, "...you could drive them from Hell to Eternity with no problems."[12] A document from June 1942 indicates that four Mk VI cars were assigned to each of the seven Motor Squadrons. Eight of the Mk VIs were dispatched to the Congo for operations there in January 1961. Although the Landsverk cars had been considered for deployment to the Congo, it was decided to send the Mk VIs instead, as they were more supportable and there were more trained crews for the Fords. Perhaps in preparation for deployment to the Congo, in January 1961, a series of tests were

---

12 Donal MacCarron, *Step Together*, page 41.

*Ford Mk VI. 1/35 scale.*

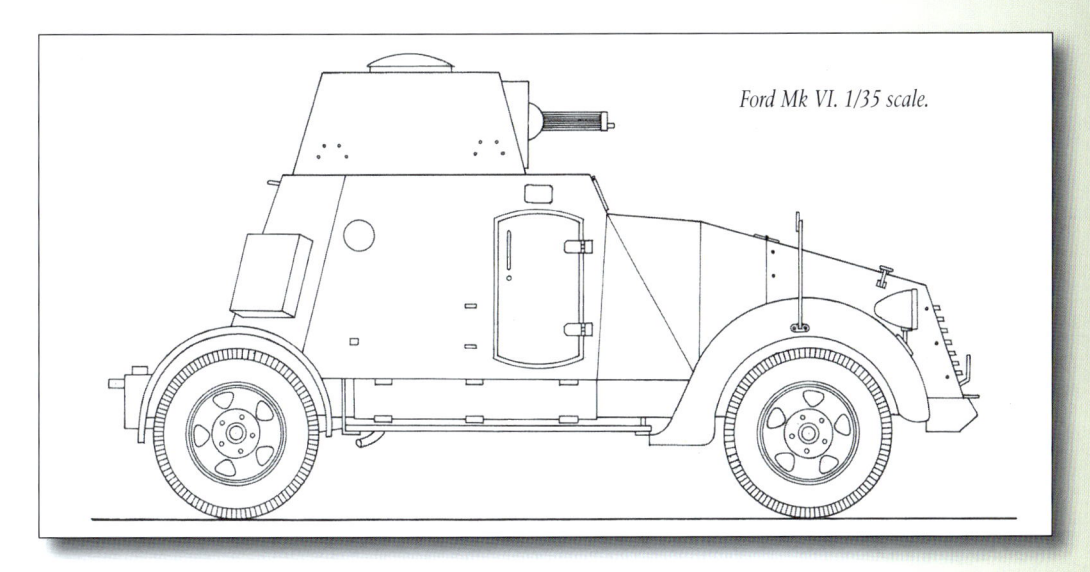

carried out at the Glen of Imaal to determine how effective the armour of the Mk VI was against various types of rifle rounds. The tests showed that the armour was proof against ordinary .303 ball ammunition at any range, and against .303 armour-piercing ammunition at any range above 200 yards, and that there was no flaking or spalling on the inner side of the plating. Prior to departure for the Congo, a number of modifications were made, including fitting a seat for the commander and providing extra storage for the machine-gun ammunition. Once in the Congo itself, additional modifications were made including installation of an interior cooling system to protect the crews from heat exhaustion, and mounting a searchlight on the roof for night operations. In June 1961, a further three Mk VIs were sent to the Congo with the 35th Battalion, for a total of eleven cars. Two of these three cars were converted to scout cars by removing their turrets and welding a steel "collar," about 6 inches high, around the roof opening. A Bren gun on a pintle mount was fixed to the collar. The Brens were later replaced by .30 caliber Browning machine-guns, but overall, the conversion was not reported as being satisfactory. Considering the age and limitations of the Mk VIs, they performed creditably in the Congo, in no small measure due to the efforts of their crews. When the Irish Army left the Congo after hostilities ceased, they handed over six operational Mk VIs to the Congolese Army. The remaining Mk VIs in Ireland were retained in service until replaced by Panhards and were used for border patrols from 1969 until retirement in the early 1970s. One of the Mk VIs was retained by the Army in the Curragh as a museum piece, the remainder were auctioned off. Three appear to have been sold to museums or collectors in England; one has subsequently been returned to Ireland and is the property of the National Museum at Collins Barracks in Dublin.

*Two Ford Mk VI cars in the Thompson yard in Carlow. The cars are complete except for their armament that still has to be fitted. The Thompson firm produced the vast majority of Ireland's domestically produced armoured cars (almost 80%); the Mark VI accounted for almost half the total of all armoured cars produced in Ireland between 1934 and 1943. (Thompson)*

*Top left: Ford Mk VI ZD 1768 at Curragh Camp in 1967. At the time of this photograph, what remained of the Mk VI fleet was either non-operational or was nearing the end of its service life. (Peter Leslie)*

*Top right: ZD 1761 in service. The Ford Mk VI cars were produced in greater numbers than any other armoured car produced in Ireland, and were a key element in the Irish Cavalry Corps inventory during World War II. (Sean O'Sullivan)*

*Right: The Cobbaton Collection's Mk VI as it appeared in olive drab livery prior to being repainted in UN white livery. Its armament is missing. This is only one of two documented surviving Mk VIs. (Preston Isaac)*

*Bottom left: The Ford Mk VI from the Cobbaton Combat Collection in North Devon, England, in white UN ONUC (Congo) livery; note that a dummy Vickers gun has been installed. (Preston Isaac)*

*Bottom right: ZD 1768 at Curragh Camp in 1967. This was one of the few remaining Mark VI cars following the deployment to the Congo. Armament is missing, and the headlights are damaged. (Peter Leslie)*

*ZD 1779 photographed in 1969. During this period, the Mk VIs that were still serviceable were pressed into duty for patrols along the border with Northern Ireland. (Peter Leslie)*

*Ford Mk VI ZD 1844 at a parade in September 2002. This vehicle belongs to the Cavalry Corps and is one of two surviving Mk VIs. It is not fitted with armament, either real or dummy. The vehicle is painted in a gloss olive drab finish rather than a more correct matte finish, primarily for ease of maintenance. (Curragh History Group)*

*Old and new: A Ford Mk VI parked next to a Mowag Piranha. Sixty years of automotive technology, design, and development stand in rather stark contrast to each other. (Paul Murphy)*

*Ford Mk VI ZD 1760 at the Cobbaton Combat Collection in white UN livery prior to its return to Ireland. This is the vehicle presently (in 2009) housed at the National Museum of Ireland's Collins Barracks, Dublin location. (Preston Isaac)*

*Right side view of ZD 1844, 2 July, 2009. The general configuration of the Ford cars is strongly reminiscent of the layout of the Rolls-Royce 1920 Pattern armoured car which in fact inspired the original design of the Ford cars. (Terry Ward)*

## Ford Mark VI Specifications:

| | |
|---|---|
| Manufacturer: | Ford chassis; Thomas Thompson and Son, Carlow, fabricated the body |
| Dates of service (Irish Defence Forces): | 1941 - 1970s |
| Number in Irish service: | 28 |
| Crew: | 3 (commander, gunner, driver) |
| Combat weight: | 12,432 lbs (5639 kg) (empty weight; estimated) |
| Armament: | Vickers .303 in. machine-gun (water-cooled) |
| Ammunition capacity: | NA |
| Engine: | Ford V-8 flathead, gasoline, 3621cc (221 cubic inches) |
| Horsepower: | 85 |
| Transmission: | 4-speed manual |
| Fuel capacity: | 15.8 Imperial gallons (19 US gallons; 72 litres) |
| Maximum speed (road): | 45 mph (72 km/h) |
| Operating radius (road): | 150 miles (241 km) |
| Armour: | .5 inch (12.7mm) mild steel |
| Length: | 178 inches (4521mm) |
| Width: | 79 inches (2007mm) |
| Height: | 96 inches (2438mm) |
| Tire size: | 7.00 x 20, 8-ply |
| Wheelbase: | 122 inches (3099mm) |
| Track: | 57 inches (1448mm) front, 65 inches (1651mm) rear |
| Ground clearance: | NA |
| Trench crossing: | No capability |

# DODGE MK VII AND DODGE MK VIII ARMOURED CARS

A contemporary of the Irish Ford armoured cars, the Dodge 4 x 2 "heavy" armoured car was developed in 1941, because of the inability to procure the additional Landsverk L 180 cars desired by the Irish Army. The car was designed by the team of Col. J.V. Lawless and Commandant A.W. Mayne who earlier had been responsible for design of the Ford Mk V armoured car. The car in fact resembled the hull of the Ford, while the turret was an Irish copy of the Landsverk turret as used on the L60, L 180, and Leyland. The chassis selected was that of the Dodge TF-37 truck whose 160-inch wheelbase had been shortened to 135 inches and whose front leaf springs had been strengthened. As with the Ford armoured cars, the body of the Dodge was built by Thomas Thompson of Carlow, who obtained the necessary plate for the cars from the Irish Sugar Company, also located in Carlow. A total of five Dodges were built, in two versions, two as the Mk VII and three as the Mk VIII. The difference between the versions was in the armament fit, which on the Mk VII consisted of a 20mm Madsen cannon (that had been supplied by the Irish Marine Service) and a Madsen .303 in. machine-gun (although some sources claim that the machine-gun was a Vickers .303), and on the Mk VIII was a Vickers .50 in. water-cooled machine-gun in addition to a Vickers .303 in. water-cooled machine-gun. Although design of the Dodges dated back to late 1941, approval and funding were not obtained until July 1942, and first of the Dodges was not completed until 29 October, 1942. Deliveries were completed in May 1943.

The Dodge cars served their entire careers, from late 1942-early 1943 until the time of their retirement, with the 1st Armoured Squadron. Effective service life seems to have ended in 1955, although it was not until 1962 that the Dodges were actually disposed of. Reportedly the Dodge was popular with its crews, but difficulty in obtaining spares made it uneconomical to keep them in continued service. A suggestion was advanced in 1950 to transfer the Dodge bodies to the chassis of the Mk IV that were being disposed of in 1950, but the proposal was shelved. None have survived.

*A Dodge Mk VIII armoured car in the yard of the Thompson works in Carlow. Note the Thompson placard on the running board. The Mark VII was armed with two Vickers water-cooled machine-guns, one in the standard .303 British small arms caliber, and the other in the heavier .50 inch caliber. It is interesting to note that although fresh from the factory assembly floor, the front fender shows signs of minor damage in two places. (Thompson)*

## Dodge Mark VII and Dodge Mark VIII Specifications:

| | |
|---|---|
| Manufacturer: | Dodge TF-37 truck chassis; body fabricated by Thomas Thompson and Son, Carlow |
| Dates of service (Irish Defence Forces): | 1942-1962 (?) |
| Number in Irish service: | 5 |
| Crew: | 4 |
| Combat weight: | 11,312 lbs (5131 kg) |
| Armament: | 20mm Madsen L.60 anti-tank gun and one Madsen .303 in. machine-gun (Mark VII); one Vickers .50 in. and one Madsen .303 in machine-gun |
| Ammunition capacity: | NA |
| Engine: | Dodge 6-cylinder 228 cubic inch (3700cc) gasoline |
| Horsepower: | 27.3 |
| Transmission: | 4-speed manual |
| Fuel capacity: | NA |
| Maximum speed (road): | 45 mph (72 km/h) |
| Operating radius (road): | 150 miles (241 km) |
| Armour: | ½ inch mild steel |
| Length: | 202 inches (5131mm) |
| Width: | 82 inches (2083mm) |
| Height: | 104 inches (2642mm) |
| Tire size: | NA |
| Wheelbase: | 135 inches (3429mm) |
| Track: | NA |
| Ground clearance: | NA |
| Trench crossing: | No capability |

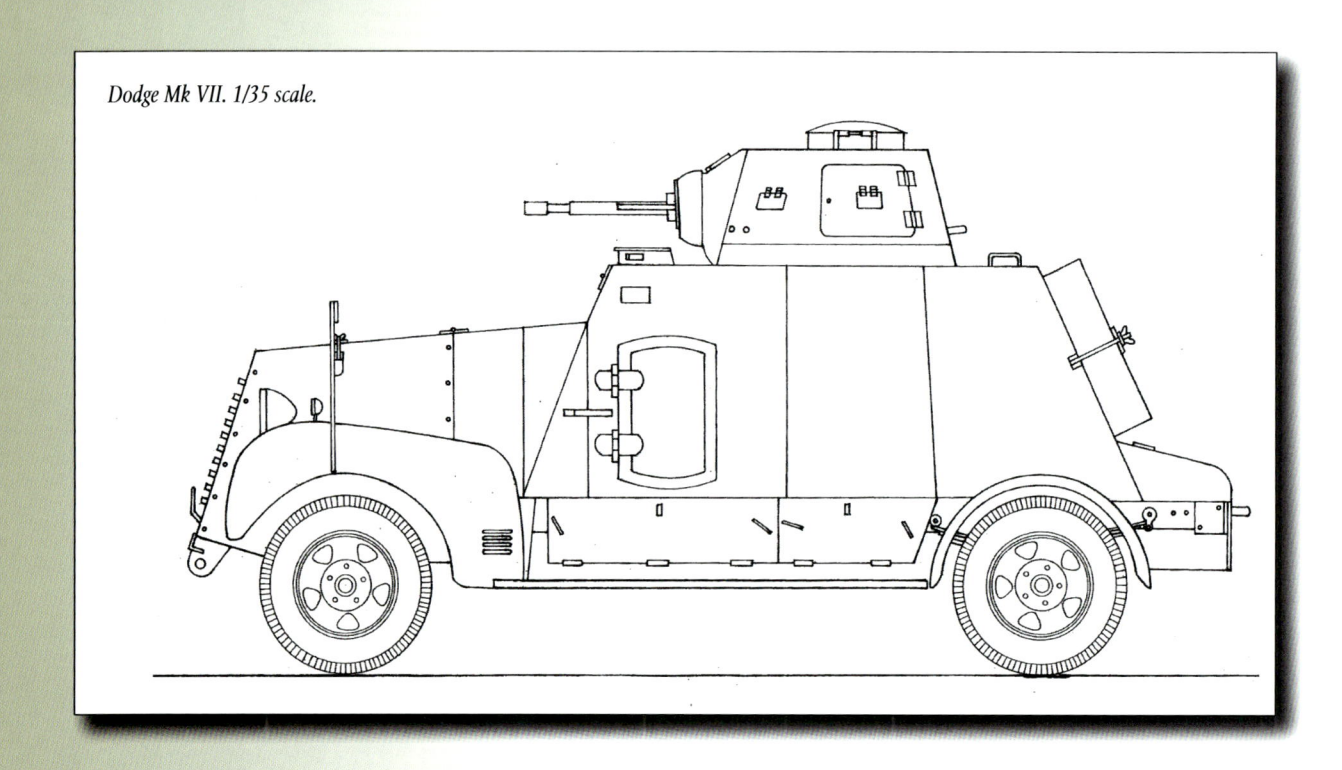

*Dodge Mk VII. 1/35 scale.*

*Dodge Mk VIII. 1/35 scale.*

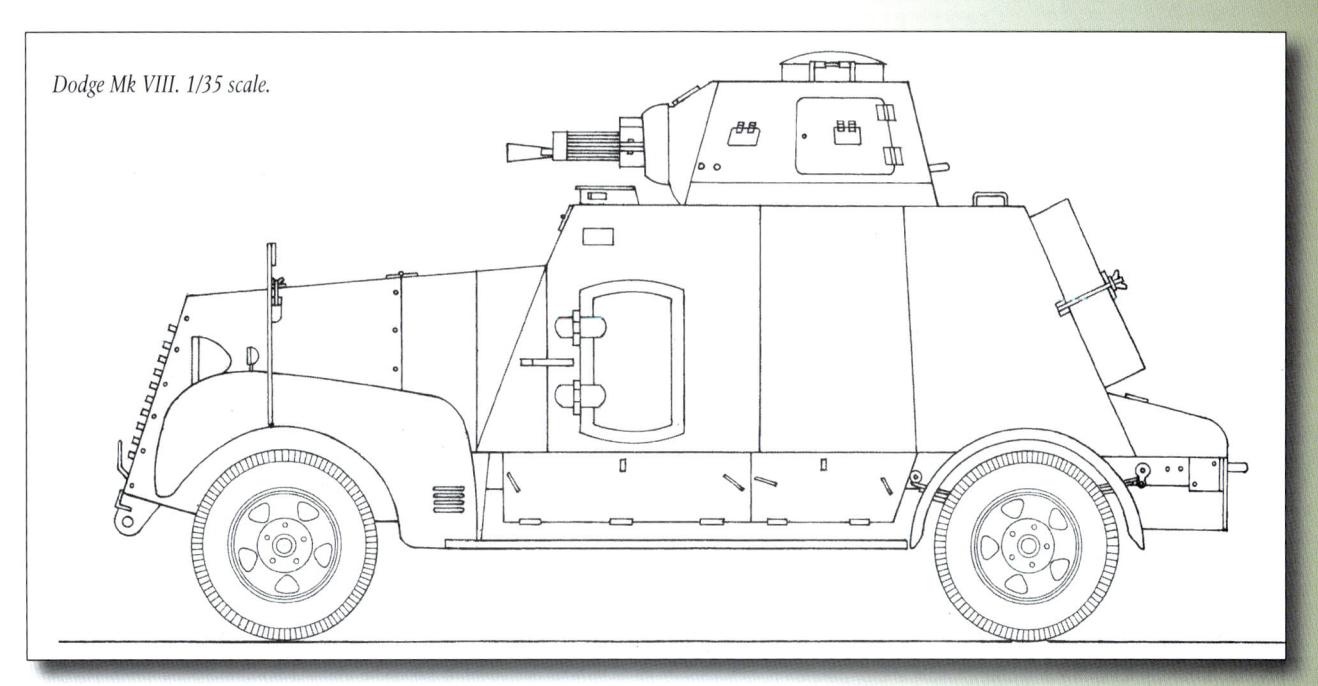

# BEAVERETTE LIGHT ARMOURED CAR SCOUT CAR

Thirty Beaverette light armoured cars were procured by Ireland in 1943 to supplement the armoured vehicle inventory. The Beaverette was a small, very rudimentary armoured vehicle based on a Standard Motor Company 4 x 2 commercial car chassis (a Standard 14 saloon), and produced at the instigation of Lord Beaverbrook (hence the name "Beaverette"), and was much used by the Home Guard in Britain. The "armour" on the Mk I and Mk II consisted of 1/8-inch mild steel plate backed by 2 to 3 inch oak planks reinforcing the frontal armour from behind, while the Mk III and Mk IV versions had more substantial armour plate. Armament normally consisted of a

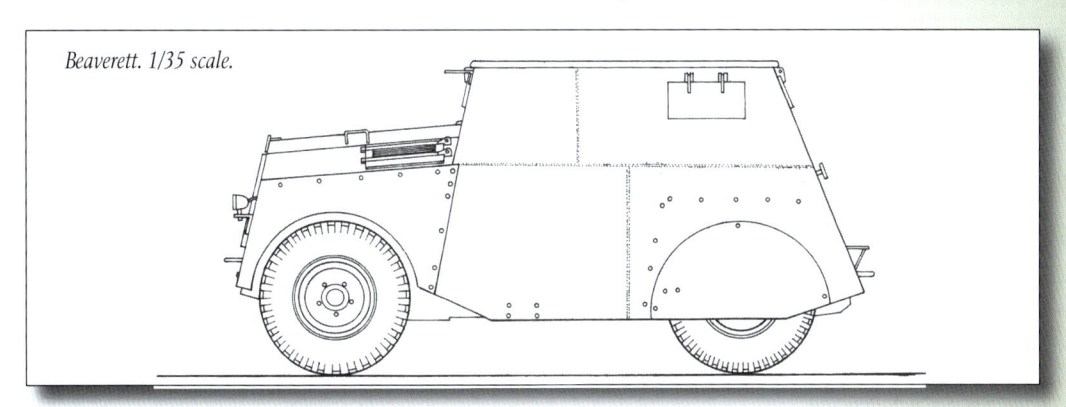

*Beaverett. 1/35 scale.*

Bren light machine-gun. Performance characteristics of the Beaverette were minimal; its top speed was only 20 mph. The vehicle was difficult to drive and handled very poorly; added to this was poor visibility for the driver. The Beaverettes were fitted with 9-inch wide tires to offset the lack of four-wheel drive, but the wider tires increased the vehicle's weight and drag which made steering unpleasant and tiring for the driver. To compensate for the weight and drag, a special reduction gear was introduced into the rear axle; while this ensured full mobility over ideal terrain, it imposed a drastic reduction in overall speed, as well as proving to be fragile and a source of trouble. However inadequate it may have been, and however marginal its capabilities were, it nevertheless was better than nothing at all. It was made in four different Marks; ten Mk III and twenty Mk IV versions were used in Irish service. Seventeen of the Beaverettes (designated as Mk IX armoured cars in Irish service) equipped the 4th Armoured Squadron, which had replaced the Carrier Squadron, and the remaining thirteen were distributed among the Motor Squadrons. The 4th Armoured

Squadron was disbanded at the end of the war, and the Beaverettes parceled out to various units to be used in a variety of training and support roles. Between 1951 and 1953, all of the Beaverettes were converted from light reconnaissance vehicles (fitted with a turret) to open-topped scout cars employed for training purposes. The conversion consisted of removal of the turret and the closed top. Following conversion, four were assigned to the 1st Armoured Car Squadron, and four each to the 3rd, 5th, and 11th Motor Squadrons, with the remaining fourteen being held at the Cavalry Depot. Although they were not held in high regard, they remained in service until 1965 for lack of anything better to fill the role.

## Beaverette Mk IV Specifications:

| | |
|---|---|
| Manufacturer: | Standard Motor Company, Coventry, England |
| Dates of service (Irish Defence Forces): | 1944–1960s |
| Number in Irish service: | 40 (mix of Mk III and Mk IV) |
| Crew: | 3 |
| Combat weight: | 5825 lbs (2642 kg) approximate |
| Armament: | .303 in. Bren gun (?) |
| Ammunition capacity: | NA |
| Engine: | Standard 4-cylinder gasoline |
| Horsepower: | 46 |
| Transmission: | 3-speed manual (?) |
| Fuel capacity: | NA |
| Maximum speed (road): | 24 mph (38 km/h) |
| Operating radius (road): | 186 miles (300 km) |
| Armour: | 12mm maximum |
| Length: | 122 inches (3100mm) |
| Width: | 68 inches (1730mm) |
| Height: | 85 inches (2160mm) |
| Tire size: | 9 inches (229mm) wide |
| Wheelbase: | NA |
| Track: | NA |
| Ground clearance: | NA |
| Trench crossing: | No capability |

*Beaverette ZD 3319 at McKee Barracks, Dublin, in 1967. This is the lone Beaverette to survive in Ireland, and is maintained by the Cavalry Corps as part of its historical vehicle collection. (Peter Leslie)*

*A Mk IV Beaverette on static display in 2006. The use of flat plates throughout bespeaks the simplicity of manufacture. By 1953 all of the Beaverettes, which originally had been fitted with turrets, had had their turrets removed, converting them to scout cars. (Bob Cantwell)*

*A Beaverette secured for transport on a trailer. The 9-inch tires provided a marginal improvement in mobility; their size actually increased drag and slowed the vehicle. (Bob Cantwell)*

*A Beaverette in August, 1974, being prepared for decommissioning. The crane is a Berliet TBU 15CLD 6x6 recovery truck. (Bob Cantwell)*

**101**

*Above: A Beaverette Mk III with its turret shown during an artillery exercise. Three Morris Quad artillery tractors in the background were the prime movers for the modernized 18-pdr field guns. (MA)*

*Right: Rear view of ZD 3319 in 1967. The cramped quarters of the vehicle can be appreciated by the fact that the driver's head protrudes above the roof line. (Peter Leslie)*

*Beaverette ZD 3319 showing its diminutive size, compared to a Willys CJ3B jeep. The short wheelbase and large tires made for difficult driving. (Bob Cantwell)*

# FERRET MK II ARMOURED CAR

Developed in 1949 as a follow-on to its World War II era Dingo scout car, the Ferret armoured car (more commonly referred to as a scout car) was produced between 1952 and 1971 by the British Daimler company. It was built with an all-welded monocque steel body; the running gear was inside the crew compartment, resulting in an extremely noisy environment for the occupants. Four-wheel drive was incorporated with "run flat" tires; the turret carried a single machine-gun. From November 1962 until June 1964, twelve Daimler Mk II Ferret armoured cars fitted with the .30 caliber Browning machine-gun were supplied by Britain to the UN, which then provided them on a loan basis to Irish Cavalry elements that were part of the UN peacekeeping operation in the Congo (ONUC). These twelve cars first served with the 2nd Armoured Car Squadron, and later with its replacement unit, the 3rd Armoured Car Squadron. The Ferrets supplemented the somewhat tired Ford Mk VI armoured cars that equipped the Irish contingent in the Congo, and were a decided improvement over the Fords in terms of overall capabilities and reliability. During their period of service the Ferrets were used for patrolling duties and saw no combat. Upon withdrawal of Irish forces from the Congo the Ferrets were relinquished to the UN

## FERRET MK II SPECIFICATIONS:

| | |
|---|---|
| Manufacturer: | Daimler Motor Company, Coventry, England |
| Dates of service (Irish Defence Forces): | 1962-? |
| Number in Irish service: | 12 (on loan from Britain, in Congo only) |
| Crew: | 2 (driver, gunner) |
| Combat weight: | 9634 lbs (4370 kg) |
| Armament: | One 7.62mm Browning machine-gun |
| Ammunition capacity: | NA |
| Engine: | Rolls Royce B60 6-cyliner gasoline |
| Horsepower: | 129 |
| Transmission: | Daimler 5-speed manual |
| Fuel capacity: | 21.1 Imperial gallons (96 litres; 25.3 US gallons) |
| Maximum speed (road): | 58 mph (93 km/h) |
| Maximum speed (cross-country): | ? |
| Operating radius (road): | 190 miles (306 km) |
| Operating radius (cross-country): | 100 miles (160 km) |
| Armour: | 12-16mm |
| Length: | 151 inches (3835mm) |
| Width: | 75 inches (1905mm) |
| Height: | 65 inches (1651mm) |
| Tire size: | NA |
| Wheelbase: | 90 inches (2286mm) |
| Track: | NA |
| Ground clearance: | 13 inches (330mm) |
| Trench crossing: | 48 inches (1220mm) with channels |
| Vertical obstacle: | 16 inches (406mm) |
| Fording depth: | 36 inches (914mm) |

*Ferret Mk II. 1/35 scale.*

*A Ferret Mk 2 parading on the occasion of the Cavalry Corps' 80th anniversary in September 2002. Although displaying UN markings, the Ferret pictured was not actually one of the cars used by the Irish contingent in the Congo, but is representative. The Ferrets were on loan by the UN; they retained their olive drab livery rather than the white livery normally applied to UN vehicles. (Sean O'Sullivan)*

*The Cavalry Corps' Ferret Mk 2 in Irish livery. The vehicle is privy of all armament, which normally consisted of a single Browning .30 calibre machine gun in the turret. (Paul Murphy)*

# SCANIA SKPF M/42 APC

During the deployment to the Congo, a small number of Scania m/42 wheeled APCs were loaned by the Swedish contingent to the Irish contingent. Subsequently, in Jadotville in 1962 an undetermined number were transferred to the Irish contingent. The m/42 was developed in Sweden during World War II. Two versions were built, designated SKPF and VKPF, the difference being that the SKPF was built on a Scania-Vabis chassis and was powered by a Scania-Vabis gasoline engine, whereas the VKPF was built on a Volvo chassis, powered by a Volvo gasoline engine. The all-welded steel hull of the m/42 has a front-mounted engine, commander and driver in the center, and troop compartment at the rear. The commander and driver each have a forward-opening side door. Personnel are seated on bench seats which run down the middle of the hull; entry and exit is through a door in the rear. The upper sides and roof of the personnel compartment are open, giving the vehicle a rather unusual appearance. The open-topped configuration is somewhat of a throwback to World War II era German and American open-topped half-track personnel carriers, and provides less than optimum protection for the troops. The troop compartment can be covered by a tarpaulin normally carried on board the vehicle. The m/42 is not amphibious. A representative Scania (not one of the vehicles actually used in the Congo) is preserved at the Cavalry Museum in the Curragh.

## Scania SKPF m/42 Specifications:

| | |
|---|---|
| Manufacturer: | Scania-Vabis, Södertälje, Sweden |
| Dates of service (Irish Defence Forces): | 1962 (on loan basis) |
| Number in Irish service: | Several |
| Crew: | 2 |
| Combat weight: | 18,739 lbs (8500 kg) |
| Armament: | NA |
| Ammunition capacity: | NA |
| Engine: | Scania Type 402 4-cylinder gasoine |
| Horsepower: | 115 |
| Transmission: | NA |
| Fuel capacity: | NA |
| Maximum speed (road): | 44 mph (70 km.h) |
| Maximum speed (cross-country): | 22 mph (35 km/h) |
| Operating radius (road): | NA |
| Operating radius (cross-country): | NA |
| Armour: | 10mm maximum |
| Length: | 272 inches (6900mm) |
| Width: | 90.5 inches (2300mm) |
| Height: | 122 inches (3100mm) |
| Tire size: | 8.25x20 |
| Wheelbase: | 150 inches (3800mm) |
| Track: | NA |
| Ground clearance: | NA |
| Trench crossing: | No capability |

*A frontal view of the Scania m/42, showing the front glacis that completely encloses the engine compartment. There is no type of grille or louver arrangement in the front of the vehicle to provide air for the radiator. (Ralph Riccio)*

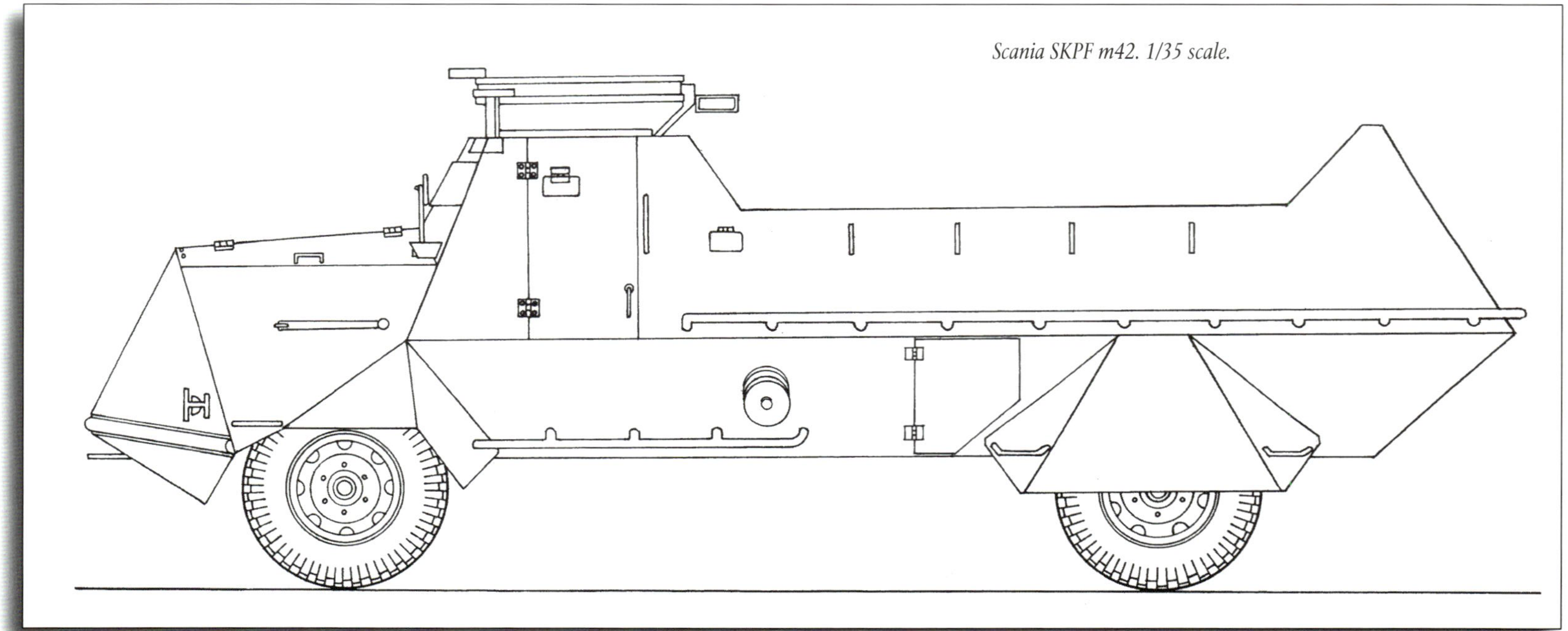

*Scania SKPF m42. 1/35 scale.*

*The SKPF m/42 in service with the Irish contingent in the Congo in 1962. Troops climb aboard through the open top. The degree of protection offered to the mounted troops was problematic, as the open top afforded no overhead protection from small arms fire from a high vantage point, or from bursting artillery or mortar shells. (MA)*

*A Scania SKPF m/42 as used by the Irish Army for a period in the Congo during the 1960's. This particular vehicle was not one of the Scanias actually used by the Irish contingent, but was acquired by the Irish Army in 1998 in exchange for a Landsverk L 180 armoured car that the Swedes desired for their historical collection. Note the rear troop compartment covered by a tarpaulin, providing only protection from the elements for the mounted infantry. (Curragh History Group)*

***Below:** The Scania m/42 at the Curragh Camp, on 2 July, 2009. The road clearance indicators are extended, and the open door to the driver's compartment shows the stark white interior that is virtually a universal feature of armored vehicles regardless of age or nationalality. (Terry Ward)*

107

# HUMBER MK I (FV 1611) PIG

In 1964, the Irish contingent in Cyprus was supplied with ten British Mk I Humber Pig armoured personnel carriers by the UN, while awaiting delivery of the Panhard AML 60 CS armoured cars which had been ordered in April 1964 from France. In 1965 the number of Humbers in the Irish contingent was reduced to seven, as by this time enough Panhards were on the island to equip the contingent's armoured element. The FV 1611 Pig is a one-ton 4 x 4 armoured personnel carrier originally built on the chassis of a Humber 1-ton truck as a stop-gap measure, as in the early 1950s insufficient numbers of Saracen APCs were available to meet British Army requirements. The chassis was supplied by Rootes in Kent, and the armoured bodies by GKN Sankey and Royal Ordnance Factory, Woolwich. The Pig has an all-welded steel hull, a front-mounted engine, a compartment for the commander and driver in the middle, and a troop compartment in the rear. Its rather uncomplimentary name allegedly was bestowed upon it because its hood somewhat resembled a pig's snout. The front portion of the Humber bore a striking resemblance, probably coincidentally, to an earlier German armoured car, the Benz Typ 21, only 24 examples of which were built in 1924 and 1925. Interestingly, in the 1950s about a dozen Pigs were placed in service with the Royal Ulster Constabulary, serving until 1970, and in 1974 three of the Mk II variant similarly were added to the RUC inventory. The disposition and fate of the Humbers in Irish Army service are unclear, but given the normal UN practice of loaning vehicles to contingents only for the duration of their commitment or as otherwise necessary, it is likely that the Humbers reverted to UN control once the Irish contingent had received its full complement of Panhards in 1965.

## HUMBER MK I PIG SPECIFICATIONS:

| Manufacturer: | Humber Motors, England |
| --- | --- |
| Dates of service (Irish Defence Forces): | 1964-1965 (on loan from UN) |
| Number in Irish service: | 10 |
| Crew: | 2 (commander/gunner, driver) (plus 8 passenngers) |
| Combat weight: | 12,765 lbs (5790 kg) |
| Armament: | None |
| Engine: | Rolls Royce B60 Mk 5A, 4.2 litre, gasoline |
| Horsepower: | 120 |
| Transmission: | 5-speed manual |
| Fuel capacity: | 31.9 Imperial gallons (38.3 US gallons; 145 litres) |
| Maximum speed (road): | 40 mph (64 km/h) |
| Operating radius (road): | 250 miles (402 km) |
| Armour: | NA |
| Length: | 196 inches (4970mm) |
| Width: | 80 inches (2040mm) |
| Height: | 83 inches (2120mm) |
| Tire size: | 11.00 x 20 Run Flats |
| Wheelbase: | 108 inches (2743mm) |
| Track: | 64.5 inches (1713mm) |
| Ground clearance: | NA |
| Trench crossing: | No capability |

*Humber Mk I. 1/35 scale.*

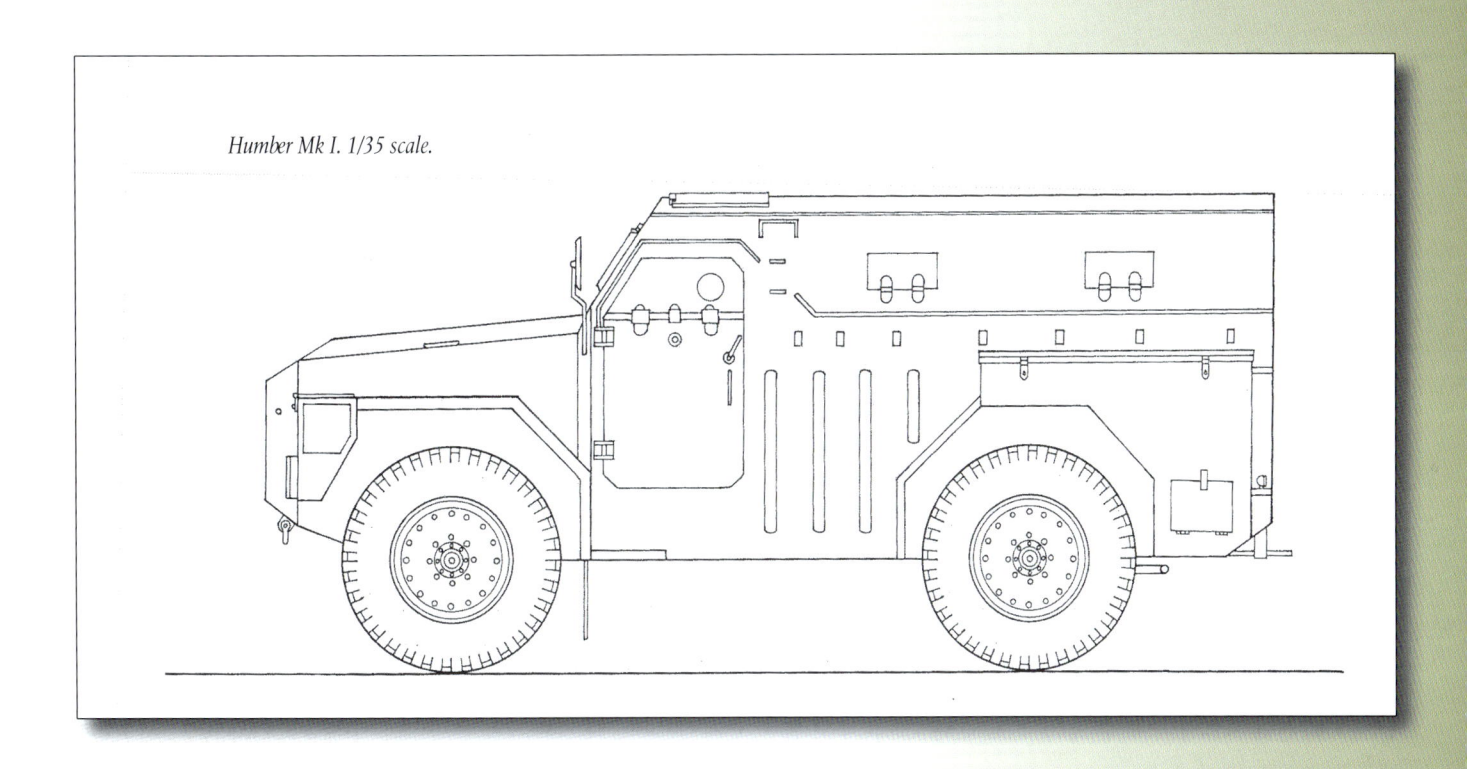

A representative Humber Mk I Pig armoured personnel carrier. Ten vehicles of this type were supplied in 1964 by the U.N. to the Irish contingent in Cyprus. The Pigs never were included in the official Irish armour establishment, serving only on a loan basis in Cyprus. (TMB 2551/B/4)

# PANHARD AML 245 ARMOURED CARS (H60 AND H90 SERIES)

The Irish deployment to the Congo in 1960 pointed out the need for a modern armoured car to replace the somewhat heterogeneous and definitely aging Irish armoured car inventory, which in 1961 consisted of the Leyland, Landsverk, Dodge and Ford Mk VI armoured cars dating back to the 1930s and 1940s. Accordingly, the Defence Forces explored various options, including the French Panhard AML (Automitrailleuse Légère, or light armoured car) 245 H90, which had been introduced into French service in 1961, and which was relatively inexpensive and, with a 90mm gun, was much more capable than any of the cars then in Irish service. The AML 245 has an all-welded steel hull divided into three compartments (driver's in front, fighting compartment in the centre, and engine in the rear). The turret, manufactured by Hispano-Suiza, is likewise all-welded.

Probably as a cost-saving measure, the AML 60-7 CS variant, armed with a 60mm DTAT CS (Cloche Special) mortar and two French Model AA52 machine-guns of 7.5mm was chosen in preference to the AML 90. An order was placed for eight vehicles, and in April 1964 the first two Panhards were delivered to Plunkett Barracks at Curragh Camp for familiarization and training; they were then shipped to the Irish contingent's Armoured Car Group deployed on UN duty in Cyprus, where on 2 May they were joined by another six Panhards shipped directly from France. These eight Panhards were joined by another batch of eight in August 1964, slated to form a second armoured car group to support the newly arrived 3 Infantry Group. There was an unusual learning curve associated with the arrival of the new cars with respect to gear changes; the Panhard engine had to be kept at high revs, even when changing gears. Failure to maintain high revs while shifting gears resulted in clutch slippage, clutch plate overheating, and clutch failure. Additionally, the clutch setup itself was markedly different from the normal foot-operated clutch. The clutch was an electrical clutch, fitted to the gear selector lever. The gear is preselected by lifting the knob, then dropping the gear lever into the appropriate gear. The drivers soon learned to adjust to these new procedures, but one must assume that some damage occurred to the clutch assemblies of the new vehicles before total proficiency was gained. In 1965 eight of the Panhards were returned to Ireland, while the remaining eight cars continued to serve in Cyprus with successive Irish UNFICYP contingents until 1972. At that time, with the worsening security situation in Northern Ireland, all of the remaining Panhards were pulled out of Cyprus, returned to Ireland, and distributed amongst the remaining Motor Squadrons (1, 2, and 4). In the 1980s, the original French Model AA 52 machine-guns were replaced by Belgian Fabrique National (FN) MAG 80 machine-guns, modified for use in the AML cars. Modifications include a shorter gas chamber, elimination of the butt and the bipod attachment, reduced pistol grip, and firing by solenoid switch (although manual fire is also possible).

The satisfactory performance of the Panhards, coupled with the deteriorating security situation along the border with the North, led the Irish Defence Forces to order a further 36 Panhards, in two variants. The order was placed in 1970, but delivery of the 36 vehicles was not completed until 1975. Of the 36 vehicles, twenty were the AML H 90 variant, armed with a low-pressure smoothbore Giat D 921 F1 90mm gun (also referred to as the CN90F1) capable of firing HE, HEAT, smoke and canister rounds; secondary armament consisted of a co-axial 7.62mm FN MAG 80. Delivery of the H 90s could be said to have ushered in a new era in Irish armour, as it introduced a very capable series-produced armoured car mounting the most potent weapons system, in the form of the largest-caliber gun ever mounted on any vehicle in Irish service. Because of the recoil forces of the gun, crews were reluctant to fire the gun with the turret traversed 90 degrees from the centerline, for fear that the vehicle would tip over due to the recoil. Common practice is to fire the gun at a halt, basically aligned with the vehicle centerline. When fired, the recoil tends to compress the rear suspension and raise the front end of the vehicle considerably. Of the 20 AML 90s, one was destroyed in an accidental fire in Lebanon with the Irish UNIFIL contingent there. The other 16 vehicles ordered in 1960 were the AML H 60-7 HB variant, armed with the improved 60mm

Hotchkiss-Brandt (HB) mortar. The HB mortar could be fired either as a breech-loaded weapon from inside the vehicle, or as a conventional mortar loaded from the muzzle. Firing in the conventional mode requires the crew to stand on the outside of the vehicle in order to drop the mortar bomb down the muzzle of the tube.

As the 1970s wore on, the 60mm main armament on 16 AML 60-7 CS cars revealed a design fault that rendered them inoperable, effectively limiting them to use of their twin 7.62mm machine-guns. In 1989 the British firm of Manroy Engineering of Beckley (Rye), East Sussex, was contracted to replace the original armament with a single Browning .50 caliber M2 HB-QCB (Heavy Barrel–Quick Change Barrel) heavy machine-gun manufactured by Manroy. This conversion is referred to as the AML 127, reflecting the metric measurement of the .50 caliber Browning gun (12.7mm bore diameter). This "quick fix" did not prove entirely satisfactory and was not popular with the crews because of cramped conditions in the turret, obliging the car commander to sit in an awkward position because of the space taken up by the gun's body. Likewise, the dimensions of the turret required that in order to mount the gun into the turret, the gun's receiver, minus its barrel, first be maneuvered into and mounted in the turret, while the barrel then had to be mounted from outside the turret. The procedure was reversed for removal of the gun for maintenance or repairs, i.e., removal of barrel, followed by removal of the body of the gun from inside. Space considerations also led to elimination of the twin MAG 80 armament in the turret.

Some interesting experiments were carried out in Ireland with the Panhard AML in 1986 and 1987, involving the fitting of turrets armed with light cannons. The first was an AML fitted with a Mecanique Creusot-Loire T25 turret mounting a 25mm M242 Bushmaster chain gun; the system was tested at the Glen of Imaal in July 1986. In April 1987, another AML, mounting a 30mm Rarden turret (the same type used on the British Scimitar tracked light armoured vehicle) was also tested at the Glen of Imaal. No further interest was shown in either of the vehicles, however, and it was not until the late 1990s that Ireland developed its own unique cannon-armed version of the AML, mounting a 20mm cannon, described more fully later in the text.

*A column of Panhard AML 60 CS cars on patrol, at a halt in the village of Zyyi, southwest of Larnaca in Cyprus. The cars have not yet been issued with Irish registration numbers; the UN logo has been applied on the turret over the factory paint scheme. The local townspeople do not seem at all intimidated by the presence of the patrol. (Sgt James "Gus" Hayle, Irish Defence Forces Ret'd, via Sgt David Nagle, An Cosantoir)*

Continuous operational use of the Panhards demonstrated that the original Panhard 4D 90 hp gasoline engine was underpowered, prone to overheating, and suffered from vapor lock problems, and therefore it was advisable that the cars be upgraded with a new, more powerful engine. Accordingly, in 1991, the ever-inventive Cavalry Workshops experimentally fitted Mercedes, Audi, and Peugeot engines in three AML 60 hulls. Extensive testing showed the 98 HP Peugeot XD3T turbocharged diesel to be the most suitable of the three, and in 1992, two AML 60s and two AML 90s were fitted with the Peugeot diesels. Eventually, all of the AML 90s and AML 60-7 CS cars were retrofitted with diesel engines by the Cavalry Workshops. Fitting the new engine required extensive modifications to the hull, suspension, and electrical systems, and the addition of an engine cooling pack. The refurbishment also included fitting new gearboxes for the AML 90s, and strengthening the gearboxes of the AML 60s, which were lighter. It is interesting to note that the body of the AML was lengthened by about 14 inches to accommodate the new engine, and inasmuch as the modifications were made in the Cavalry Workshops and new engine housings were individually fabricated for each car, even though they were made to a common pattern individual lengths can vary slightly between the cars. As a consequence of these modifications, although braking and handling were improved at lower speeds due to redistribution of weight, paradoxically overall performance in these areas suffered because of the higher speeds attainable (i.e. stopping distances lengthened and handling at higher speeds required more skill and attention by the driver). Brakes were particularly susceptible to overheating. In the late 1990s all of the AML cars were temporarily sidelined due to concerns regarding asbestos in the braking systems, which however proved to be unfounded.

The modified AML 90s and AML 60-7 CS cars served satisfactorily until the late 1990s (the 16 AML 60-7 HB cars were not modified), when the Army instituted an upgrade program for the AML 90s that included fitting a South African fire direction system with a laser rangefinder and night image intensifier, both of which contain externally and internally mounted elements. The upgrade was carried out by the Cavalry Workshops, using kits supplied by South Africa. More or less contemporaneously, the 16 AML 60 CS cars that had previously been modified by replacing the original 60mm main armament with the .50 caliber Manroy Browning weapon (resulting in the previously described AML 127) were again upgraded by replacing the .50 caliber Browning with new armament consisting of a South African Denel/Vektor 20mm G12 cannon and new fire direction systems; the resulting vehicle has been dubbed the AML 20, and is unique to Irish service. Because the work involved to fit the new 20mm cannon in place of the .50 caliber Browning was extensive, the turrets were shipped to South Africa for modification, then shipped back to Ireland

*AML CS 60 NZH 12, minus its 60mm CS mortar, at the Curragh Vehicle Workshops in 1967. NZH 12 served in Cyprus from 1964 to 1965, and was one of the first eight Panhards in Irish service. (Peter Leslie)*

*Panhard AML 245 60 CS. 1/35 scale.*

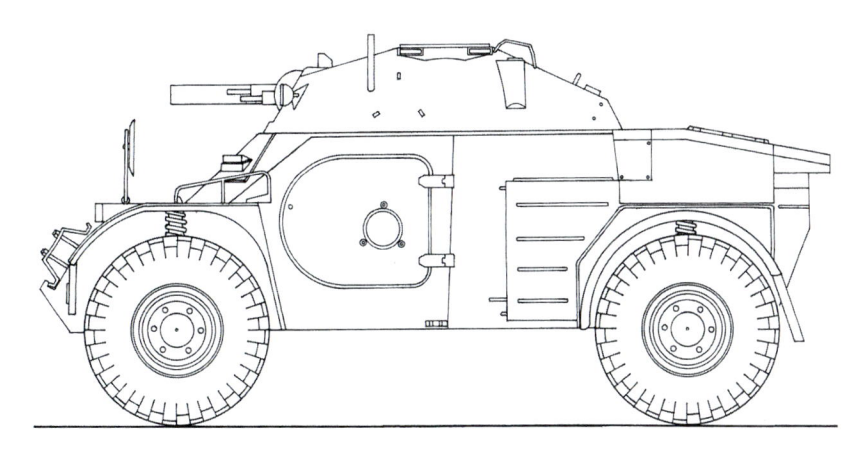

*Panhard AML 245 60 HB. 1/35 scale.*

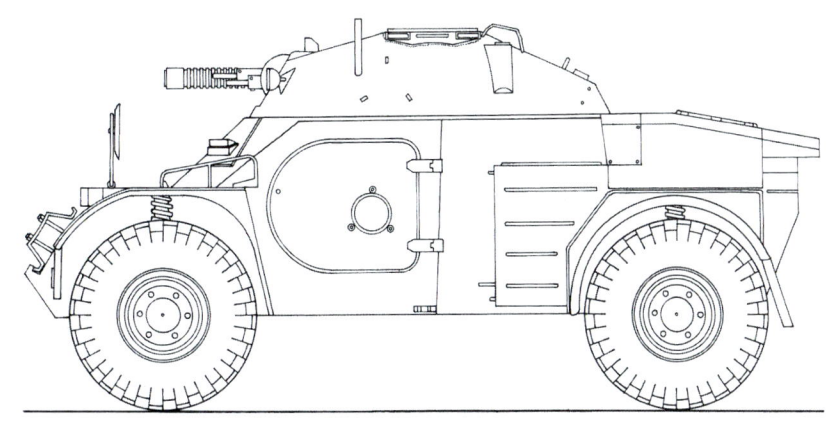

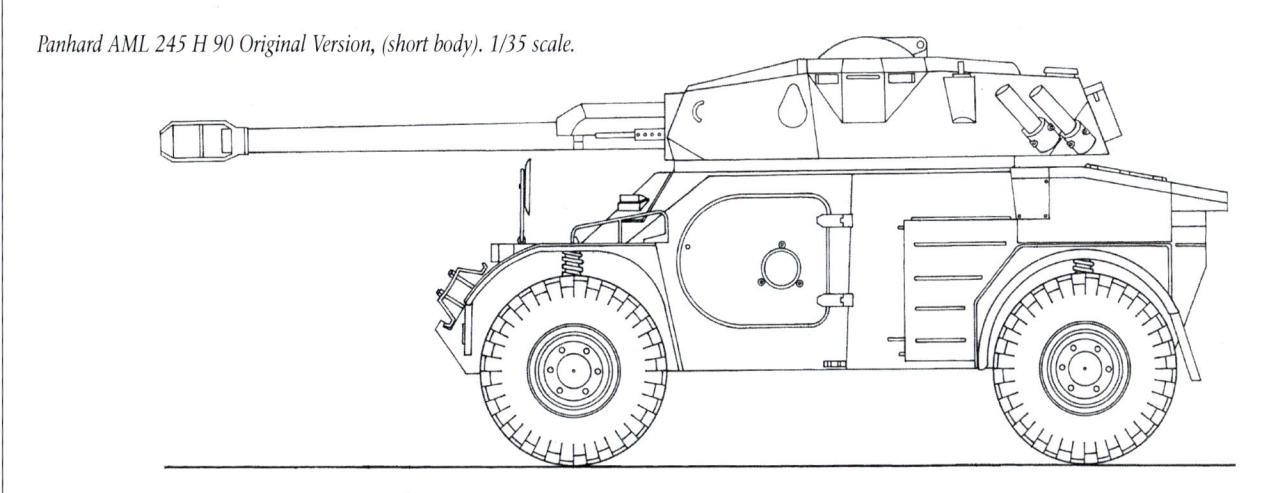

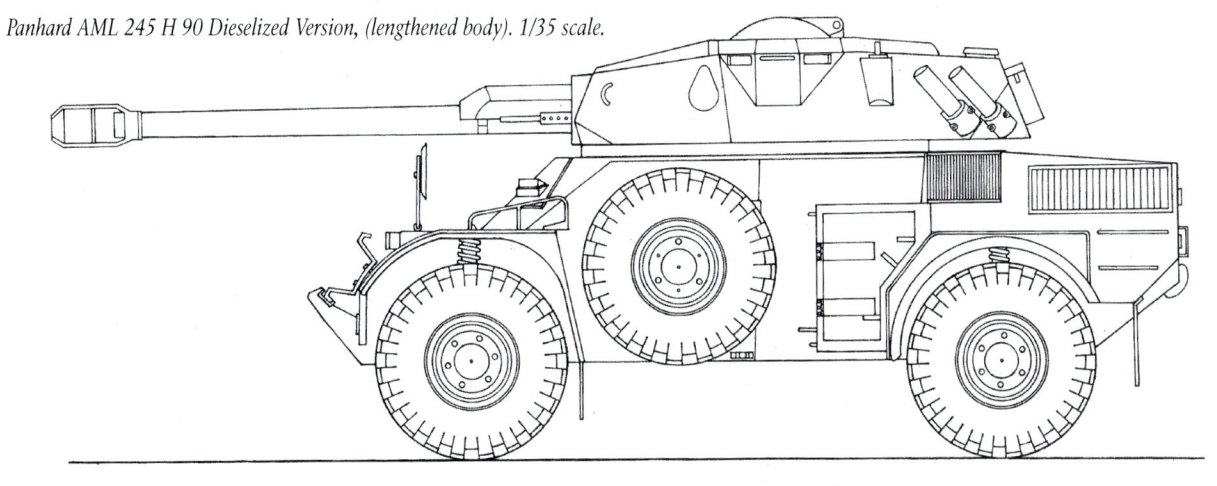

*Panhard AML 245 H 90 Original Version, (short body). 1/35 scale.*

*Panhard AML 245 H 90 Dieselized Version, (lengthened body). 1/35 scale.*

113

upon completion, where they were again mated with their respective hulls. The 20mm cannon is installed upside down in the turret, and a micro switch lockout feature prevents the weapon from being fired unless the ejection opening flap on the roof of the turret is first opened. Ammunition is belted, and two 140-round belts are normally carried. Of the sixteen HB variant, fourteen were withdrawn from service and, as of 2005, stored at Coolmoney Camp for use as hard targets on the Glen of Imaal ranges. As of mid-2009, 318 RRI and 6459 ZE were maintained in running condition at Curragh Camp, another, with no registration number, was on static display at the camp, and a fourth, apparently rescued from being used as a target, was in deplorable condition, also at Curragh Camp

## PANHARD AML 245 60 CS/HB SPECIFICATIONS:

| | |
|---|---|
| Manufacturer: | Panhard, Marolles-en-Hurepoix, France |
| Dates of service (Irish Defence Forces): | 1964–2009. The CS version were modified as AML 127 in 1989, and further upgraded to AML 20 in the late 1990s. The HB version were in service from 1970 until the 1990s, when all but two were scrapped. |
| Number in Irish service: | 32 (16 AML 245 60 CS, and 16 AML 245 60 HB) |
| Crew: | 3 |
| Combat weight: | 10,582 lbs (4800 kg) |
| Armament: | 60mm CS mortar (AML 60 CS); 60mm Brandt breech-loading mortar (AML 60 HB); two 7.62 MAG machine-guns |
| Ammunition capacity: | 53 x 60mm rounds; 3800 x 7.62mm rounds |
| Engine: | Panhard Model 4 HD 4-cylinder air cooled, gasoline |
| Horsepower: | 90 HP @ 4700 rpm |
| Transmission: | Selective sliding gear; electrical clutch mounted on gearshift lever; 4-speed transmission; transfer case low-range and high-range;permanent 4-wheel drive |
| Fuel capacity: | 34.3 Imperial gallons (41.2 US gallons; 156 litres) |
| Maximum speed (road): | 56 mph (90 km/h) |
| Maximum speed (cross-country): | NA |
| Operating radius (road): | 373 miles (600 km) |
| Operating radius (cross-country): | NA |
| Armour: | 8-12mm |
| Length: | 149 inches (3790mm) |
| Width: | 78 inches (1970mm) |
| Height: | 74 inches (1890mm) |
| Tire size: | 11.00 x 16 |
| Wheelbase: | 98 inches (2500mm) |
| Track: | 64 inches (1620mm) |
| Ground clearance: | 13 inches (330mm) |
| Trench crossing: | 32 inches (800mm) |
| Vertical obstacle: | 12 inches (300mm) |
| Fording depth: | 43 inches (1100mm) |

*A Panhard 60 CS, date unknown. The truck behind and to the left of the AML is a Bedford MR2, and behind the AML is what appears to be the front of a Leyland armoured car. (Denis McCarthy)*

*Closeup of 60mm CS mortar and twin 7.62mm MAG 80 machinegun armament. (Denis McCarthy)*

115

# Panhard AML 245 H90 Specifications:

| | |
|---|---|
| Manufacturer: | Panhard, Marolles-en-Hurepoix, France |
| Dates of service (Irish Defence Forces): | 1970-2011 |
| Number in Irish service: | 20 |
| Crew: | 3 |
| Combat weight: | 12,125 lbs (5500 kg) |
| Armament: | GIAT F1 90mm gun; one 7.62mm MAG machine-gun |
| Ammunition capacity: | 20 rounds main gun |
| Engine: | Panhard Model 4 HD 4-cylinder air cooled, gasoline, 1997cc (original); upgraded with Peugeot XD3T turbocharged Diesel beginning in 1992 |
| Horsepower: | 90 HP @ 4700 (Panhard); 98 HP (Peugeot) |
| Transmission: | Electrical clutch mounted on gearshift lever; 4-speed transmission; transfer case low-range and high-range; permanent 4-wheel drive |
| Fuel capacity: | 34.3 Imperial gallons (41.2 US gallons, 156 litres) |
| Maximum speed (road): | 56 mph (90 km/h) |
| Maximum speed (cross-country): | NA |
| Operating radius (road): | 373 miles (600 km) |
| Operating radius (cross-country): | NA |
| Armour: | 8-12mm |
| Length: | 201 inches (5110mm) with gun forward; hull length 149 inches (3790mm) for original version; Dieselized version in service since 1992 have extended rear deck resulting in hull length of 163 inches (4150mm) and overall length of 215 inches (5470 mm) with gun forward. |
| Width: | 78 inches (1970mm) |
| Height: | 82 inches (2070mm) |
| Tire size: | 11.00 x 16 |
| Wheelbase: | 98 inches (2500mm) |
| Track: | 64 inches (1620mm) |
| Ground clearance: | 13 inches (330mm) |
| Trench crossing: | 32 inches (800mm) |
| Vertical obstacle: | 12 inches (300mm) |
| Fording depth: | 43 inches (1100mm) |

*These two photographs allow an easy comparison of the striking difference between the appearance of the main armament on the AML 60 CS and AML 60 HB cars. The upper photo of the HB version shows the distinctive rings on the mortar barrel as well as the muzzle counterweight; the lower picture of the AML 60 CS instead shows the smooth tube of the 60mm CS mortar. (Bob Cantwell)*

# Panhard AML 127 and AML 20 Specifications:

| | |
|---|---|
| Manufacturer: | Panhard, Marolles-en-Hurepoix, France; modified by Manroy Engineering, East Sussex, England, for Irish Defence Forces and by Cavarly Workshops |
| Dates of service (Irish Defence Forces): | 1989–late 1990s (in AML 127 configuration); late 1990s to 2009 (in AML 20 configuration) |
| Number in Irish service: | 16 |
| Crew: | 3 |
| Combat weight: | 10,582 lbs (4800 kg) approximate |
| Armament: | Manroy Browning HB M2 .50 caliber heavy machine-gun (AML 127); 20mm Denel/Vektor G12 cannon and one 7.62mm MAG coaxial machine-gun (AML 20) |
| Ammunition capacity: | 1500 rounds .50 caliber (AML 127); 280 rounds 20mm and 1000 rounds of 7.62mm (AML 20) |
| Engine: | Peugeot XD3T turbocharged Diesel |
| Horsepower: | 98 HP |
| Transmission: | Electrical clutch mounted on gearshift lever; 4-speed transmission; transfer case low-range and high-range; permanent 4-wheel drive |
| Fuel capacity: | 34.3 Imperial gallons (41.2 US gallons; 156 litres) |
| Maximum speed (road): | 56 mph (90 km/h) |
| Maximum speed (cross-country): | NA |
| Operating radius (road): | 373 miles (600 km) |
| Operating radius (cross-country): | NA |
| Armour: | 8-12mm |
| Length: | 163 inches (4150mm) |
| Width: | 78 inches (1970mm) |
| Height: | 74 inches (1890mm) |
| Tire size: | 11.00 x 16 |
| Wheelbase: | 98 inches (2500mm) |
| Track: | 64 inches (1620mm) |
| Ground clearance: | 13 inches (330mm) |
| Trench crossing: | 32 inches (800mm) |
| Vertical obstacle: | 12 inches (300mm) |
| Fording depth: | 43 inches (1100mm) |

*An AML 60 HB in convoy. The 60mm Hotchkiss-Brandt breech-loading mortar is normally fired from within the vehicle, but can also be loaded from the muzzle. Note the cover, complete with windshield wiper, over the driver's position. The vehicle behind the AML is a MAN 8:150 4 x 2 truck. (Bob Cantwell)*

*An AML 60 HB participating in a parade in Clonmel. The unmistakable shape of the HB mortar is clearly evident in this photograph. The vehicle does not have its spare tire mounted on the side. (Bob Cantwell)*

*A May 2005 photo of the Cavalry Corps' AML 60 HB at a display in the Curragh. Immediately to its right is a Landsverk L 180 armoured car. (Terry Ward)*

119

*AML 60 HB 6456ZE photographed with armament removed at Curragh Camp in 2005. Despite its apparently good state of repair, the car was consigned to use as a range target shortly afterward. (Paul Murphy)*

*An AML 60 HB at Coolmoney Camp in 2005 awaiting its turn as a hard target at the Glen of Imaal firing range. It has been stripped of its armament, and lacks the trench crossing channels, allowing a good view of the angle and slope of the front glacis. (Paul Murphy)*

*The Panhard logo as applied to the rear of AML series cars. (Paul McMenamin)*

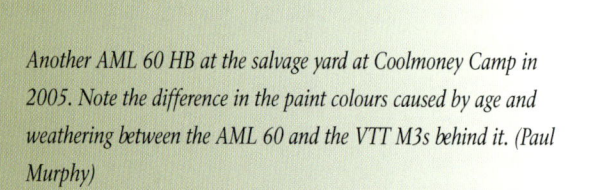

*Another AML 60 HB at the salvage yard at Coolmoney Camp in 2005. Note the difference in the paint colours caused by age and weathering between the AML 60 and the VTT M3s behind it. (Paul Murphy)*

*Above:* A side view of the original configuration of the AML 90 hull. The rear sponsons above the wheels ended just behind the wheels, and the engine compartment cover was angled and had access doors. The device above the barrel is a Weston SIMFIRE gunnery training system, no longer in service. A rack has been fitted to carry a jerrycan on the door, in lieu of the spare wheel and tire normally mounted in that position. Also of note is what appears to be a camouflage net draped over the front of the vehicle; the re-engined AML 90s were fitted with a large wire basket on the turret rear that could carry such items. (By kind permission of Karl Martin).
*Below:* The elongated rear deck of the Dieselized version of both the AML 90 and AML 20, comprising the engine compartment and rear fender sponsons. The Cavalry Workshop designed and fabricated all of the components. The ribbed sponsons incorporate a forward storage compartment, and the engine compartment is surmounted by a grilled vent. Other changes include brackets for jerrycans, towing shackles, and revised taillights covered by protective mesh cages. (By kind permission of Karl Martin)

*An AML 90 (190 AZI) and an AML 120 (NZH 16) parked side by side in June 2007. Note the different rear turret stowage arrangements; the AML 90 has an open wire mesh basket, while the AML 20 has a much shallower enclosed storage box that was included when the turret was upgraded for the 20mm cannon. (Paul McMenamin)*

*A side by side frontal view of an AML 90 and an AML 20 from 4th Cavalry Squadron. In addition to the obvious difference in main armament, there are other details in difference between the two vehicles, such as the turret cupola configuration, the long and short brackets and stowage orientation of the ditching channels, and the size and shape of the side view mirrors. (Terry Ward)*

*An AML 90 of the Irish UNIFIL contingent in a revetted position at An Tri, Lebanon, 1 May 1980. (UN 122915)*

*A pair of AML 90s halted during a rest stop at a petrol station. The AMLs have sufficient range to accomplish most road marches within Ireland without having to stop to refuel. Petrol station parking areas afford the crews an opportunity to rest and to eat before proceeding on the next leg of the march. (Paul Murphy)*

*Rear of a 1st Cavalry Squadron AML 90, September 2005. Two center-mounted brackets for jerrycans are in the folded position. The Panhard logo is also clearly visible. The storage basket has significant capacity for bulky items. (Paul Murphy)*

*Coolmoney Camp, July 2007. A pair of AML 90s, with behind them another pair of AML 20s lacking their armament. The crews of the AML 90s have chosen different locations to stow their canvas. The AML 90 in the background has a protective cover over the muzzle baffle. (Seamus Corcoran, via Paul Murphy)*

*A freshly painted AML 90 in 2008. To the side is a 40mm Bofors EL/70 anti-aircraft gun. (Paul McMenamin)*

*One of the AML 90s deployed with the Irish UN peacekeeping contingent in Liberia, with the obligatory white UN livery. (Roy Kinsella)*

*An unusual colour scheme on an AML "hybrid". The hull is from an AML 20, and the turret obviously from an AML 90. This was a temporary mating, as the proper AML 90 hull was not available and the vehicle was jury-rigged in order to participate in a shoot at the Glen of Imaal. The hull belonged to an AML 20 (converted from the AML 60CS) that had been deployed on a UN assignment, and hence had been painted white, and had not yet been repainted in the regulation green livery. (Paul Murphy)*

*An AML 90 in convoy, led by a motorcycle outrider. Following the AML 90 is an AML 20, in turn followed by a Leyland DAF T244 troop carrier. (Sean O'Sullivan)*

*Gun muzzle and electronic gear on this AML 90 are protected by appropriate coverings. (Sean O'Sullivan)*

*Close-up of the so-called "long front supports" for the ditch crossing channels. The tow bar can also be seen behind the ditch crossing channels. Some AML 90s retained the older short supports. (Roy Kinsella)*

*Close-up view of the older short front supports for the ditch crossing channels. Note the difference in stowage position from channels carried on the newer long supports. (Roy Kinsella)*

*The updated rear wheel well of the Dieselized AML 90. The extensions to accommodate the larger Peugeot Diesel engine for the modernized AML 90s and AML 20s were designed and fabricated by the Cavalry Workshop. (Roy Kinsella)*

*An interesting comparison between these two AML 90s. The closer car is fitted with the electronic range finding gear, while the second car is not. The ditch crossing channels are also stowed differently. (Roy Kinsella)*

**Right:** *Close-up of one of the components of the electronic range-finding and fire control equipment mounted on the AML 90. (Roy Kinsella)*

**Bottom:** *Glen of Imaal, September 2006. 90-mm rounds being loaded on an AML 90 prior to deployment for range firing. Normal stowage capacity for the AML 90 is 20 rounds. (Bob Cantwell)*

125

*An AML 90 on the firing line at the Glen of Imaal range in September 2006. Note the spent brass casings to the left of the vehicle, and the jerrycans mounted on the brackets on the rear of the vehicle. (Bob Cantwell)*

*St. Patrick's Day, 2002. 3rd Cavalry Squadron AML 90 leading a group of vehicles. The gunner is armed with a Steyr AUG assault rifle. (Bob Cantwell)*

Head-on view of the AML 90's main armament. The GIAT F1 90mm smoothbore gun is a very potent weapon for an armoured car of modest size. In terms of bore diameter, it is the largest gun ever mounted on an amored vehicle in Irish service. (Bob Cantwell)

A mixed group of AML 90 and AML 20 cars in open storage at Curragh Camp, 27 May, 2009. These vehicles returned from Liberia some two years previously. The AML 20s have had their 20mm cannons removed; one of the AML 90s has a cover on its muzzle, while the other, minus a cover and with its barrel elevated, likely has suffered significant barrel corrosion. The tarpaulins covering some of the vehicles provide only minimal protection against the usually damp Irish weather. (Ralph Riccio)

A Diesel engined AML 90 wading a stream during an exercise. The car has entered the stream from the steep slope to the rear. The pioneer tools on the front glacis are seldom seen fitted. Note that the turret and hull are slightly different shades of green. (Bob Cantwell)

*An AML 127 participating in a St. Patrick's Day parade in 1997. The AML 127 (also referred to as the AML .50) was a unique Irish transitional model between the AML 60 CS and the AML 20. The short rear deck houses the original Panhard engine; the AML 127 cars were later updated with a Peugeot Diesel engine, requiring extending the rear engine compartment. (Paul Murphy)*

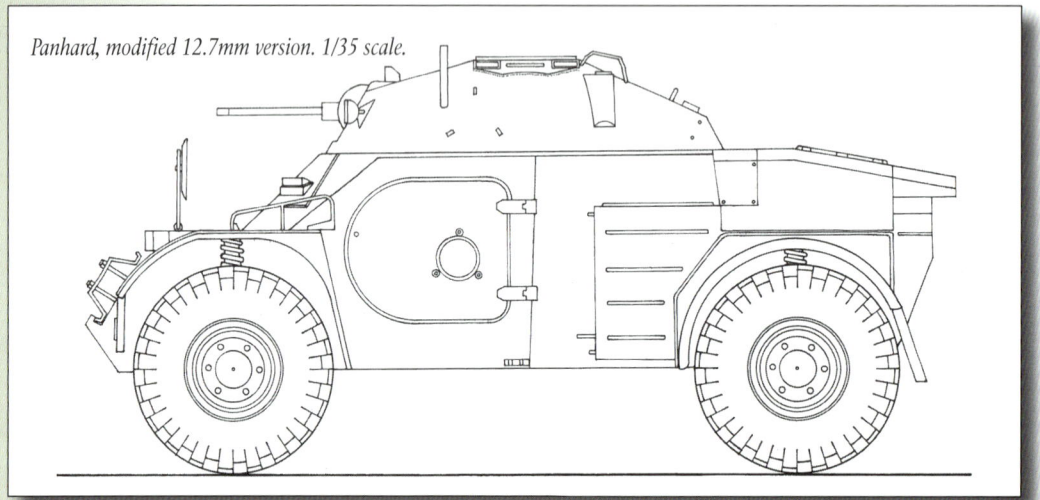

*Panhard, modified 12.7mm version. 1/35 scale.*

*NZH 13 minus its .50 caliber armament in September 1999 as the 1st Cavalry Squadron is departing Fermoy for its new location at Collins Barracks, Cork. Note the commander and gunner carrying the Steyr AUG assault rifles, now standard issue in the Irish Army, but at the time of this photograph issued in lieu of the FN FAL normally carried by Cavalry crews. Also note the short rear deck of the car ahead of NZH 13 indicating that it was one of the unmodified AML 60 HB's, and the AML 60 HB behind NZH 13. (Sean O'Sullivan)*

128

*An AML 127 with its .50 caliber armament elevated. The AML 60 CS cars were modified by Manroy Engineering of East Sussex, England, by modifying the gun mantlet and installing a Browning HB (Heavy Barrel) machinegun manufactured by Manroy. (Bob Cantwell)*

*The photogenic NZH 13 on St. Patrick's Day, Clonmel, 1995. The car commander is Cpl Paul Murphy, the gunner is Derek Hackett, and the driver is John Fitzpatrick. NZH 13 was the first AML 60 to be converted to the AML 127 configuration, mounting the .50 caliber machinegun as main armament, replacing the 60mm CS mortar. (Bob Cantwell)*

*This AML 20, complete with spare tire, was at an air show in Baldonnel in 2008. Judging from the litter of discarded water bottles in front of the vehicle, the weather was warm. (Seamus Corcoran)*

*An AML 20 parading in 2002 on the 80th anniversary of the Irish Cavalry corps. All of the original AML 60 CS cars were modified as AML 127 cars (mounting the .50 caliber heavy machinegun), then further upgraded to AML 20 standard by fitting with a South African 20mm G12 cannon and new fire control equipment. (Curragh History Group)*

*NZH 14 on exercise in the Glen of Imaal in March 2008. The car appears to be supporting the infantry deployed to the side of the road. (Paul Murphy)*

*NZH 14 during an exercise break at the Glen of Imaal in March 2008. The open driver's hatch allows the white painted interior to be seen; white interiors are the norm for most armoured vehicles. (Roy Kinsella)*

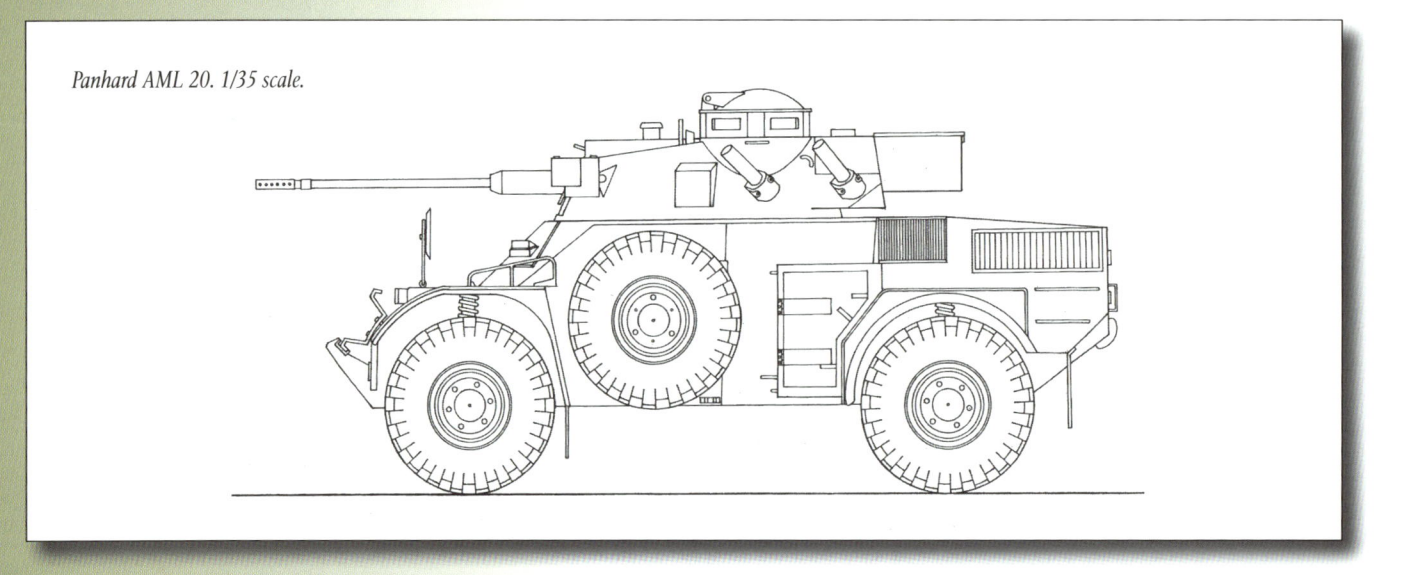

*Panhard AML 20. 1/35 scale.*

# LANDSVERK UNIMOG SCOUT CAR

*A Unimog in Irish service. The well-sloped armour surfaces provided enhanced protection from small arms fire. The shield for the machinegun was designed and fabricated by the Cavalry Workshops. (Sean O'Sullivan)*

In 1971 the Irish Army purchased 15 Landsverk Unimog scout cars as a stop-gap measure while awaiting delivery of the Panhard M3 armoured personnel carriers it had ordered. The sense of urgency was prompted by the deteriorating security situation in Northern Ireland, leading to fear of trouble along the border with Northern Ireland. The Landsverk SH, known as the Pansarbil Unimog in Swedish, was based on the Mercedes-Benz 4 x 4 Unimog S404 truck (Unimog is a German acronym for Universal Motor Gerät, or Universal Motor Machine); the chassis was modified for the purpose by moving the engine from the front to the rear of the vehicle. Its armoured body was well angled and sloped, with armour ranging from 7.5mm to 10mm thick. In addition to the driver, there was accommodation for four other personnel in the car. These particular vehicles originally had been ordered by Belgium for use by its gendarmerie forces in the Congo, but when hostilities broke out there in 1960 the Swedish government embargoed the vehicles. They remained in storage at Landsverk in Sweden until 1971, when the Irish Army was able to acquire them at

*A group of Unimogs on the move on a rather rainy day. Note the addition of the spot lights to the gun shields of all three vehicles. (Bob Cantwell)*

131

*A Unimog on a Hino 6 x 4 equipped with a Boughton Ampliroll system. The Ampliroll allowed the truck's platform to be lowered to the ground, enabling the vehicle to be transported to drive onto the platform, which was then winched onto the truck along with the platform. (Bob Cantwell)*

a bargain price. The fifteen Unimogs, plus two prototypes that were also purchased as a source of spare parts, arrived in Dublin in February 1972. Prior to being issued to units, the cars were fitted by the Cavalry Workshops with a shield for the 7.62mm MAG machine-gun carried as armament. Road handling suffered due to a high center of gravity and very sensitive power steering. The Unimogs served with 1st Armoured Squadron for a time, and in April 1978 were assigned to 1, 2 and 4 Motor Squadrons until May 1980, when they were transferred to 3, 5, and 11 FCA (An Forsa Cosanta Áitùil, or Reserve Defence Force) Motor Squadrons. Upon transfer, the 7.62mm MAG GPMGs were replaced by .30 caliber Browning machine-guns or .303 in. Bren guns. The last of the Unimog scout cars were withdrawn from service with the FCA in 1984 and boarded (definitively withdrawn from service) on 24 February 1987. One of the Unimogs is preserved at the National Transport Museum in Howth, another by the Cavalry Corps, and two others are owned by private collectors in Ireland but are not in running condition

*Rear view of a Unimog showing engine grille covering and exposed muffler. The registration number, 2259 ZC, is the lowest registration number for the Unimogs. (Sean O'Sullivan)*

*The Unimog preserved under cover at the National Transport Museum in Howth. Another Unimog is maintained by the Cavalry Corps at the Curragh, and two other Unimogs are in the hands of private collectors in Ireland, but neither is in running order. (Terry Ward)*

## Unimog Scout Car Specifications:

| | |
|---|---|
| Manufacturer: | AB Kockums Landsverk, Landskrona, Sweden |
| Dates of service (Irish Defence Forces): | 1972-1987 |
| Number in Irish service: | 15 |
| Crew: | 5-6 |
| Combat weight: | 11,465 (5200 kg) approximate weight |
| Armament: | 7.62mm MAG 80 machine-gun |
| Ammunition capacity: | NA |
| Engine: | Daimler-Benz 6-cylinder gasoline, 2200cc |
| Horsepower: | 90 HP |
| Transmission: | 4-speed manual |
| Fuel capacity: | 26.4 Imperial gallons (31.7 US gallons; 120 litres) |
| Maximum speed (road): | 50 mph (80 km/h) |
| Maximum speed (cross-country): | NA |
| Operating radius (road): | NA |
| Operating radius (cross-country): | NA |
| Armour: | 7.5mm-10mm |
| Length: | 181 inches (4600mm) |
| Width: | 89 inches (2250mm) |
| Height: | 83 inches (2100mm) |
| Tire size: | 10.5 x 20 |
| Wheelbase: | 94 inches (2380mm) |
| Track: | 65 inches (1660mm) |
| Ground clearance: | 16 inches (405mm) |
| Trench crossing: | No capability |
| Vertical obstacle: | 14 inches (350mm) |
| Fording depth: | 39 inches (1000mm) |

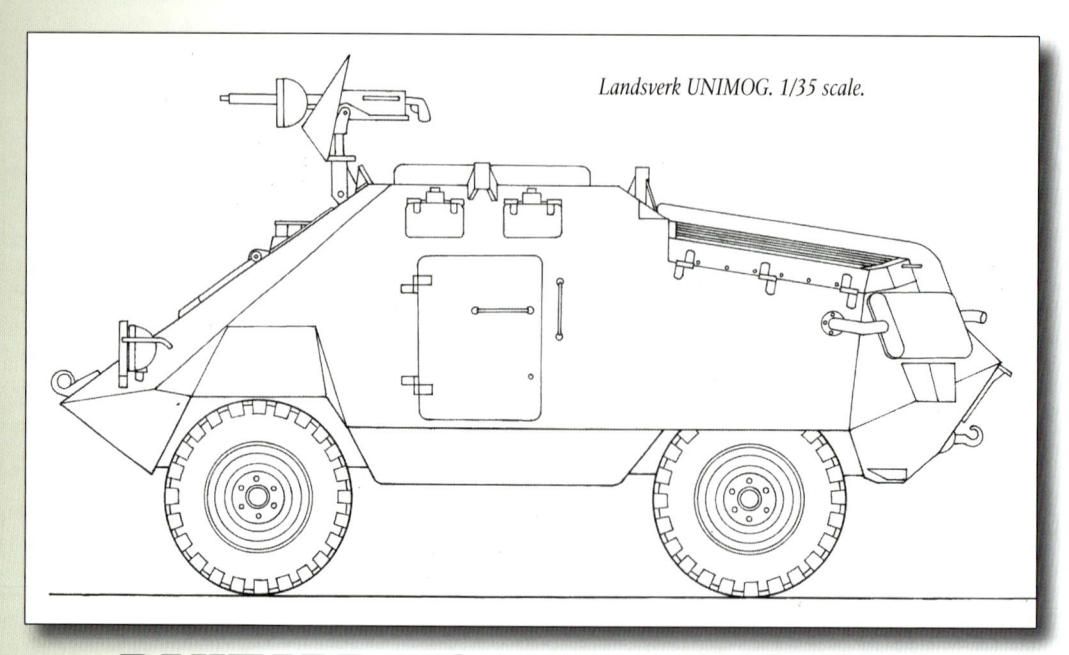

*Landsverk UNIMOG. 1/35 scale.*

# PANHARD M3 VTT ARMOURED PERSONNEL CARRIER

The Panhard M3 VTT (Véhicule Transport de Troupes – Troop Transport Vehicle) is an armoured personnel carrier developed in 1969 by Panhard et Levassor, utilizing some 95% of the AML 245's components, thus making it very attractive from a standardization standpoint. The hull of the M3 is made of all-welded steel armour with the driver seated at the front of the vehicle. The engine is immediately behind the driver with air inlet louvers above and to the rear of the driver, air outlet louvers on either side of the roof, and exhaust pipes running along the side of the hull on each side. The Irish Army ordered 60 VTT M3s, the first 17 of which were delivered in 1972. Irish M3s were fitted with a TL 2.1.80 turret armed with twin 7.62mm machine-guns. Although initially well received because of its characteristics which suited it well to Irish operational conditions, faults soon began to emerge. The vehicle was tiring on drivers because steering was unassisted, and its drum brakes could not be counted on to stop the vehicle as quickly as might be needed at times. The vehicle was also quite cramped. As with the AML armoured cars, the M3 suffered from being underpowered and engine reliability problems developed as a result. Due to the greater size and weight of the VTT compared to the AML cars, its power-to-weight ratio was even worse than that of the AML. In an attempt to rectify this, in 1983 the Army fitted a Peugeot 140 HP V6 engine in an M3, and tests were very successful. This led to rebuilding 14 M3s by a Panhard affiliate near Dublin, installing, in addition to the Peugeot V6 engine, a new power-assisted braking system, new electrical system, and an uprated 6-speed manual gearbox; the upgraded version was referred to as the Buffalo. In addition to being issued to the Motor Squadrons and later to the cavalry squadrons (one troop per squadron), the M3 was also issued to the infantry battalions, on the scale of one mechanized company per battalion. By 1989, the upgraded M3s were issued to the 27th and 28th Infantry Battalions serving along the border with Northern Ireland. At about the same time, the 14 M3s that had been deployed to Lebanon with UNIFIL were replaced by the much more capable Finnish SISU XA-180 armoured personnel carriers, supplied by the UN. The M3s began to be withdrawn from service and scrapped in July 1996. The last of the upgraded M3s served with the 28th Infantry Battalion along the border and were withdrawn from service in 2001. The upgraded Buffalo variant may still be in storage at Finner Camp for possible use along the border with Northern Ireland, as the roads along the border are too narrow for effective use by the much larger Mowags. In 2005 almost all the remaining early models (the pre-Buffalo conversions) were in Coolmoney Camp awaiting their turn to be used as targets. A number have survived as gate guardians, in museums and in the hands of private collectors

*The best preserved and running VTT M3 in Ireland is 6156 ZH, which is maintained by a private collector. One other M3 is displayed at the National Museum of Ireland's Collins Barracks facility in Dublin. Several other M3s are displayed as gate guardians at various Irish military installations. This photograph is from the 2000 celebration of the 80th anniversary of the Cavalry Corps. (Curragh History Group)*

*A VTT M3 clearly showing the firing ports on the upper hull slope, as well as the folded brackets for the fuel cans. The utility of a fire extinguisher on the outside of the vehicle may be somewhat questionable. (MA, Cavalry Collection)*

## Panhard AML M3 Specifications:

| | |
|---|---|
| Manufacturer: | Panhard, Marolles-en-Hurepoix, France; modified by Irish Defence Forces |
| Dates of service (Irish Defence Forces): | 1972-2001 |
| Number in Irish service: | 60 |
| Crew: | 2, plus 10 infantrymen |
| Combat weight: | (6100 kg) |
| Armament: | Two 7.62mm MAG machine-guns |
| Ammunition capacity: | NA |
| Engine: | Panhard Model 4 HD 4-cylinder air cooled gasoline |
| Horsepower: | 90 HP @ 4700 rpm |
| Transmission: | 4-speed manual; 2-speed transfer case |
| Fuel capacity: | 36.3 Imperial gallons (43.6 US gallons; 165 litres) |
| Maximum speed (road): | 62 mph (100 km/h) |
| Maximum speed (cross-country): | NA |
| Operating radius (road): | 373 miles (600 km) |
| Operating radius (cross-country): | NA |
| Armour: | 8mm |
| Length: | 175 inches (4450mm) |
| Width: | 95 inches (2400mm) |
| Height: | 90 inches (2280mm) |
| Tire size: | 11.00 x 16 |
| Wheelbase: | 98 inches (2500mm) |
| Track: | 64 inches (1620mm) |
| Ground clearance: | 13 inches (330mm) |
| Trench crossing: | 32 inches (800mm) |
| Vertical obstacle: | 12 inches (300mm) |
| Fording depth: | 43 inches (1100mm) |

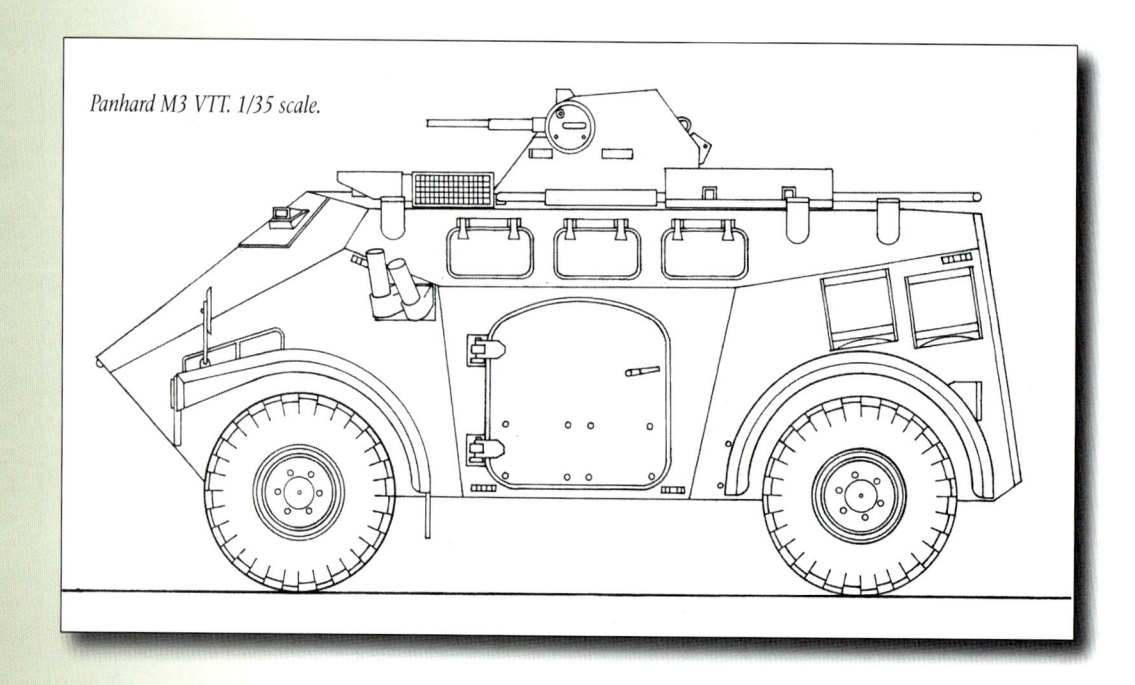

*Panhard M3 VTT. 1/35 scale.*

*A VTT M3 en route from Ireland to Lebanon in 1982 aboard the Irish patrol vessel L.E. Aiofe. Note that the mudguards have been removed for the voyage, that the wheels have been chocked, and that the vehicle has been braced with wooden supports. The rear door hinges have been liberally daubed with grease to protect them against corrosion. (Anonymous, via Paul Murphy)*

*Left side view of 6156 ZH. The collector's degree of care in maintaining this vehicle is noteworthy. An ACMAT truck belonging to the same collector follows the M3. (Sean O'Sullivan)*

*M3 6156 ZH parked in front of the collector's garage which houses several other ex-Irish Army vehicles. (Sean O'Sullivan)*

*Above*: This photograph of a VTT M3 taken at the Curragh in April 2008 provides an excellent comparison to the preceding photograph. Note the brackets for the jerrycans on the rear doors, missing from the vehicle at Coolmoney. (Sean O'Sullivan)

*Above, right*: Another decrepit M3 at Coolmoney Camp in 2005. The side door was very ample, and the upper firing ports themselves are larger than those normally found on armoured fighting vehicles. (Paul Murphy)

*Above*: A Panhard M3 gate guardian at Cathal Brugha Barracks, Rathmines, Dublin. It is fitted with dummy armament. The M3 was issued to infantry as well as cavalry units, and had a service life of almost thirty years with the Irish Army. (Roy Kinsella)

*Above*: One of the VTT M3s at Coolmoney Camp in 2005, awaiting its turn as a target on the Glen of Imaal firing range. The front end of the vehicle shows a different paint colour than the rear portion of the vehicle, which appears to have been sprayed at a later date. Both show the effects of age and weather. Some, but not all of the vehicles awaiting disposition have been painted with prominent red Xs on them. (Paul Murphy)

*Right*: This photograph of an M3 awaiting disposition at Coolmoney Camp provides an excellent view of the twin rear doors to the troop compartment of the vehicle. Note the circular firing ports in each door. (Paul Murphy)

# TIMONEY MK I APC

In response to the escalating violence in Northern Ireland that had begun as early as 1968 and reached a crescendo in 1972, the government of the Republic of Ireland, fearing a possible spread of violence to the Republic or even possibly a British incursion into the Republic, decided to expand the Defence Forces. It was in this context that Technology Investments Ltd (Timoney) of Navan, north of Dublin, offered to provide a new armoured personnel carrier. Although at the time there was some indication that the government might order between 100 and 200 vehicles, the passing of the crisis and decrease in tension with Northern Ireland led to abandonment of any such plans. Nonetheless, three prototypes were built, designated the Mk I, Mk II, and Mk III. The Mk I originally was planned to be built with a wooden mockup body, but instead it was decided that in order to gain experience the body would be fabricated from armour plate. This first prototype brought to light a number of shortcomings and it was found unsuitable as a personnel carrier, but did provide experience that was used in successive prototypes and marks. The Mark I prototype was delivered to the Defence Forces in October 1973 and was maintained on the IDF rolls until 1974 when it was finally retired.

## TIMONEY MARK I SPECIFICATIONS:

(Note: reliable specifications are not available)

| Manufacturer: | Timoney Technology, Navan, County Meath, Ireland |
| --- | --- |
| Dates of service (Irish Defence Forces): | 1973-1974 |
| Number in Irish service: | 1 (prototype) |
| Crew: | 2, plus 10 troops |
| Tire size: | 11.00 x 20 or optional 12.00 x 20 |

# TIMONEY MK II APC

The Mk II was a follow-on prototype to the Mk I and incorporated lessons learned from the Mk I prototype. The Mk II was powered by a Chrysler 360 CID V8 gasoline engine, as were the Mk I and the subsequent Mk III and Mk IV models. The Mk II was delivered to the IDF in April 1974. It was withdrawn from service in 1977.

## TIMONEY MARK II SPECIFICATIONS:

(Note: reliable specifications are not available)

| Manufacturer: | Timoney Technology, Navan, County Meath, Ireland |
| --- | --- |
| Dates of service (Irish Defence Forces): | 1974-1977 |
| Number in Irish service: | 1 (prototype) |
| Crew: | 2, plus 10 troops |
| Tire size: | 11.00 x 20 or optional 12.00 x 20 |

*The Timoney Mk II undergoing trials. The Mk II was characterized by the large air intake on the top of the hull roof, and the inwardly sloping lower sides. (Timoney, via Sean O'Sullivan)*

*The Timoney Mk II prototype in 1999 in a salvage yard. The Mk II was built in prototype only. Although the inwardly sloping sides offered some degree of ballistic protection, they were eliminated in favor of straight sides on later Marks in order to increase internal space. Although there were some hopes that this vehicle would be restored, sadly it has since been scrapped. (By kind permission of Karl Martin)*

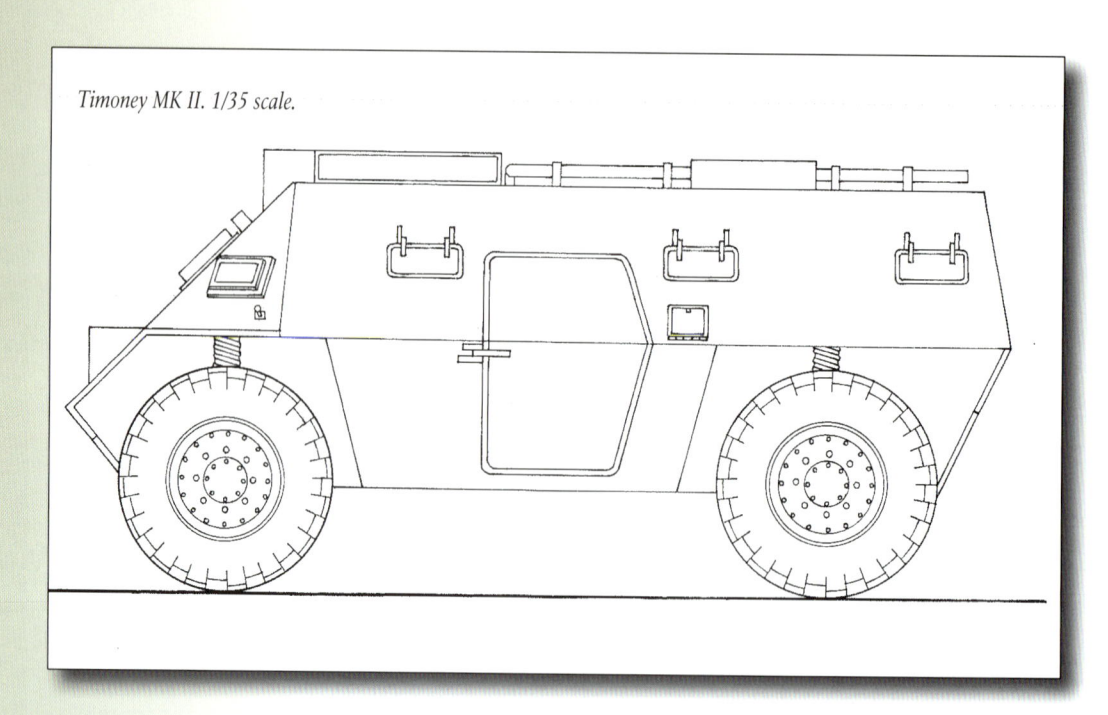

Timoney MK II. 1/35 scale.

# TIMONEY MK III APC

The Mk III incorporated lessons learned from the first two Timoney prototypes, incorporating such improvements as a full width front air intake and bottom side panels that were more vertical than on the predecessors. It also incorporated a turret fitted with twin machine-guns. It was delivered to the IDF in July 1974 and remained in service until at least 1980. Although this third prototype did not result directly in an order for vehicles, it was the vehicle upon which the following Mk IV was based, and which eventually was purchased by the Irish Army.

## Timoney Mark III Specifications:

| | |
|---|---|
| Manufacturer: | Timoney Technology, Navan, County Meath, Ireland |
| Dates of service (Irish Defence Forces): | 1974-1980 |
| Number in Irish service: | 1 (prototype) |
| Crew: | 2 (driver, gunner/commander) plus 10 troops |
| Combat weight: | 14,000 lbs (6350 kg) (empty weight) |
| Armament: | Twin 7.62mm machine-guns |
| Ammunition capacity: | NA |
| Engine: | Chrysler V-8, gasoline, 5900cc (360 cubic inches) |
| Horsepower: | 180 HP |
| Transmission: | Allison AT-540, 4-speed automatic; Timoney 2-speed transfer box |
| Fuel capacity: | 53.5 Imperial gallons (64 US gallons; 243 litres) |
| Maximum speed (road): | 55 mph (88 km/h) |
| Maximum speed (cross-country): | NA |
| Operating radius (road): | 398-597 miles (640-960 km) |
| Operating radius (cross-country): | NA |
| Armour: | NA |
| Length: | 195 inches (4950mm) |
| Width: | 95 inches (2410mm) |
| Height: | 80 inches (2030mm) to hull roof; 98 inches (2480mm) to turret roof |
| Tire size: | 11.00 x 20 or optional 12.00 x 20 |
| Wheelbase: | 113 inches (2870mm) |
| Track: | 76 inches (1930mm) |
| Ground clearance: | 16 inches (400mm) |
| Trench crossing: | NA |
| Vertical obstacle: | 30 inches (760mm) |
| Fording depth: | Amphibious without preparation; speed in water 3 mph (4.8 km/h) |

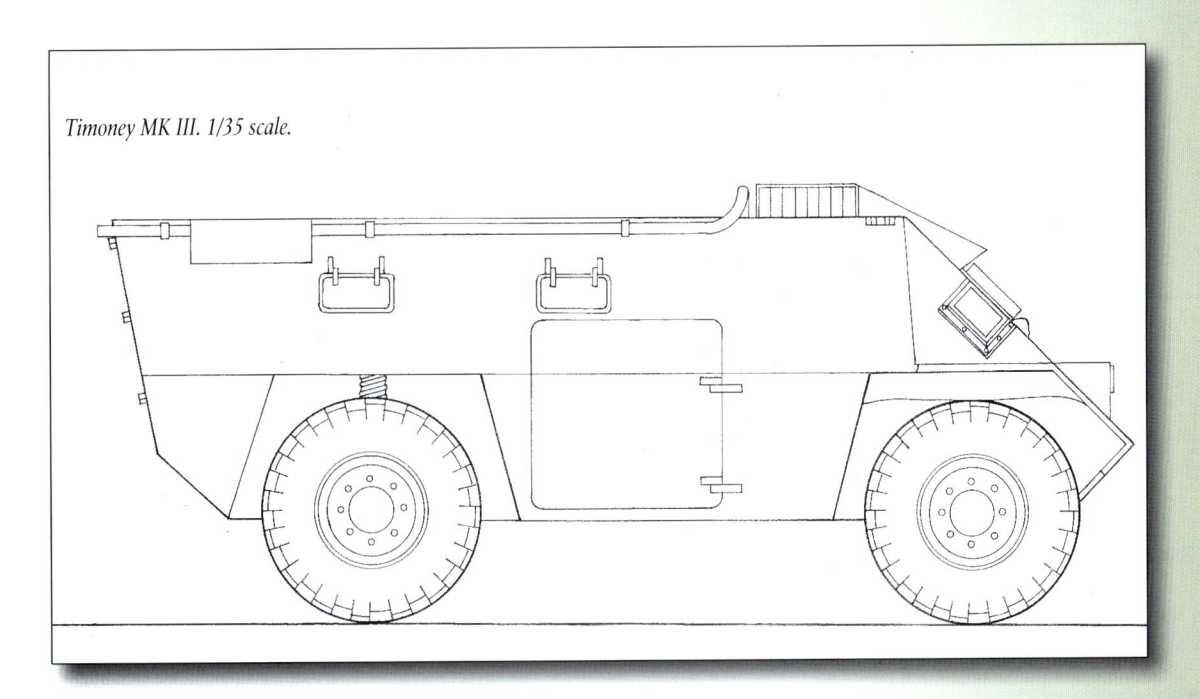

*Timoney MK III. 1/35 scale.*

*The remains of the Timoney Mk III, identifiable by the position of the firing ports. The hulk, which has obviously sustained severe damage as a range target, was photographed at the Glen of Imaal in 2005. (Paul Murphy)*

*Left side view of the same Timoney Mk III hulk. In a relative sense, this side of the vehicle has sustained considerably less damage than has the right-hand side. (Paul Murphy)*

# TIMONEY MK IV APC

*The National Transport Museum's Timoney Mk IV taken in February 2008. It has been primed in gray primer preparatory to further refurbishment. (Terry Ward)*

It was not until December 1977 that the Department of Defence ordered five APCs from Timoney, based on the third prototype (the unofficially designated Mk III). The five APCs, officially designated as the Timoney Mk IV, were delivered during the course of 1978. As with the Mk III predecessor, the Mk IV was fitted with a Timoney designed turret armed with two 7.62mm MAG80 machine-guns. The Mk IVs were used primarily for patrolling along the border with Northern Ireland. In service, the Mk IVs experienced a number of teething problems, especially with their brakes, but the problems were eventually corrected. The MK IVs served until 1988. One example is preserved at the National Transport Museum in Howth, and one is maintained by the Cavalry Corps at Curragh Camp.

## Timoney Mark IV Specifications:

| | |
|---|---|
| Manufacturer: | Timoney Technology, Navan, County Meath, Ireland |
| Dates of service (Irish Defence Forces): | 1978-1988 |
| Number in Irish service: | 5 |
| Crew: | 2 (driver, commander/gunner) plus 10 troops |
| Combat weight: | 17,999 lbs (8164 kg) |
| Armament: | Twin 7.62mm MAG 80 machine-guns |
| Ammunition capacity: | NA |
| Engine: | Chrysler V-8 gasoline, 5900 cc (360 cubic inches) |
| Horsepower: | 180 HP |
| Transmission: | Allison AT-540, 4-speed automatic, with Timoney two-speed transfer box |
| Fuel capacity: | 53.5 Imperial gallons (64 US gallons; 243 litres) |
| Maximum speed (road): | 55 mph (88 km/h) |
| Maximum speed (cross-country): | NA |
| Operating radius (road): | 398-597 miles (640-960 km) |
| Operating radius (cross-country): | NA |
| Armour: | NA |
| Length: | 199 inches (5050mm) |
| Width: | 96 inches (2440mm) |
| Height: | 80 inches (2030mm) to top of hull roof |
| Tire size: | 12.00 x 20 Michelin with run-flat inner tubes |
| Wheelbase: | 118 inches (3003mm) |
| Track: | 76 inches (1930mm) |
| Ground clearance: | NA |
| Trench crossing: | NA |
| Vertical obstacle: | 30 inches (760mm) |
| Fording depth: | Amphibious without preparation |

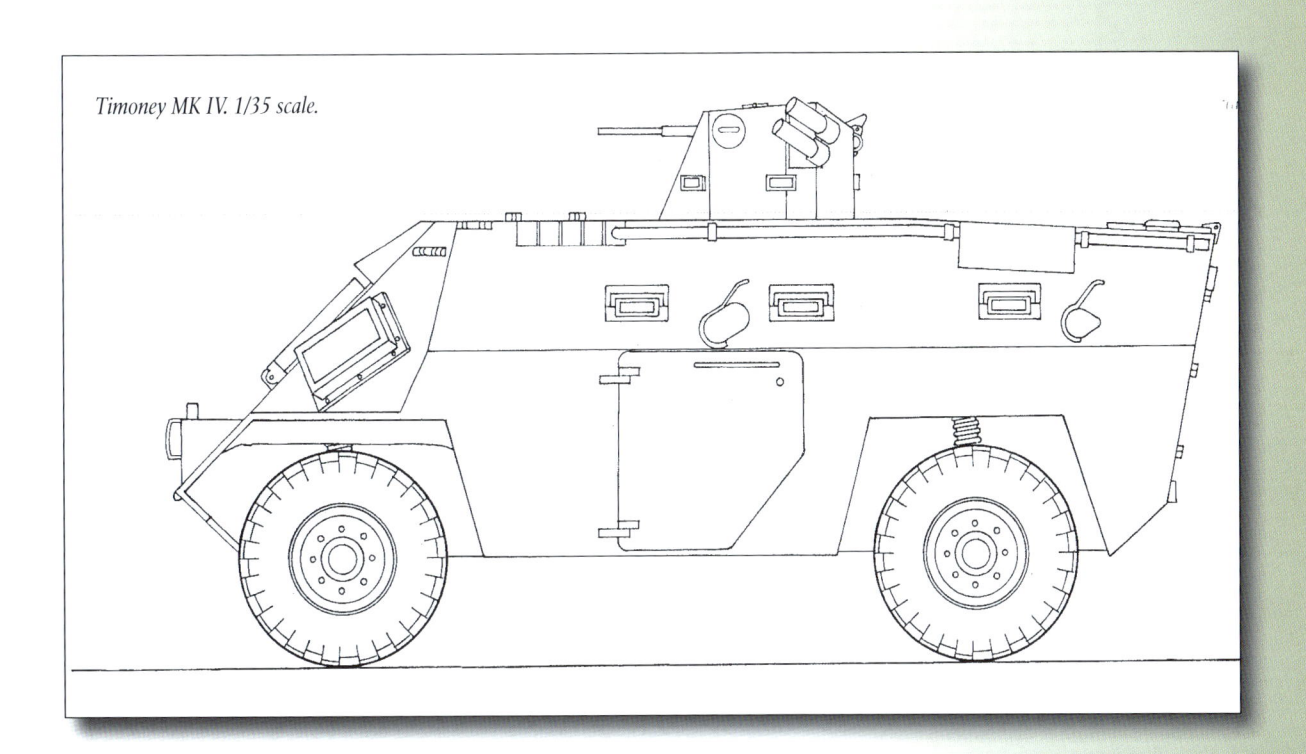

*Timoney MK IV. 1/35 scale.*

*Rear view of the Timoney Mk IV at the National Transport Museum in Howth. The rear plate is slightly angled, providing an increased passive ballistic protection. (Howth)*

# TIMONEY MK VI APC

*Below: Timoney Mk VI, ASI 127, in 1983, the year of its introduction into Irish service. To the left in the picture is a Scorpion tracked reconnaissance vehicle in olive drab livery. The Mk VI served alongside the Scorpion until 1999. Although the Creusot-Loire turret was very compact and presented a somewhat rakish appearance, its angulation provided an undesirable shot trap. (By kind permission of Karl Martin)*

The Mk VI was a much improved version of the Mk IV (there was no Mk V designation; an improved version of the Mk III was built by the Belgian firm of Beherman Demoen and designated the BDX, a further improved version of which, the Valkyr, was manufactured in the UK by Vickers Defence Systems). Five Mk VIs were ordered in June 1981, with deliveries occurring in 1983. The Chrysler gasoline engine of the earlier Timoney models was replaced by a Detroit Diesel model 4-53T turbocharged diesel engine developing 170 HP. The Mk VI was fitted with a Creusot-Loire TLi 127 turret armed with a .50 caliber Browning heavy machine-gun and a 7.62mm MAG 80. The Mk VI was more reliable than the Mk IV, in part due to the diesel engine. However, although it was assigned to the 1st Tank Squadron along with the Scorpion light tank and had excellent cross-country performance for a 4 x 4, it was unable to keep up with the very agile tracked vehicle in a cross-country environment. It did, however, remain in service alongside the Scorpion until 1999. One Mk VI was fitted experimentally with an AML 90 turret but no production resulted. Three Mk VI vehicles have survived and are maintained in Ireland.

## Timoney Mark VI Specifications:

| | |
|---|---|
| Manufacturer: | Timoney Technology, Navan, County Meath, Ireland |
| Dates of service (Irish Defence Forces): | 1983-1999 |
| Number in Irish service: | 5 |
| Crew: | 2 (driver, commander/gunner) plus 10 troops |
| Combat weight: | 22.002 lbs (9980 kg) |
| Armament: | One 12.7mm (.50 caliber) machine-gun; one 7.62mm machine-gun |
| Ammunition capacity: | NA |
| Engine: | Detroit Diesel Model 4-53T diesel |
| Horsepower: | 170 HP @ 2800 rpm |
| Transmission: | Allison AT-545, 4-speed automatic with Timoney two-speed transfer box |
| Fuel capacity: | 66 Imperial gallons (79.25 US gallons; 300 litres) |
| Maximum speed (road): | 65 mph (105 km/h) |
| Maximum speed (cross-country): | NA |
| Operating radius (road): | 305 miles (490 km) |
| Operating radius (cross-country): | NA |
| Armour: | Hull front, back and sides 14mm; roof 12mm; floor 10mm |
| Length: | 195 inches (4950mm) |
| Width: | 98 inches (2500mm) |
| Height: | 108 inches (2746mm) |
| Tire size: | 12.00 x 20 Michelin with run-flat inner tubes |
| Wheelbase: | 118 inches (3003mm) |
| Track: | 87 inches (220mm) |
| Ground clearance: | NA |
| Trench crossing: | NA |
| Vertical obstacle: | 24 inches (600mm) |
| Fording depth: | Amphibious without preparation |

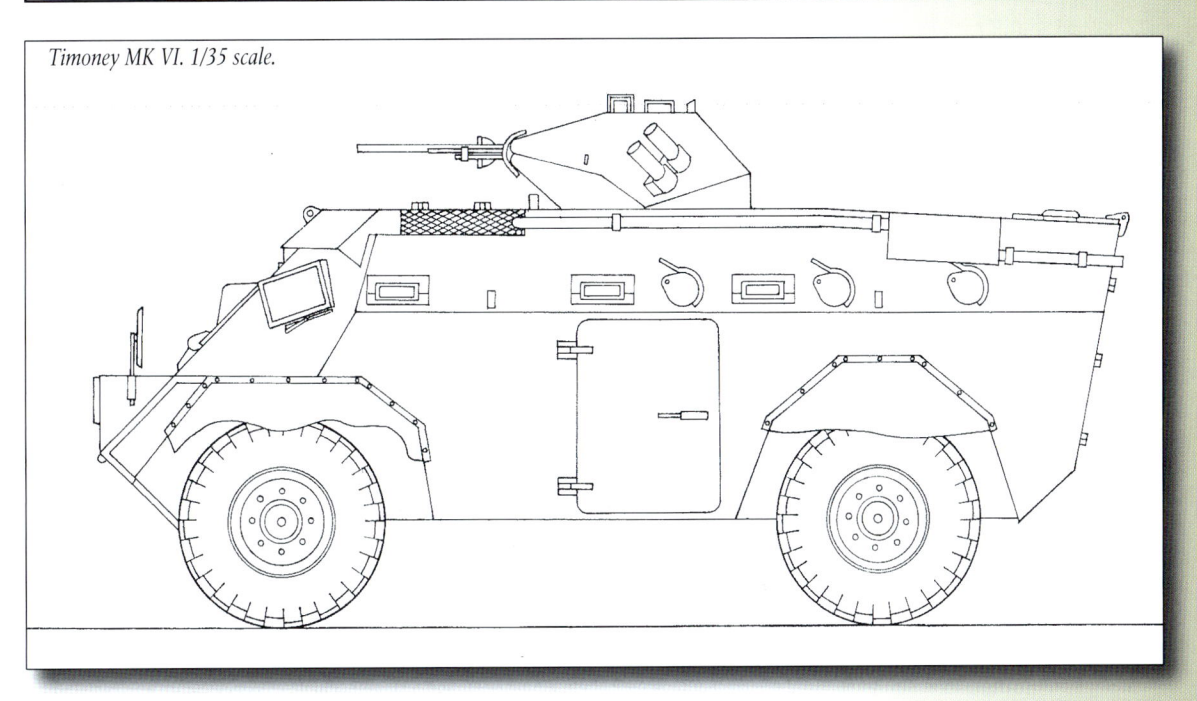

*Timoney MK VI. 1/35 scale.*

Timoney ASI 124 with a Scorpion in the background. This photograph was taken while the Mk VIs were assigned to the 1st Tank Squadron. (Paul Murphy) One of the two surviving Timoney Mk VI personnel carriers (ASI 125), sporting a three-tone camouflage scheme. (Sean O'Sullivan)

¾ front view of ASI 125 in camouflage scheme. Note the rusting Unimog car behind the Timoney. (Sean O'Sullivan)

ASI 125, now part of the Cavalry Corps vintage vehicle collection, in solid green livery. Curragh Camp, 27 May, 2009. (Ralph Riccio)

*A second surviving Mk VI (ASI 128) shown in its original olive drab livery. The shot trap produced by the undercut shape of the Creusot-Loire turret is clearly evident. (Paul Murphy)*

*Timoney Mk VI ASI 128 with an updated three-colour camouflage scheme. The .50 caliber Browning main armament and 7.62mm secondary armament are missing. (Paul Murphy)*

*A Timoney Mk VI at the salvage yard at Coolmoney Camp in September 2005. Although the vehicle appears to be in good condition externally, nevertheless ultimately it was used as a range target. (Paul Murphy)*

*Front view of the Mk VI at Coolmoney Camp, showing evidence of severe damage to its vision blocks, due either to vandalism or possibly to small arms fire. (Paul Murphy)*

**147**

# SISU XA-180 APC

Originally developed by the Finnish state-owned Vammaskosken Tehdas, the SISU XA-180 6 x 6 APC is built by SISU Defence (now part of the Patria Group) of Karjaa, Finland. The XA-180 is based on the SISU SA-150 6 x 6 truck, with which it shares many components. The chassis and wheel arrangement, however, differ markedly from that of the truck. The layout of the XA-180 is somewhat unusual in that the engine is located on the left-hand side of the vehicle, to the rear of the driver. The XA-180 has a crew of two and can carry ten troops. Troops enter and exit the troop compartment via two doors in the rear of the hull. In 1989-1990 the UN supplied the Irish UNIFIL contingent with ten SISUs to replace the 14 Panhard VTT M3 APCs that had been deployed with the contingent. While in Irish service, the Polish 12.7mm NSV heavy machine-gun originally mounted on the XA-180 was replaced by a .50 caliber Browning M2 heavy machine-gun. In 1990 two SISUs were purchased by Ireland, and until 2001 were used for training crews and infantry prior to their departure for duty with the UNIFIL battalion. In 1993, the two SISUs were sent to Somalia to provide additional protection for UNOSOM II convoys, and remained there until September 1994. In 1993-94, the Irish SISUs were fitted with Creusot-Loire turrets from ex-M3 Panhard APCs; these turrets have since been removed, and the SISUs present a "clean" appearance. Although in many respects a satisfactory vehicle (it was easy to drive, had good cross-country mobility, and had good resistance to mines), it was not without its shortcomings. Driver visibility to the right was poor, and lack of a rear access ramp made entering and exiting through the doors somewhat difficult. The two SISUs that were purchased are still (2009) in service with the Combat Service Support College in the Curragh and are used as command cars for AML shoots at the Glen of Imaal.

*Opposite page: SISU 91-D-2347 in white U.N. livery loading aboard a Russian-built Mi-26 Halo helicopter during a U.N. deployment in Somalia. The blackened middle wheel due to exhaust emissions is particularly evident against the white livery. (SISU)*

## SISU XA-180 Specifications:

| | |
|---|---|
| Manufacturer: | SISU Defence (Patria Group), Karjaa, Finland |
| Dates of service (Irish Defence Forces): | 1989-2001 (on loan basis from UN); 1990–present in permanent service in training role |
| Number in Irish service: | 10 (on loan from UN); 2 purchased by Ireland |
| Crew: | 2, plus 10 troops |
| Combat weight: | 33,069 lbs (15,000 kg) combat laden |
| Armament: | 12.7mm Polish NSV heavy machine-gun, replaced by .50 caliber Browning M2 heavy machine-gun on SISUs loaned by the UN to the Irish UNIFIL contingent; the two Irish-owned SISUs were fitted with Creusot-Loire turrets with two 7.62mm MAG machine-guns in 1993-1994, but the turrets have since been removed and the SISUs no longer mount armament |
| Ammunition capacity: | NA |
| Engine: | Valmet 611 DBSJ 6-cylinder in-line turbocharged Diesel |
| Horsepower: | 236 HP |
| Transmission: | Allison MT 643 automatic, with TL380 torque converter |
| Fuel capacity: | 66 Imperial gallons (79.25 US gallons; 300 litres) |
| Maximum speed (road): | 62 mph (100 km/h) |
| Maximum speed (cross-country): | NA |
| Operating radius (road): | 497 miles (800 km) |
| Operating radius (cross-country): | NA |
| Armour: | NA |
| Length: | 291 inches (7390mm) |
| Width: | 114 inches (2900mm) |
| Height: | 104 inches (2650mm) |
| Tire size: | 14.00 x 20 |
| Wheelbase: | 150 inches (3800mm); 75 inches (1600mm) between first and second axle; 75 inches (1600mm) between second and third axle |
| Track: | 79.5 inches (2020mm) front; 60.2 inches (1530mm) rear |
| Ground clearance: | 16 inches (400mm) |
| Trench crossing: | NA |
| Vertical obstacle: | 20 inches (500mm) |
| Fording depth: | Amphibious |

*One of the SISUs acting as a command post on an exercise in the Glen of Imaal, September 2006. The white interior of the open rear troop compartment door provides stark contrast to the olive drab livery. (Bob Cantwell)*

*SISU XA-180. 1/35 scale.*

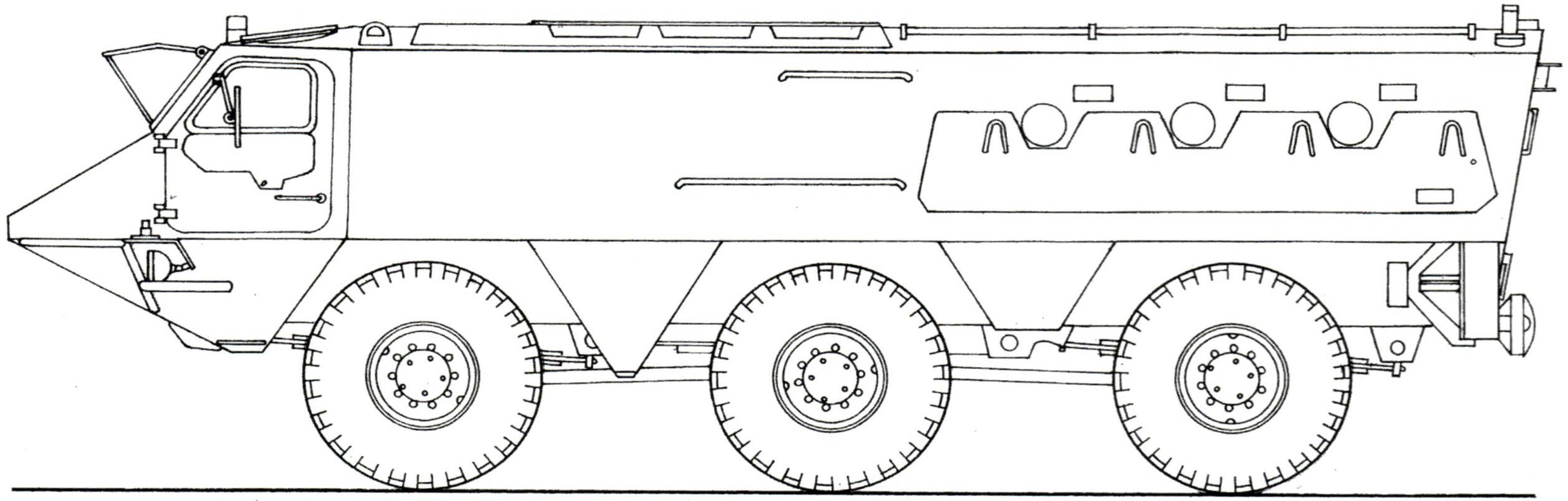

Rear view of the pair of SISUs allowing a clear view of the double rear troop doors and the vanes for the propellers to allow swimming. The propellers, however, are not fitted on the Irish versions. (Bob Cantwell)

Right-side view of both of the Irish SISUs in August 2005. The SISUs are used for training purposes, although they have also been deployed for U.N. peacekeeping duties. (Bob Cantwell)

The second SISU in the Irish inventory, 91-D-2350, showing the effects of having been on a field exercise. Note the difference in paint tones between the SISU and the van parked beside it. (Paul Murphy)

150

SISU XA-180 registration 91-D-2347 parked for a static display. The middle wheel is dirtier than the leading and trailing wheels because the exhaust is vented through the middle wheel well, inevitably blackening the wheel. (Bob Cantwell)

*200: SISU 91-D-2347 in spotless white U.N. livery as it parades in September 2002 on the 80th anniversary of the Cavalry Corps. (Curragh History Group)*

*The driver's station of the SISU. The XA-180 is one of the few vehicles in the Irish inventory to have the driver's position on the left-hand side of the vehicle rather than on the right. The large windows, which are fitted with moveable protective shields, provide excellent vision for the driver. (Roy Kinsella)*

*Interior of the troop compartment of the SISU as seen from the front passenger position. The troop seating area is spacious. Note the firing ports above the seats. (Roy Kinsella)*

*The very photogenic 91-D-2347 while on exercise. The SISU is fitted with smoke dischargers on both sides of the front of the vehicle. (Bob Cantwell)*

# RG-31 MK 3 NYALA

The RG-31 Nyala (the Nyala is a species of antelope found in South Africa) armoured personnel carrier is manufactured in South Africa by BAE Land Systems South Africa (formerly Olifant Manufacturing Company, South Africa). The RG-31 is based on the TFM Industries (South Africa) Mamba APC, which in turn was based on the Mercedes-Benz Unimog truck; it has permanent 4-wheel drive. The vehicle has a V-shaped monocque welded steel hull and high suspension designed to resist powerful mine blasts. The Nyala carries a driver plus nine troops. Around March 1996, three RG-31s were lent to the Irish UNIFIL Battalion by the UN; all of the thirty RG-31s provided to the UN by BAE Land Systems in early 1995 were the Mk 3 version. The RG-31s reverted to UN control upon departure of the battalion to Ireland. In US Army service the RG-31, powered by a Detroit Diesel engine, is known as the Charger.

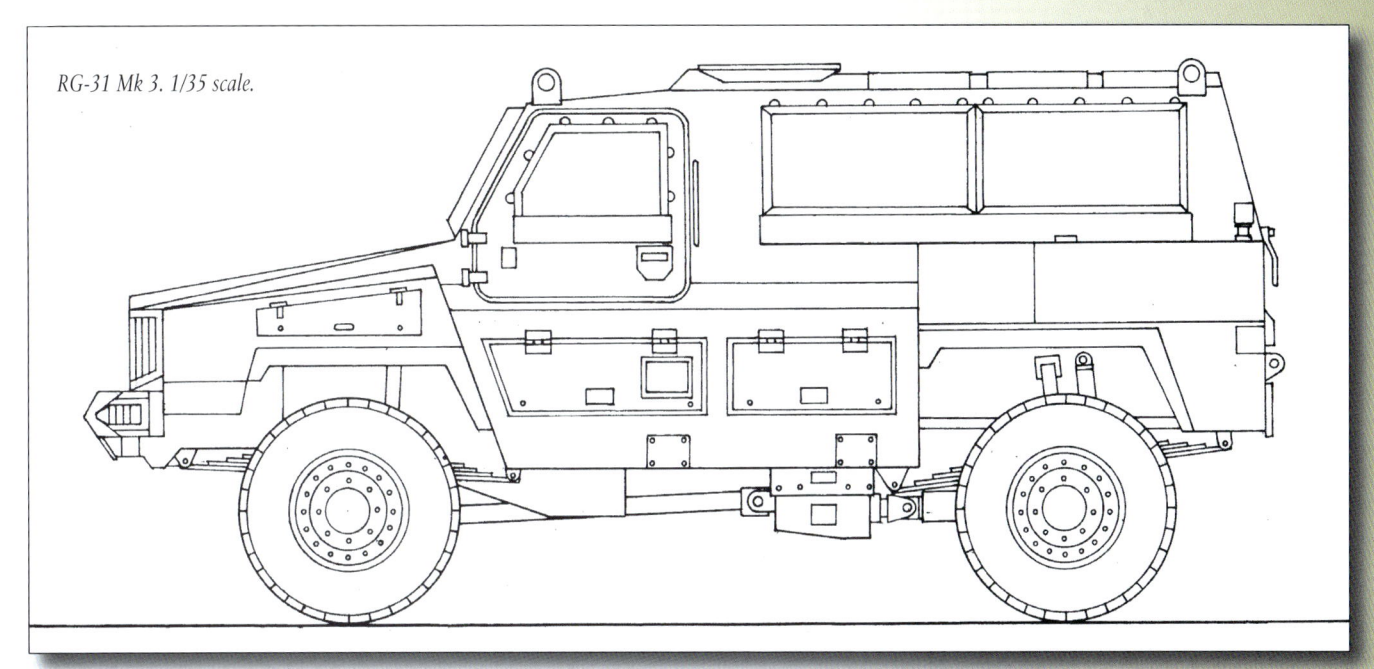

*RG-31 Mk 3. 1/35 scale.*

*An RG 31Mk 3. This is a representative factory photo of the type of vehicle supplied to the Irish UNIFIL contingent in Lebanon by the UN. It provides a high degree of protection and survivability to the occupants. (BAE OMC)*

## RG-31 Mk 3 Nyala Specifications:

| Manufacturer: | BAE Systems Land Systems, Benoni, South Africa |
|---|---|
| Dates of service (Irish Defence Forces): | 1989-199? |
| Number in Irish service: | Three (on loan from UN) |
| Crew: | 10 (driver plus 9 troops) |
| Combat weight: | 18,519 lbs (8400 kg); tare weight 16,244 lbs (7368 kg) |
| Armament: | NA |
| Ammunition capacity: | NA |
| Engine: | Mercedes Benz OM 366 A, 6-cylinder Diesel, 5895cc |
| Horsepower: | 167 HP @ 2800 rpm |
| Transmission: | Allison AT-545, 4-speed automatic, with Rockwell BT 232 2-speed transfer box (permanent 4-wheel drive) |
| Fuel capacity: | NA |
| Maximum speed (road): | 62 mph (100 km/h) |
| Maximum speed (cross-country): | NA |
| Operating radius (road): | NA |
| Operating radius (cross-country): | NA |
| Armour: | NA |
| Length: | 252 inches (6400mm) |
| Width: | 97 inches (2470mm) |
| Height: | 107 inches (2720mm) |
| Tire size: | NA |
| Wheelbase: | 134 inches (3400mm) |
| Track: | 73 inches (1854mm) |
| Ground clearance: | 13 inches (322mm) |
| Trench crossing: | NA |
| Vertical obstacle: | NA |
| Fording depth: | NA |

# MOWAG PIRANHA III H ARMOURED PERSONNEL CARRIER/ARMOURED INFANTRY FIGHTING VEHICLE

In 1999 the Irish Army tested both the Austrian Steyr-Daimler-Puch Pandur 6 x 6 and the Swiss Mowag III 8 x 8 APCs at the Curragh. Despite (or perhaps because of) the fact that the Irish army already had two SISU XA-180 6 x 6 APCs, the SISUs were not considered for acquisition. The tests resulted favorably for the Mowag, and an initial order was placed for 40 Piranhas, subsequently increased to 65, and ultimately (as of 2009) to 80. The Mowag Piranha family of wheeled armoured vehicles was designed, developed and manufactured by the Swiss Mowag Corporation, which is now part of General Dynamics European Land Combat Systems. The Mowag family includes 4x4, 6x6, 8x8, and 10x10 versions. The Mowag III H in service with the Irish Army is a modern 8 x 8 armoured vehicle available in several variants. The Mowag III has been adopted by almost twenty countries other than Ireland, among them the United States, where it is known as the Stryker in the Army and the LAV 25 in the Marine Corps. The Irish Army took delivery of the first tranche of 65 Piranhas beginning in early 2001; this delivery consisted of four different variants, including 54 armoured personnel carriers, eight command vehicles, two ambulances, and one recovery vehicle. Costing well over two million US dollars each, this purchase represents a somewhat radical departure from the long-standing parsimonious attitude of the Irish government towards purchase of military equipment. Although there was the ritual comparison shopping for a new armoured vehicle capable of fulfilling ever expanding Irish requirements, especially in the peacekeeping arena, selection of a state-of-the-art vehicle at the outset was in several respects a first for the Irish Army (although it could be argued that selection and introduction of the FV 101 Scorpion CVR(T) and the Panhard cars could also be considered ground-breaking). In 2007, a further fifteen Piranha variants were delivered, nine of which are the CRV (Close Reconnaissance Vehicle) and six of which are the MRV (Medium Reconnaissance Vehicle) versions. The Mowag APC versions are Infantry assets, whereas the six CRV and nine MRV are Cavalry assets. The CRVs are armed with an Overhead Weapon Station (OWS) fitted with a .50 caliber Browning HB M2 heavy machine-gun and/or a Heckler and Koch (H&K) 40mm automatic grenade launcher (AGL), also referred to as a grenade machine-gun (GMG); the MRVs are fitted with an OTO Melara HITFIST turret mounting a 30 mmm Mk 44 fully stabilized cannon and were delivered in June 2008, and it appears that they will be assigned to the 1st Armoured Cavalry Squadron and integrated with the Scorpion CVR(T)s.

The Mowag APCs are retained under centralized control in the Curragh rather than being issued to individual infantry units. The overriding reason for storing all of the APC version in the Curragh seems to be that the support facilities needed to service them are located there; the facilities also include heated hangers that have enough storage capacity to accommodate all of the Mowags. Although the Mowags originally were supplied with a spares package, the package was not appropriate for Irish operational requirements, and as a result, some vehicles have been cannibalized to keep others running. This has had the unfortunate effect of negating the manufacturer's warranty and exacerbating maintenance problems because, although highly capable machines, they are also very complex and very dependent on skilled maintenance support. To attenuate maintenance problems, the Mowags are transported by flatbed whenever possible, although the army's

*A Mowag III H Piranha undergoing testing by Mowag in Switzerland prior to delivery to Ireland. It is in three-tone leather brown and tar black over bronze green. The initial order to Mowags by Ireland was for 65 vehicles, with deliveries beginning in 2001. (Mowag)*

*A Mowag III H being prepared for deployment on a U.N. peacekeeping mission, December 2007. The vehicle's Irish registration number appears to have been masked off as the vehicle was repainted in U.N. white livery. Although the hull has been painted white, the wheels themselves remain in the original bronze green livery. (Sean O'Sullivan)*

*The Irish Mowag 8 x 8 fitter's vehicle at the Mowag factory prior to delivery to the Irish Army. This is the only repair version of the Piranha in the Irish inventory; cost considerations dictated that only a basic fitter's vehicle be purchased instead of a considerably more expensive, and more capable, fully equipped recovery vehicle (Mowag)*

156

flatbed inventory can handle only moves of a limited number of the APCs at one time. They are also deployed overseas with Irish peacekeeping contingents as the need arises; the first Mowag overseas deployment was with the UN Mission in Ethiopia and Eritrea (UNMEE) in late 2001-early 2002.

## MOWAG PIRANHA III H SPECIFICATIONS:

| | |
|---|---|
| Manufacturer: | Mowag Motorwagenfabrik AG, Kreuzlingen, Switzerland |
| Dates of service (Irish Defence Forces): | 2001- |
| Number in Irish service: | 65 (54 APC, 8 command vehicles, 2 ambulances, 1 recovery vehicle) |
| Crew: | 2 (driver, commander/gunner) plus 9 troops |
| Combat weight: | 40,785 lbs (18,500 kg) |
| Armament: | None |
| Engine: | MTU/Mercedes 6V 183 TE2 Diesel |
| Horsepower: | 400 HP |
| Transmission: | ZF 7 HP 600, 7-speed automatic |
| Fuel capacity: | Two tanks, totaling 70.4 Imperial gallons (2 x 35.2); 84.5 US gallons (2x 42.23) (320 litres; 2 x 160) |
| Maximum speed (road): | 65 mph (105 km/h) |
| Maximum speed (cross-country): | NA |
| Maximum swim speed: | 6.2 mph (10 km/h) |
| Operating radius (road): | 373 miles (600 km) |
| Operating radius (cross-country): | NA |
| Armour: | NA |
| Length: | 274 inches (6960mm) |
| Width: | 105 inches (2660mm) |
| Height: | 85 inches (2170mm) |
| Ground clearance: | 23.5 inches (595mm) |
| Trench crossing: | 79 inches (2000mm) |
| Vertical obstacle: | 24 inches (600mm) |
| Fording depth: | 59 inches (1500mm) |

*A Mowag CRV prior to delivery to the Irish Army. It is fitted with an Overhead Weapons Station (OWS) that can be armed interchangeably with either a .50 caliber Browning HB M2 heavy machinegun or a 40mm Heckler and Koch automatic grenade launcher. The OWS on this CRV is fitted with the Browning machinegun. (Mowag)*

## Mowag Piranha III MRV Specifications:

| | |
|---|---|
| Manufacturer: | Mowag Motorwagenfabrik AG, Kreuzlingen, Switzerland |
| Dates of service (Irish Defence Forces): | 2008 - |
| Number in Irish service: | 9 |
| Crew: | Three (commander, gunner, driver) plus room for four - man dismountable reconnaissance detachment |
| Combat weight: | 47,179 lbs (21,400 kg) |
| Armament: | 1 x 30mm ATK Bushmaster cannon; 2 x 7.62mm machine-guns (one co-axial, one pintle-mounted) |
| Ammunition capacity: | NA |
| Engine: | MTU/Mercedes 6V 183 TE2 Diesel |
| Horsepower: | 400 HP |
| Transmission: | ZF 7 HP 600, 7-speed automatic |
| Fuel capacity: | Two tanks, totaling 70.4 Imperial gallons (2 x 35.2); 84.5 US gallons (2x 42.23) (320 litres; 2 x 160) |
| Maximum speed (road): | 65 mph (105 km/h) |
| Maximum speed (cross-country): | NA |
| Maximum swim speed: | 6.2 mph (10 km/h) |
| Operating radius (road): | 373 miles (600 km) |
| Operating radius (cross-country): | NA |
| Armour: | NA |
| Length: | 274 inches (6960mm) |
| Width: | 105 inches (2660mm) |
| Height: | 134 inches (3400mm) |
| Tire size: | NA |
| Wheelbase: | NA |
| Track: | NA |
| Ground clearance: | 23.5 inches (595mm) |
| Trench crossing: | 79 inches (2000mm) |
| Vertical obstacle: | 24 inches (600mm) |
| Fording depth: | 59 inches (1500mm) |

*A factory image of an Irish Mowag MRV fitted with the Italian OTO Melara 30mm HITFIST turret. The two man OTO turret is welded aluminum armour with additional appliqué armour to meet higher threat levels and mounts a 30mm Mk44 cannon and 7.62mm machinegun. Turret traverse and weapon elevation are all electric with manual backup, and a roof-mounted meteorological sensor is standard. (Mowag)*

*Mowag Piranha III H. 1/35 scale.*

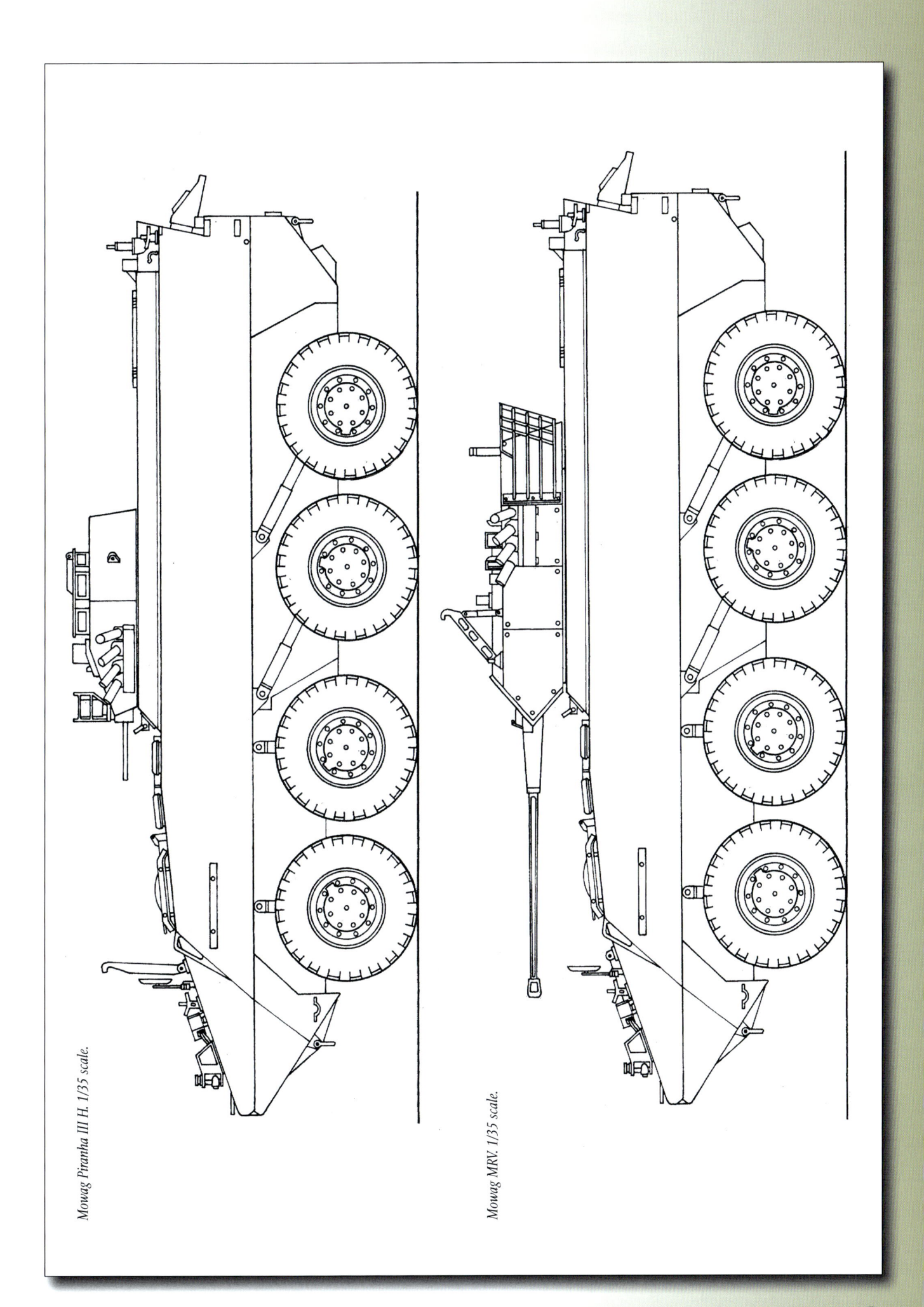

*Mowag MRV. 1/35 scale.*

*A Mowag that appears to have returned from service with a U.N. contingent. Its white paint has been worn in several places indicating field use. Note that the Mowag logo on the leading corner has not been painted over, and that the headlights as well as the wheels retain the factory bronze green colour. (Paul Murphy)*

*A Mowag returned from U.N. duties undergoing maintenance and repairs at the Combined Vehicles Base Workshop, Curragh Camp, 27 May, 2009. (Roy Kinsella)*

*An accident staged for training purposes during the International Military Police Course held in July 2008. This course is held annually in the Curragh, sponsored by the Irish Defence Forces Military Police School, and invites military and civil police authorities internationally, and runs 4-5 weeks. The Piranha obviously has come off as the winner in this encounter with a Toyota Cynos, supplied by the Garda in Kildare that had impounded it in connection with a police operation. (Roy Kinsella)*

*An MRV at speed, with the undercut glacis nicely deflecting the bow wave. The HITFIST turret incorporates a laser rangefinder and a thermal night vision camera. The barrel of the 30mm OTO-Melara cannon is fluted for strength and for cooling. (Irish Defence Forces)*

*Right side view of a Mowag MRV driving along a stream bed. The three-tone camouflage pattern is fairly effective against the backdrop of trees in this setting. (Irish Defence Forces)*

*A Piranha in the Curragh in 2008. A windscreen has been provided to protect the driver while driving with the hatch open and his head exposed. (Roy Kinsella)*

*The Mowag ambulance version. Of the 65 Mowags in the Irish Army inventory, there are two of the ambulance version. There is also one fitter's vehicle version in the inventory. (Roy Kinsella)*

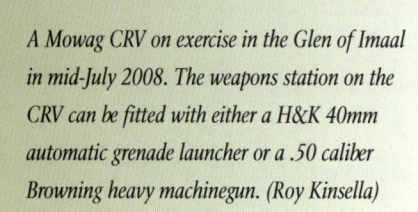

*A Mowag CRV on exercise in the Glen of Imaal in mid-July 2008. The weapons station on the CRV can be fitted with either a H&K 40mm automatic grenade launcher or a .50 caliber Browning heavy machinegun. (Roy Kinsella)*

*Mowag CRV interior, Glen of Imaal, July 2008. Note the camera screen over the front left seat. An H&K grenade launcher is secured on floor on the left, and a spare .50 caliber heavy machinegun barrel is on floor on right, next to the ammunition box. (Roy Kinsella).*

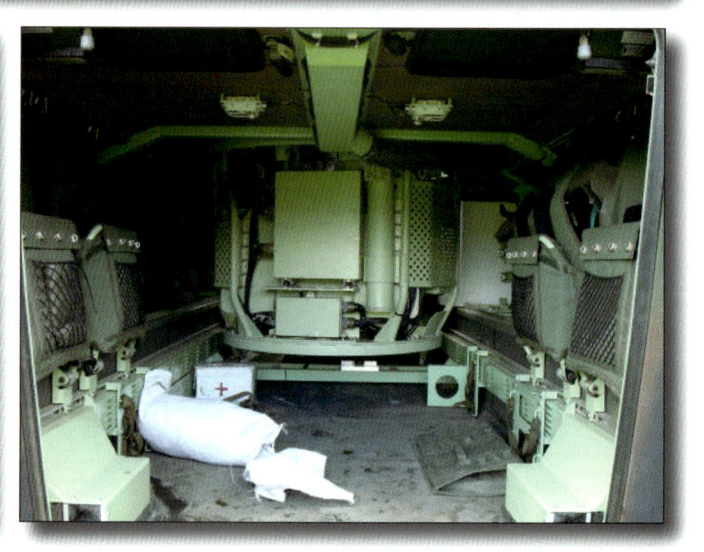

*Interior of a Mowag MRV showing the prominent turret basket. The large white box ahead and to the right of turret contains equipment for chemical attack. (Roy Kinsella)*

The CRV's weapons station fitted with the Heckler and Koch 40mm automatic grenade launcher. The station also has two banks of four smoke grenade launchers. The grenade launcher can be replaced with a .50 caliber Browning heavy machinegun depending on mission requirements. (Roy Kinsella)

The H&K automatic grenade launcher seen from the right-hand side. The automatic grenade launcher, also referred to as a grenade machine gun, can fire single rounds or continuous fire and has a range of 2,200 meters. (Roy Kinsella)

Detail of the open rear ramp of a Piranha, with its integral door. The raised ribs are designed to provide better traction for entering and exiting troops than would a smooth surface. (Roy Kinsella)

The Mowag driver's compartment. (Roy Kinsella)

A Mercedes MTU Diesel engine as used in the Mowag Piranha III. (Roy Kinsella)

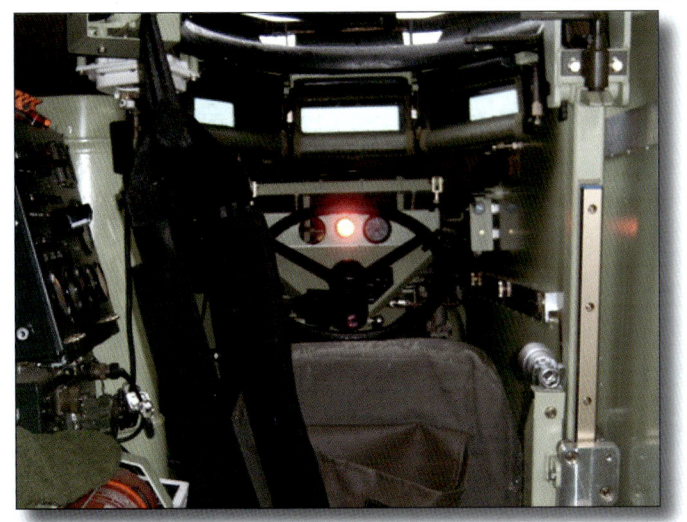

163

# BAE RG 32M LTV LIGHT TACTICAL VEHICLE (LTV)

Since at least 2005, in light of its increasing commitments to peacekeeping operations, the Irish Army has been interested in acquiring a light tactical armoured vehicle (LTAV) for patrol duties. The first attempt to choose a LTAV, which called for acquisition of 66 vehicles, was cancelled in September 2005. A new tender competition was initiated by the Department of Defence in May 2008; tenders were received in July and were evaluated by a military/civilian project team. In September 2008 the three finalists were announced, these being the Swiss Mowag Eagle 4, the Italian IVECO Panther LMV, and the BAE Systems South Africa RG 32M. A standard vehicle from each company was delivered to Curragh Camp for trials, which continued until early November 2008. In December 2008, selection was made and a decision was announced to purchase the BAE Systems RG 32. In accordance with the terms of the original proposal, a 19.6 million Euro contract was awarded for 27 vehicles (17 for deployment on overseas missions, and ten to remain in Ireland for training purposes), with an option to buy a similar number as a follow-on order. The RG 32M, described as a "mine-hardened patrol vehicle," will operate alongside the Irish Mowag armoured personnel carrier fleet. The Irish variant offers more internal crew space than the initial variant of the vehicle, due to a 200mm wider hull and 50mm increased headspace. Windows are externally mounted, providing improved side-blast protection while also freeing up space inside the cabin. Other features are an improved 2-ton payload capability and a newly designed load bay that can accommodate a variety of mission-specific equipment. The vehicles will be delivered over a three-year period, beginning in 2009. They will be used in a variety of roles, including surveillance, communication, target acquisition, and carrying the Javelin anti-armour missile. Armament will consist of a remotely operated turret similar to that fitted to the Mowag CRV, with a .50 caliber heavy machine-gun or a 40mm grenade launcher.

*Manufacturer's photo of an RG 32M LTV. The RG 32M LTV was one of the three vehicles tested by the Irish Army in late 2008, and was selected over the competing vehicles. The other contenders were the Swiss Mowag Eagle 4, and the Italian IVECO Panther LMV. (BAE OMC)*

*RG 32M. 1/35 scale.*

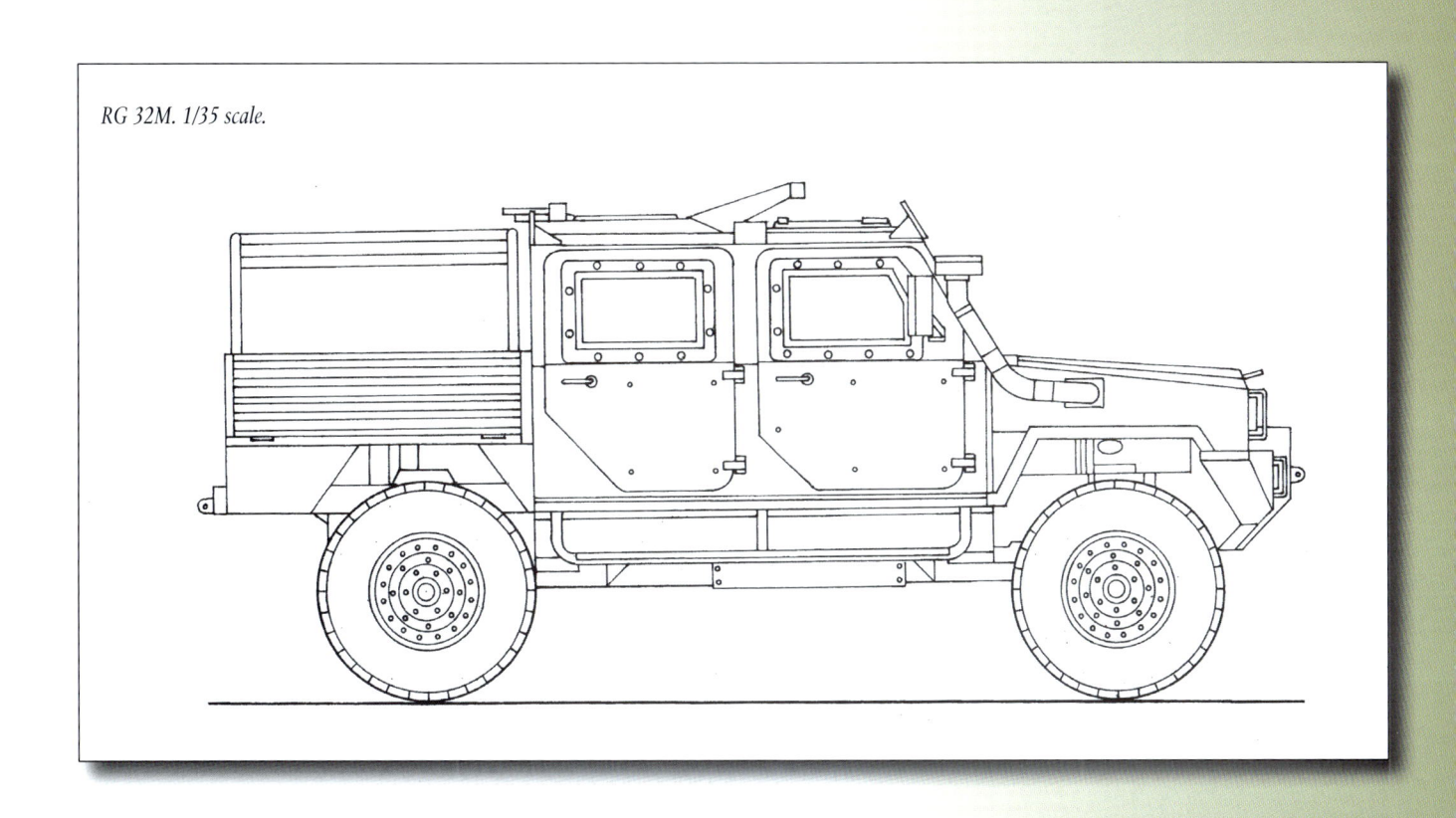

## BAE RG 32M LTV Light Tactical Vehicle (LTV) Specifications::

| | |
|---|---|
| Manufacturer: | BAE Systems Land Systems OMC, Benoni, South Africa |
| Dates of service (Irish Defence Forces): | 2009- |
| Number in Irish service: | 27 (initial contract; 27 additional possible) |
| Crew: | Driver, plus four troops |
| Unladen weight/Combat weight: | 16,755 lbs (7600 kg)/19,842 lbs (9000kg) |
| Armament: | .50 caliber Browning heavy machine-gun or 40mm automatic grenade launcher |
| Ammunition capacity: | NA |
| Engine: | Steyr M16 SCI 6-cylinder inline, 3.2 litre, sequential turbo, intercooled, direct injected |
| Horsepower: | 268 @ 4000 rpm (200 kW) |
| Transmission: | Allison S1000. 5-speed automatic with Atlas II two-speed gear driven syncrhonised transfer case |
| Fuel capacity: | NA |
| Maximum speed (road): | 81 mph (130 km/h) |
| Operating radius (road): | 466 miles (750 km) |
| Armour: | All steel, welded (thickness NA) |
| Length: | 211 inches (5360mm) |
| Width: | 101.5 inches (2580mm) |
| Height: | 85 inches (2150mm) |
| Tire size: | Hutchinson 11 x 20 forged aluminum 3-piece split rim with Michelin 335/80 R20 XZL tires; Hutchinson VFI run flat insert |
| Wheelbase: | 132 inches (3345mm) |
| Track: | 71 inches (1810mm) |
| Ground clearance: | 17 inches (440mm) |

*A pair of newly arrived RG 32M LTVs. The vehicle in the foreground mounts the 40mm grenade launcher, while that in the background has a small shielded enclosure for a GPMG. (Irish Defence Forces)*

*Two recently delivered RG 32M LTVs on the move in Ireland. Although barely visible, the driver is on the left-hand side; this option was selected in view of the presumed employment in peacekeeping missions overseas in environments where driving is on the right-hand side of the road. (Irish Defence Forces)*

# VICKERS MK D TANK

The first tracked vehicle to enter the Irish armour inventory was the Vickers-Armstrongs Mark D medium tank, based on the Vickers Mk II which had been in service with the British Army since 1925. Except for the fitting of a turret cupola for the commander, it was essentially was the same tank as the Mark C, one example of which had been purchased by Japan and which led to development of their own Type 89 Medium Tank. The Mark D was acquired in 1929 and was stationed at the Curragh, where a small cadre was formed to maintain the Vickers, to conduct training and to demonstrate its capabilities to other Army units. In addition to its main armament of a 6-pdr gun, the tank fairly bristled with machine-guns; one was mounted in the front plate, one was mounted in the rear of the turret, and there was one on each side of the hull. In 1940 the Vickers was badly damaged during anti-tank defence trials and was withdrawn from service because it would not have been economically feasible to repair it. Although the tank was scrapped, its turret was salvaged and used as part of a pillbox in the static defences of Curragh Camp.

*The Vickers Mk D was the first tank in Irish service. It mounted a 6-pdr gun, which was a respectable main armament for the times. The Mk D was not series produced, and remained the only tank in the Irish inventory until delivery of the two Swedish Landsverk L 60s in 1935-1936, tripling the size of the Irish armour force. (Matt McNamara)*

*Instruction on the workings of the Mk D. The pool of cadre and personnel familiar with the operation and maintenance of the Mk D was extremely small. The Mk D was used primarily to train soldiers in anti-tank measures; it did not constitute a viable armour force for the Irish Army. (MA)*

167

*Vickers Mk D. 1/35 scale.*

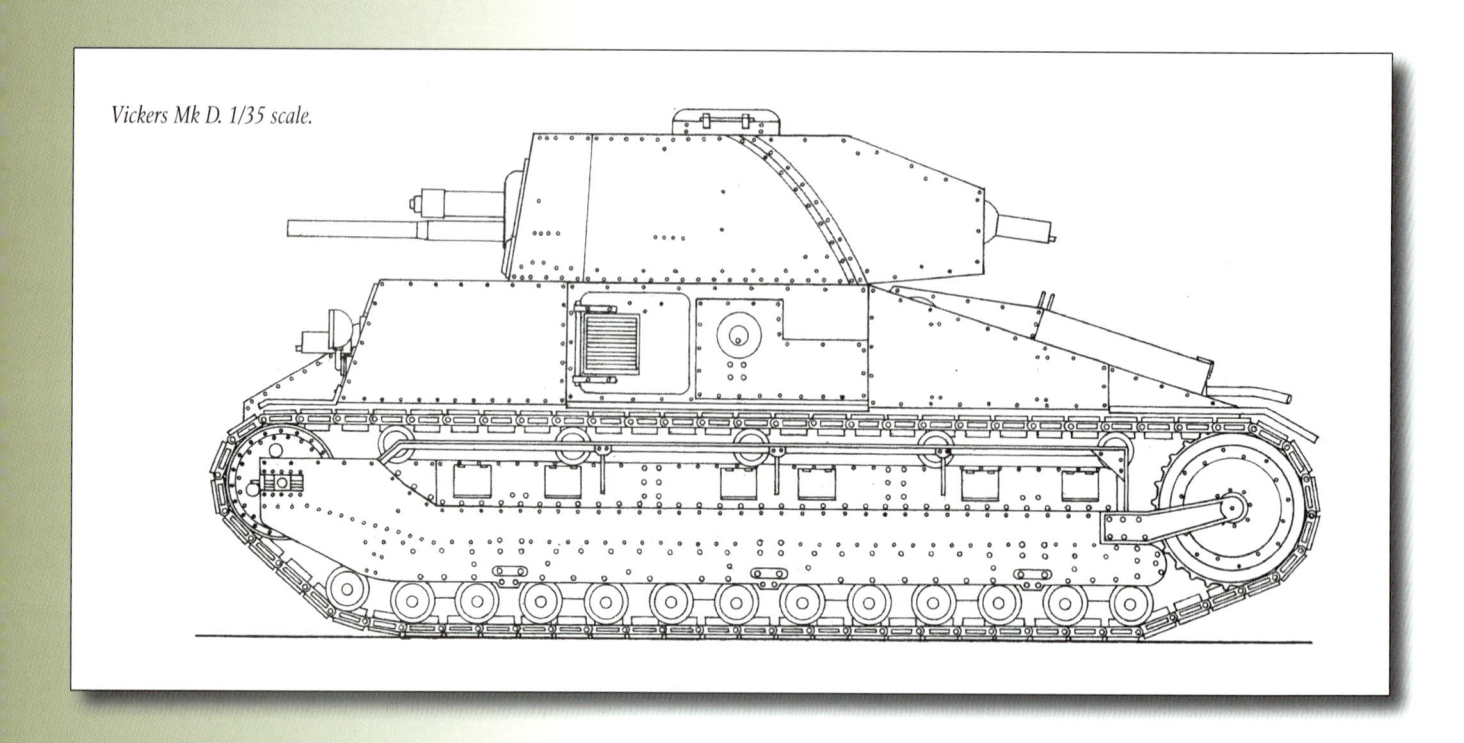

## Vickers Mark D Specifications:

| | |
|---|---|
| Manufacturer: | Vickers-Armstrongs |
| Dates of service (Irish Defence Forces): | 1929-1940 |
| Number in Irish service: | 1 |
| Crew: | 5 |
| Combat weight: | 27,216 lbs (12,345 kg) |
| Main armament: | 6-pdr gun |
| Secondary armament: | Four Vickers .303 in. machine-guns |
| Ammunition capacity: | 20 rounds (?) main gun; 1500 rounds .303 in. |
| Engine: | Sunbeam Amazon 6-cylinder gasoline |
| Horsepower: | 170 @ 2100 rpm |
| Transmission: | NA |
| Fuel capacity: | Three tanks totaling 88.5 Imperial gallons (106.3 US gallons, 402.5 litres). Two tanks held 31 Imperial gallons (37.25 US gallons, 141 litres) each, and one tank held 26.5 Imperial gallons (31.8 US gallons, 120.5 litres) |
| Maximum speed (road): | 20 mph (32 km/h) |
| Maximum speed (cross-country): | 15 mph (24 km/h) |
| Operating radius (road): | 130 miles (209 km) |
| Armour: | NA |
| Length: | 210 inches (5334mm) |
| Width: | 100 inches (2540mm) |
| Height: | 96 inches (2438mm) |
| Track width: | 12 inches (305mm) |
| Trench crossing: | 78 inches (1981mm) |
| Vertical obstacle: | 30 inches (762mm) approximate |

# LANDSVERK L60 TANK

Not long after the Irish Army had taken delivery of the Vickers Mk D, Irish Army authorities realised that one tank was hardly better than no tanks at all, and that in order to conduct any kind of effective tank or anti-tank training, more tanks would have to be acquired. The financial constraints that seemed to have been a constant consideration for the Army enabled the purchase of only two additional light tanks, and the choice fell upon the Swedish L 60 tank. The L60 was an interwar German design produced in Sweden by Aktiebolaget (AB) Landsverk of Landskrona. AB Landsverk began life in 1872 as Firman Pettersen & Ohlsen, manufacturing railroad cars, harbour cranes, and agricultural machinery. By 1920 it was on the verge of bankruptcy, and through a Dutch intermediary, German investors acquired 50% of its shares. In 1923 the company began manufacturing tracked agricultural tractors based on an American design, and by 1925, 61% of the company was German-owned, and in 1928 the name was changed to AB Landsverk. In 1929 a German engineer named Otto Merker was taken on by Landsverk to design armoured vehicles, eventually developing the L 180 armoured car and the L 60 light tank. At the time of its introduction in 1934 the L 60 was considered to be an advanced design, incorporating innovative torsion bar suspension, and was used not only by Sweden but by Hungary as well, where it was designated the Toldi 38.M (the Hungarian designation was 38.M Toldi I könnyű harckocsi, or 38.M Toldi I light tank). The armament on the Hungarian Toldi 38.M consisted of a 20mm Solothurn anti-tank rifle and an 8mm Gebauer machine-gun in lieu of the 20mm Danish Madsen anti-tank gun and .303 in. Madsen machine-gun as fitted on the Irish L60s. In 1935-36, two L60s were delivered to Ireland where they joined the Vickers Mk D and were attached to the Cavalry School. One source suggests that there were plans to build additional L 60s under license at the Great Northern Railway Works in Dundalk, but that these plans never materialized.[13] During World War II the L 60s were based at the Curragh Camp as part of the camp's local defence force. The L60s continued

*The first of the two Landsverk light tanks in Irish service, complete with pioneer tools. It bears the number L.6 01. Its 20mm Madsen anti-tank cannon was the precursor of similar armament on the Landsverk L 180 armoured cars and Irish-built Leyland armoured cars that subsequently served in the Irish Army. The L 60s, along with the Vickers Mk D tank, were used for training purposes only. (MA/N/358)*

13  Adrian J. English, Irish Army Orders of Battle, 1923-2004, page 20.

in use, mainly in a training role, until the early 1960s. From early 1953 onwards, the L 60s became increasingly difficult and expensive to maintain. A proposal to fit the tanks with the same Ford V-8 engine used to upgrade the Landsverk L 180 armoured cars was not pursued due to the prohibitively high cost, and at the same time obtaining replacement tracks became a problem. By late 1968 both tanks were designated as of no operational value. They were not sold or scrapped; one has been preserved at the Cavalry Museum at Curragh Camp, and the other is now on display at the National Museum of Ireland, Collins Barracks, Dublin.

## LANDSVERK L60 SPECIFICATIONS:

| Manufacturer: | AB Landsverk, Landskrona, Sweden |
|---|---|
| Dates of service (Irish Defence Forces): | 1935-1960s (?) |
| Number in Irish service: | 2 |
| Crew: | 3 (commander, gunner, driver) |
| Combat weight: | 15,212 lbs (6900 kg) |
| Armament: | 20mm Madsen L.60 anti-tank gun; one .303 in. Madsen machine-gun |
| Ammunition capacity: | NA |
| Engine: | Büssing-Nag V-8 gasoline, 7913cc |
| Horsepower: | 160 |
| Transmission: | Manual |
| Fuel capacity: | NA |
| Maximum speed (road): | 28 mph (45 km/h) |
| Operating radius (road): | 180 miles (290 km) |
| Armour: | 13-15mm (6mm roof and bottom) |
| Length: | 181 inches (4600mm) |
| Width: | 79 inches (2000mm) |
| Height: | 82 inches (2080mm) |
| Track width: | NA |
| Ground clearance: | NA |
| Trench crossing: | NA |
| Vertical obstacle: | NA |
| Fording depth: | NA |

*Both of the Landsverk L 60s at Tintown, the Curragh, date unknown. The angle of the track guard on the second tank seems to be much steeper than that on the lead tank, perhaps due to acceleration of the vehicle at the moment the photograph was taken, thus raising the front end of the vehicle. (MA, Cavalry Collection)*

*Landsverk L60. 1/35 scale.*

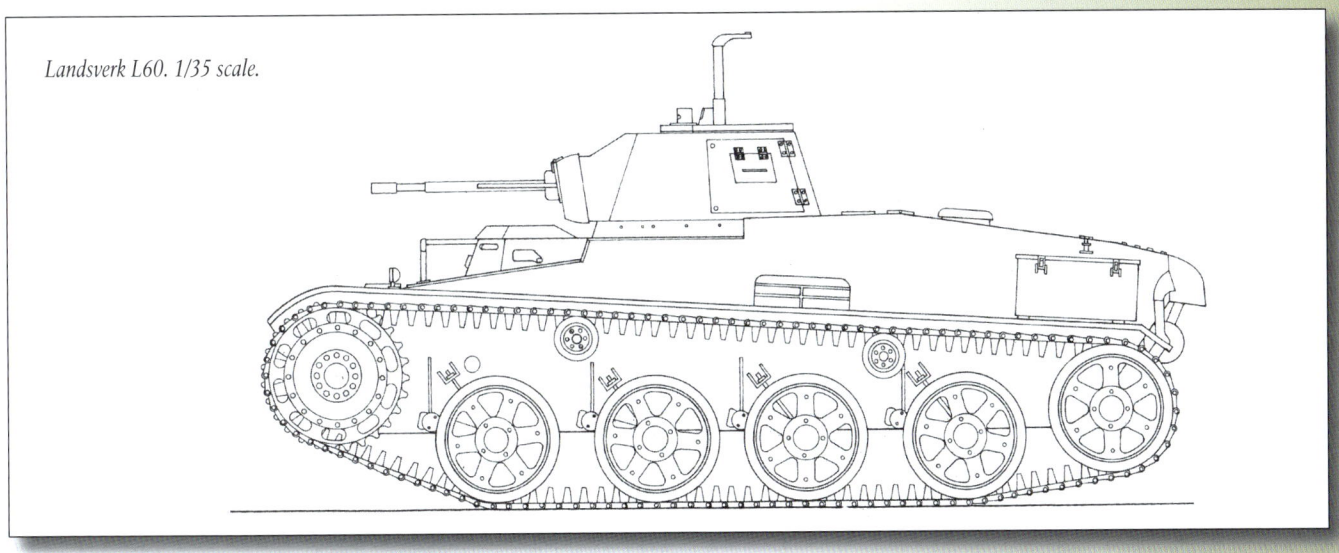

*Rear view of the restored L 60 belonging to the Cavalry Corps. The muffler's oxidized condition in contrast to the fresh paint is evidence of at least occasional running of the vehicle. (Sean O'Sullivan)*

*Both of the Landsverk L 60s in Irish service have survived. Although pictured here as a gate guardian at Curragh Camp, this vehicle has since been cosmetically refurbished and as of 2009 is on display at the National Museum of Ireland, Collins Barracks, Dublin. Its grey livery here is weathered from exposure to the elements, but otherwise it remains essentially complete and intact except for headlights and rear fender stowage boxes. (Paul Murphy)*

*A close-up of the L 60 gate guardian. From this angle and at this distance, the tank appears much more imposing than it actually was. Although considered an advanced design for its time, it nevertheless remained a light, and lightly armed, tank. (Bob Cantwell)*

**171**

*The Cavalry Corps' restored L 60 in September 2006 at a display in the Curragh. Its 20mm main armament is not fitted. (Bob Cantwell)*

*This photograph of an L 60 parked next to a jeep provides a frame of reference as to the relative size of the tank. (Bob Cantwell)*

# UNIVERSAL CARRIER (BREN GUN CARRIER)

During the inter-war period, it became somewhat the vogue to experiment with very small tanks, often described as "tankettes" or machine-gun carriers, with one or two-man crews. The British were the principal developers of this type of vehicle, producing the Carden-Loyd carrier (further developed by the Italians into the L.3 series of light tanks that formed the majority of Italy's armoured force at the outset of World War II, and which enjoyed some modest export success as well), as well as the 1934 Vickers machine-gun carrier that ultimately morphed into the Universal Carrier, commonly referred to as the Bren Carrier in reference to the armament with which it was fitted. The hull of the vehicle was a simple steel box with the engine compartment located in the center. The driver and gunner sat in a front compartment, with the radiator grill mounted in a bulkhead between them. Behind the crew were two rectangular compartments, one on each side of the engine, used to carry supplies or personnel. In mid-1940, 26 Universal Carriers Mk I were acquired from Britain and were formed into a Carrier Squadron in October of the same year. The carriers were armed with the .303 in. Bren light machine-gun. In January 1943 the Carrier Squadron was disbanded and the carriers were turned over to infantry battalions. In order to fully equip the infantry battalions with carriers, a further two hundred carriers were purchased during the war, one hundred of which were Mk I mortar carriers, and one hundred of which were the Mk II version. The two Marks differed slightly in design and manufacture; the Mk I was riveted, while the Mk II was both riveted and welded. The mortar carrier had brackets on the rear plate for carrying a 3-inch or 81mm mortar tube; the baseplate was carried on the front of the vehicle. Most battalions received nine Universal Carriers (one for the battalion CO, four for the mortar platoon, and four for the reconnaissance platoon), although some may have received as many as thirty seven carriers in a support company with a mortar platoon, two medium machine-gun carrier platoons, and possibly an anti-tank platoon with towed two-pounder guns. Two of the carriers were modified by adding flamethrowers. Sometime during the 1950s a number of the carriers were returned to the Cavalry Corps, assigned on a scale of eight carriers per Motor Squadron. In the early 1960s a reserve of carriers was stationed at McKee Barracks for defence of Dublin Airport. By 1965 the carriers had been broken up and sold as scrap. One Universal Carrier has been preserved at the Cavalry Museum, a second is on display at Collins Barracks, Dublin, and another is owned by a private collector in Clonmel, but it is not in running condition.

*The restored Cavalry Corps Universal Carrier at a static display at the Curragh in 2006. In the late 1940s, some carriers were pressed into the role as prime movers for 6-pdr anti-tank guns. (Bob Cantwell)*

# CHURCHILL MK VI TANK

Following the end of World War II, Ireland decided to acquire a more modern and capable tank than the Landsverk L60s that were still in service. The choice fell upon the British Churchill infantry tank, originally designated the A20, four prototypes of which were produced by Harland and Wolff in Belfast by June 1940. The A20 was not accepted, but a follow-on design based on the A20, designated the A22, was prepared by Vauxhall Motors as the "production parent," with production beginning in June 1941. At least a dozen different variants of the basic gun-armed tank were produced, each incorporating successive improvements or modifications. The earliest versions suffered significant teething problems, but these were remedied in the later versions. Four Churchills were acquired by Ireland, with the first two being delivered on 20 December 1948; the other two were delivered on 24 December and on 28 January 1949. The tanks, taken from the British Army inventory, had very low mileage and were in excellent condition. Initially they were leased from the British War Office and were purchased outright in 1954, despite the fact that spare parts for maintenance had almost run out. Experiments were subsequently carried out involving replacement of the original Bedford engine with a salvaged Rolls-Royce Merlin engine (a variant of which powered the Comet tanks later acquired by the Irish Defence Force), but the experiment was unsuccessful. The Churchills were retired in 1969, although by 1967 only one remained serviceable. In 1981 the last of the surviving Churchills, which had been used for firing practice at the Glen of Imaal until 1970, was buried to prevent curiosity-seekers from possibly being injured. It was disinterred in 2002-2003 and then presented by the Republic of Ireland to the "North Irish Horse", a wartime regiment of the British Army from the North of Ireland. It has been refurbished and is a gatekeeper at Dunmore Park in Belfast. One Churchill also remains preserved at Plunkett Barracks at Curragh Camp.

*Driver training for the Churchill Mk VI in the Curragh in 1950. The 1D marking on the turret identified this Churchill as ZD 5054. The engine air intake jutting out from the side of the hull seems to have been a convenient place for crews to chalk names on; this one bears the barely visible name VAMPIRE. The Churchill in the background marked 1B on the turret is ZD 5055. The four Churchills in the Irish Army inventory were marked 1A through 1D, and bore registration numbers ZD 5052 through ZD 5055. (MA IAC D48/5)*

Churchill Mk VI. 1/35 scale.

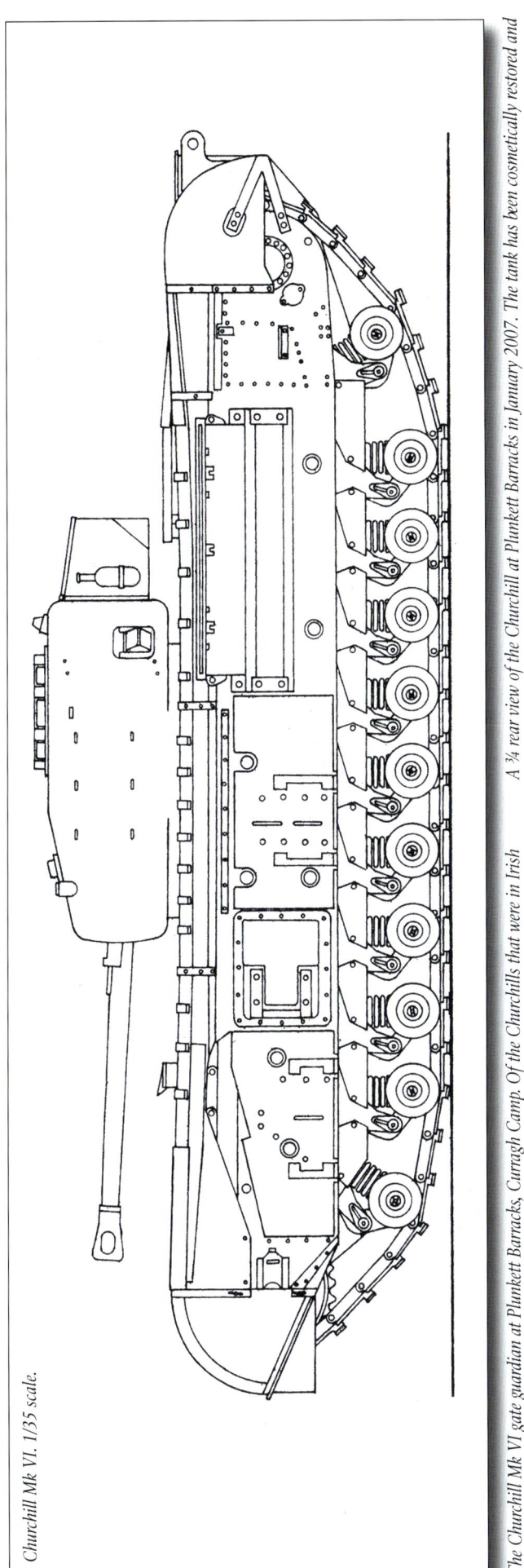

The Churchill Mk VI gate guardian at Plunkett Barracks, Curragh Camp. Of the Churchills that were in Irish service, two have survived, but neither is in running condition. In addition to the example pictured here, one is now on display in Belfast, Northern Ireland. (Bob Cantwell)

A ¾ rear view of the Churchill at Plunkett Barracks in January 2007. The tank has been cosmetically restored and is essentially complete, although the track guards seem to be an improvisation. (Bob Cantwell)

## Churchill Mk VI Specifications:

| | |
|---|---|
| Manufacturer: | Vauxhall Motors, Luton, England (prime developing contractor). Other manufacturers included Birmingham Railway Carriage and Wagon Company, Leyland Motors Lancashire, Dennis Brothers Guildford, Broome & Wade Ltd., Newton Chambers Ltd., and Metro-Cammell Carriage and Wagon Company Birmingham. |
| Dates of service (Irish Defence Forces): | 1948-1969 |
| Number in Irish service: | 4 |
| Crew: | 5 (commander, gunner, loader, driver, co-driver/hull gunner) |
| Combat weight: | 86,240 lbs (39,118 kg) |
| Armament: | 75mm OF Mk.5 gun, plus coaxial 7.92mm BESA machine-gun, and 7.92mm BESA machine-gun in hull |
| Ammunition capacity: | 74 rounds |
| Engine: | Bedford Twin Six, 12-cylinder gasoline, 21,237cc |
| Horsepower: | 350 @ 2200 rpm |
| Transmission: | Merritt-Brown, 4-speed gearbox, epicyclic |
| Fuel capacity: | 150 Imperial gallons (180 US gallons, 682 litres) |
| Maximum speed (road): | 15 mph (24 km/h) |
| Maximum speed (cross-country): | 8 mph (13 km/h) |
| Operating radius (road): | 90 miles (145 km) |
| Armour: | 16-102mm |
| Length: | 293 inches (7300mm) |
| Width: | 130 inches (3000mm) |
| Height: | 98 inches (2800mm) |
| Track width: | 22 inches (559mm) |
| Ground clearance: | 21 inches (533mm) |
| Trench crossing: | 120 inches (3048mm) |
| Vertical obstacle: | 48 inches (1219mm) |
| Fording depth: | 36 inches (914mm) |

*The Churchill gate guardian prior to being repainted in olive drab livery. It is being towed by one of the three 6 x 6 Berliet TBU 15 CLD Diesel recovery vehicles. The registration of this vehicle, 8820 ZO, identifies it as the Berliet assigned to the Cavalry Depot in Curragh Camp. This photograph would have been taken in 2000 or earlier, as the Berliets were all retired in that year. (Sean O'Sullivan)*

This Churchill was being towed on a Dyson trailer by the Irish Army's lone ex-British Diamond T 981 recovery vehicle in 1961 when it overturned on the road between Kilcullen and Dunlavin. The Diamond T was purchased in 1951 to tow the Churchills from the Curragh to the firing ranges at the Glen of Imaal because the tanks had caused damage during road marches, prompting complaints from the Kildare and Wicklow County Councils. (Matt McNamara)

The overturned Churchill in the process of being winched into the upright position. The sandbags have been placed on the road surface both to protect the road surface as well as to cushion the fall of the tank once it passes the tipping point. (Matt McNamara)

RChurchill ZD 5055 broaching the crest of a hill at Curragh Camp, date unknown. The Churchill's large size made it an impractical choice of vehicle for the Irish road system, consisting largely of narrow roads and lanes. (Matt McNamara)

*The Churchill that had been buried in the Glen of Imaal in 1981 shown as it was being disinterred in 2002. Its gun and gun mantlet are missing. It has since been refurbished and is now located in Dunmore Park, Belfast, Northern Ireland. (Sean O'Sullivan)*

*A Diamond T of the type in service with the Irish Army from 1951 to 1980, used to tow the Churchill tanks to and from the ranges at the Glen of Imaal. The original Diamond T was scrapped in 1980; the vehicle pictured was acquired by a collector in Ireland from another collector in Northern Ireland, and subsequently traded to the Irish Army in 2001 in exchange for a Panhard VTT M3 and a Berliet recovery vehicle. As of the date of this photograph, 27 May, 2009, the vehicle was still in open storage awaiting eventual restoration in the proper livery. (Ralph Riccio)*

# COMET A34 TANK

The Comet (also designated the A34) was originally fielded by Britain in 1944, and was powered by a modified version of the famous Rolls-Royce V-12 Merlin engine used in the Spitfire fighter and many other aircraft. Four Comets were purchased and were delivered to Ireland in December 1958; the Irish Army planned to acquire a further lot of eight Comets in order to bring the Tank Squadron to full strength (sixteen tanks, including the four Churchills), but plans were scaled back, likely due to the chronic budgetary problems experienced by the Army, and delivery of a further four was taken in early 1960. There were no Mark numbers assigned to the Comet, although two different "types" were designated, the Type A, whose exhaust vented through two spaced exhaust deflector cowls on the rear deck, and the Type B, in which the deflector cowls were replaced by "fish tail" exhaust pipes on the rear plate itself. Both types saw service with the Irish Army. These vehicles, like all previous tanks in Irish service, were used in the training role and for demonstration purposes, both in the Curragh and the Glen of Imaal through the 1960s and early 1970s. The service life of the Comets was relatively short, for although the vehicle was capable and had many characteristics to recommend it in the Irish operational environment, not enough foresight had been shown in purchasing vital spare parts with the initial acquisition package. Added to the lack of spares was the fact that the Comet's main gun was in a non-standard caliber, and ammunition procurement eventually became a problem, especially after it was discovered that fuses for the HE ammunition were defective. In 1969, due to dwindling stocks of 77mm ammunition for the main gun, the turret of one of the Comets that had been severely damaged by a fire was replaced by a 90mm Bofors PV 1110 recoilless rifle in an open mounting. This tank was known as the "Headless Coachman". Although the tests using the recoilless rifle were successful and approval was given to further improve and develop the concept, lack of funds ultimately precluded any further work on the project. The armament was removed from the "Headless Coachman", and the hull was used as a target in the Glen of Imaal. In the late 1970s, due to their unserviceability, it was decided to retire the Comets from service and to replace them with a much smaller tracked vehicle, the Scorpion CVR(T). One Comet has been preserved at the Curragh Museum and is in running order and three others have survived as gate guardians, two at the Curragh, and another at Custume Barracks, Athlone, having been moved from Connolly Barracks, Longford, in March 2009.

*Two of the three surviving Comets at Plunkett Barracks in 1983. Although essentially intact, both tanks show the effects of weather and neglect. The paint is flaking badly, and the track guards and fender stowage box on the closer Comet are badly damaged. (By kind permission of Karl Martin)*

## Comet A34 Specifications:

| | |
|---|---|
| Manufacturer: | Leyland Motors Ltd., Leyland, England |
| Dates of service (Irish Defence Forces): | 1958-1970s |
| Number in Irish service: | 8 |
| Crew: | 5 (commander, gunner, loader, driver, co-driver) |
| Combat weight: | 74,400 lbs (33,747 kg) |
| Armament: | 77mm HV gun, plus two 7.92mm BESA machine-guns (one coaxial and one hull mounted) |
| Ammunition capacity: | NA |
| Engine: | Rolls Royce Meteor V-12 gasoline |
| Horsepower: | 600 |
| Transmission: | Merritt-Brown Z5 mark G, 5-speed manual |
| Fuel capacity: | 120 UK gallons |
| Maximum speed (road): | 32 mph (51 km/h) |
| Operating radius (road): | 155 miles (250 km) |
| Armour: | 76-102mm |
| Length: | 258 inches (6554mm) |
| Width: | 121 inches (3073mm) |
| Height: | 105 inches (2673mm) |
| Track width: | 18 inches (457mm) |
| Ground clearance: | 18 inches (457mm) |
| Trench crossing: | 96 inches (2430mm) |
| Vertical obstacle: | 36 inches (914mm) |
| Fording depth: | 41 inches (1040mm) |

*The registration plate (TYI 499) identifies this as the last tank of the second batch to be acquired by Ireland in the 1960s. The turret is reversed, and the clearly visible large rear exhaust cowls mark this as a Comet Type A. A lieutenant is providing instruction to a group of officer trainees. (MA68)*

*The Bofors 90mm recoilless rifle experimentally mounted on the Comet whose turret had been damaged by fire and removed. Although this experiment initially met with some enthusiasm, the project was soon abandoned. (MA)*

*A Comet negotiating a steep downward slope. The turret is reversed and the gun is in the locked travel position, aiding in shifting weight to the rear of the tank. Nonetheless, the steep angle has caused the rearmost road wheel to lift completely off the ground. The crew also are leaning to the rear to maintain their own balance. (Matt McNamara)*

*A Comet undergoing maintenance inside the Base Workshop facility, date unknown. There are at least three different shades or colours of paint visible: the hull, gun tube, and muzzle brake differ noticeably. (Matt McNamara)*

*Comets being inspected, date unknown. The main armament is nearly level rather than being raised. The wheeled vehicles in the background appear to be Beaverette scout cars. (Matt McNamara)*

**183**

*Of the Irish Army's four surviving Comets, three are gate guardians, and the fourth has been meticulously restored. The restored Comet is shown at a display at the Curragh in 2006, with a Landsverk L 180 in the background. This is one of the handful of running Comets in the world. (Bob Cantwell)*

*Below: A 2 July, 2009 photograph of the same Comet in the earlier photograph at Plunkett Barracks, now repainted in proper olive drab that shows signs of weathering, on a hardstand at Ceannt Barracks. Close inspection reveals that damage to the forward portion of the track skirt remains as in the earlier photograph. (Terry Ward)*

*Comet A34. 1/35 scale.*

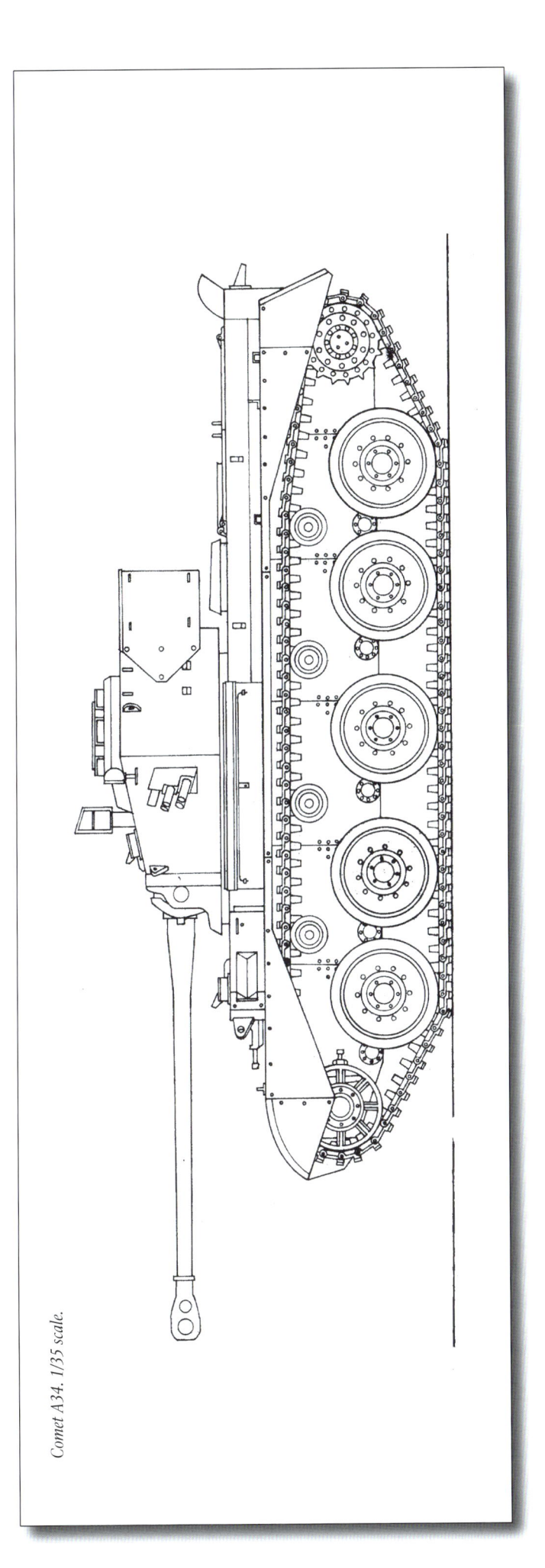

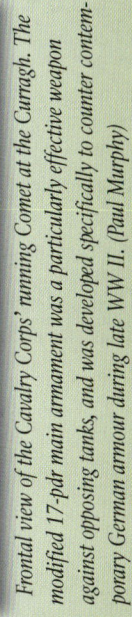

*The restored Comet returning to its vehicle shed on 7 September, 2002, following a parade in the Curragh commemorating the Irish Cavalry Corps' 80th anniversary. (Sean O'Sullivan)*

*Frontal view of the Cavalry Corps' running Comet at the Curragh. The modified 17-pdr main armament was a particularly effective weapon against opposing tanks, and was developed specifically to counter contemporary German armour during late WW II. (Paul Murphy)*

*One of the Irish Comets in badly weathered condition at Plunkett Barracks in 2005, prior to cosmetic restoration. This tank, since repainted, now stands as a gate guardian at Ceannt Barracks, Curragh Camp. (Paul Murphy)*

**185**

# M113 APC

During its deployment to the Congo, the Irish contingent obtained six M113 APCs on loan. These tracked armoured vehicles were a quantum improvement in mobility and protection for the Irish contingent. The M113, produced by Food Machinery Corporation (FMC) of San Jose, California, was the iconic American tracked armoured personnel carrier, and first entered American service in 1960. Early M113s were powered by a Chrysler Model 75M 209 hp gasoline engine mated to an Allison 4-speed transmission; the hull was made of aluminum armour that provided protection against small arms fire and shell splinters. The M113 had a crew of two (the track commander and driver), and could carry a complement of 11 infantrymen. Although it is not known for certain, it appears that the M 113s were part of an armoured vehicle inventory belonging to the UN, who loaned them to the Irish contingent for the duration of its stay in the Congo. At the end of the Irish deployment, the APCs reverted back to UN control.

*One of the M113 armoured personnel carriers used by the Irish contingent in the Congo, parked alongside the venerable Ford Mk VI cars. (Internet, via Paul Murphy)*

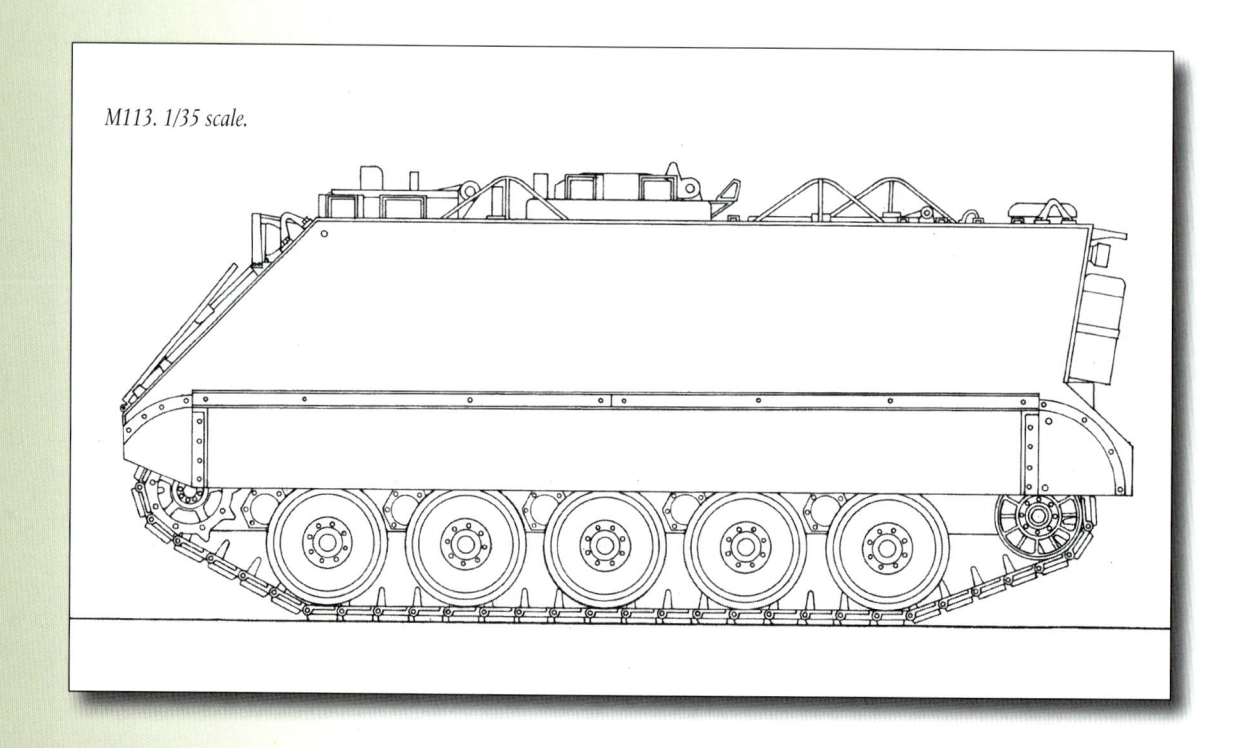

*M113. 1/35 scale.*

## M113 Specifications:

| | |
|---|---|
| Manufacturer: | Food Machinery Corporation, San Jose, California |
| Dates of service (Irish Defence Forces): | Late 1962-early 1963 (?) |
| Number in Irish service: | 6 |
| Crew: | 2 (track commander, driver), plus 11 infantrymen |
| Combat weight: | 22,900 lbs (10,387 kg) |
| Armament: | .50 caliber browning HB M2 heavy machine-gun |
| Ammunition capacity: | 2000 rounds (typical load) |
| Engine: | Chrysler 75M 8-cylinder gasoline |
| Horsepower: | 209 HP |
| Transmission: | Allison TX-200 series, 4-speed |
| Fuel capacity: | 80 US gallons; 66 Imperial gallons (301 litres) |
| Maximum speed (road): | 40 mph (64 km/h) |
| Maximum speed (cross-country): | 15 mph (25 km/h) |
| Operating radius (road): | 200 miles (322 km) |
| Operating radius (cross-country): | NA |
| Armour: | 5083/5086 H3 aluminum |
| Length: | 192 inches (4856mm) |
| Width: | 106 inches (2688mm) with track shrouds |
| Height: | 72 inches (1830mm) to top of hull |
| Track width: | NA |
| Ground pressure: | 7.5 psi (0.53 kg/cm2) |
| Ground clearance: | 16 inches (410mm) |
| Trench crossing: | 66 inches (1680mm) |
| Vertical obstacle: | 24 inches (610mm) |
| Fording depth: | 40 inches (1020mm); amphibious with minimal preparation |

## ALVIS SCORPION CVR(T)

Design and development of the Scorpion CVR(T), or Combat Reconnaissance Vehicle (Tracked), began in 1960 in response to a British Army requirement for what was then termed an AVR (Armoured Vehicle Reconnaissance), which was to mount either a 76mm or 105mm gun. An experimental vehicle, the TV 15000, was designed and built in 1965. The first actual prototype was delivered in January 1969, and following extensive testing under extreme climatic conditions, the Scorpion (or FV 101) was accepted for service with the British Army in May 1970; the first production Scorpion was completed in 1971. The Scorpion was a compact, highly mobile, air transportable light tank designed primarily for battlefield reconnaissance. It had a crew of three, was powered by a Jaguar J60 engine de-rated from 265 bhp to 195 bhp for military use, and was armed with a 76mm L23 A1 gun and a coaxial 7.62mm L43 A1 GPMG. The Scorpion's small size, weight, low ground pressure, and relatively powerful armament made it an attractive candidate for Irish requirements, and accordingly a decision was made to acquire the first tracked vehicle since the purchase of the Comets more than twenty years previously. The Irish Army acquired a total of fourteen Scorpions between March 1980 and December 1985. The Scorpions as originally issued in Irish service were of the same configuration as British vehicles, i.e., were armed with the 76mm L23 A1 gun and were also fitted with flotation gear, which was subsequently removed. However, the gun proved to be somewhat of a problem as it had no fume extractor, and when the vehicle was closed down, the crew could suffocate from the fumes (and for that reason was withdrawn from service with the British and Australian armies). The British and several other armies that had the

*Scorpion CVR (T). 1/35 scale.*

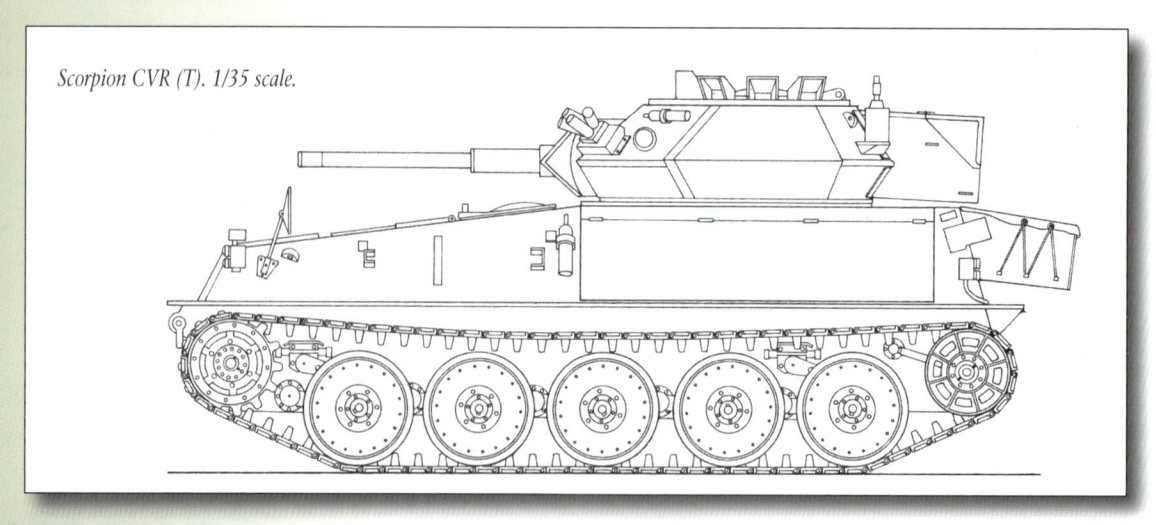

*A pair of Scorpions during the vehicle review on the 80th anniversary of the Cavalry Corps on 7 September, 2002. Because of its compact size, the Scorpion is better suited to the Irish operational environment than other tracked vehicles previously in the inventory, such as the Churchill and Comet, which were not well suited for the usually narrow Irish roads. (Sean O'Sullivan)*

*A pair of Scorpions on Dame Street, Dublin, 16 April 2006. Although the camouflage scheme follows a generally similar pattern on both vehicles, the colours are not applied to a rigid pattern or specification, although all hull corners always are painted in matte black. (Sean O'Sullivan)*

Scorpion in their inventories solved the problem by removing the 76mm gun turret and replacing it with the Scimitar turret that mounts the 30mm Rarden cannon. The Irish Army chose a different solution and experimented with and developed a fume extraction system (FES), which has worked out to the satisfaction of the Irish Army authorities. This has enabled the Irish Army to retain the 76mm gun, as it represents a powerful system for its size and cost. Scorpions assigned as troop commander's vehicles were fitted with a .50 caliber Browning HB machine-gun for anti-aircraft use, but these were subsequently removed as the gun raised the profile of the vehicle above acceptable limits. The Scorpions were incorporated into the re-established 1st Tank Squadron in 1980 and served in that squadron until 1998, when it was disestablished and formed the basis of the 1st Armoured Cavalry Squadron, equipped with the Scorpions.

*Static display of a Scorpion. The three-tone camouflage scheme has been standard on the Scorpions since about 1977; prior to that, the livery was matte olive green. The Scorpions frequently are seen with the heavy tow rope carried. (Terry Ward)*

*A Scorpion and three AML 90s parked in front of the weapons stores in Cooolmoney Camp in July 2007. This ad hoc grouping is an amalgamated unit used for Corps assessment exercises, with vehicles drawn from all cavalry units. This particular exercise was a week-long exercise. (Seamus Corcoran, via Paul Murphy)*

*Rear view of a Scorpion during a break in the conduct of a field exercise. The accumulated dirt, mud and debris will be cleaned during the inevitable ritual post-exercise vehicle cleanup. (Seamus Corcoran, via Paul Murphy)*

## Alvis Scorpion Specifications:

| | |
|---|---|
| Manufacturer: | Alvis Ltd., Coventry, England |
| Dates of service (Irish Defence Forces): | 1980-2011 |
| Number in Irish service: | 14 |
| Crew: | 3 |
| Combat weight: | 17,500 lbs (7938 kg) |
| Armament: | 76mm L23 A1 gun; 7.62mm L43A1 coaxial machine-gun |
| Ammunition capacity: | 40 rounds 76mm; 3000 rounds 7.62mm |
| Engine: | Jaguar 4.2 litre, 6-cylinder gasoline |
| Horsepower: | 195 HP |
| Transmission: | TN 15Z crossdrive, 7-speed semi-automatic |
| Fuel capacity: | 88 Imperial gallons (106 US gallons; 400 litres) |
| Maximum speed (road): | 50 mph (80 km/h) |
| Operating radius (road): | 370+ miles (595+ km) |
| Length: | 172.75 inches (4388mm) |
| Width: | 86.6 inches (2200mm) |
| Height: | 82.5 inches (2096mm) |
| Track width: | 17 inches (432mm) |
| Ground clearance: | 14 inches (356mm) |
| Trench crossing: | 81 inches (2057mm) |
| Vertical obstacle: | 20 inches (509mm) |
| Fording depth: | 42 inches (1067mm) without flotation screen |

*This Scorpion is part of a military vehicle display in June 2007. It is parked between a Mowag III H and an AML car whose rear corner is barely visible to the left. The turret is fitted with side-mounted panniers for extra stowage. It is somewhat unusual to see road wheels on the Scorpions painted in more than one colour; normally they are a matte olive green monotone. (Paul McMenamin)*

# Appendieces

## Appendix 1:

### Colour Equivalents for Modelers

The attached colour equivalent chart is provided courtesy of Roy Derek Kinsella.

|  | HUMBROL | TAMIYA | VALLEJO | MR.COLOR |
|---|---|---|---|---|
| ARMY TRANSPORT & VEHICLES 1946 ||||
| Varying shades of grey known as both; BATTLESHIP GREY or Grey Green | 164 & 165 Mixed 50/50% Or 60/40% Or 40/60% | XF076 | | |
| FIELD ARTY, TANKS & AFVs 1954+ ||||
| QUAKER GREY | 35 parts 34<br>42 parts 94<br>12 parts 109<br>5 parts 186 | | Matt White<br>128 (824)<br>61 (943)<br>143 (983) | |
| GREY GREEN | | XF076 (This can be mixed with various greys) | | |
| TRANSPORT & ARMOR 1960s to 2002 ||||
| OLIVE DRAB | 1 part 22<br>25 parts 9<br>10 parts 15<br>5 parts 21 | XF02<br>?<br>XF03<br>XF01 | 3 (842)<br>119 (914)<br>50 (899)<br>170 (861) | 316<br>44<br>5<br>2 |
| NISSAN GREEN | 116 | | | |
| MODERN IRISH UNIFORM PATTERN COLORS ||||
| NATO GREEN | | XF-67 | | |
| NATO BROWN | | XF-68 | | |
| NATO BLACK | | XF-69 | | |
| SCORPION ARMOURED RECCE VEHICLES ||||
| GREEN | | 90% XF-67<br>10% XF-58 | | |
| BROWN | | 98% XF-68<br>2% XF-64 | | |
| BLACK | | XF-69 | | |
| MORTARS, ARTILLERY, ROCKET LAUNCHERS ETC ||||
| OLIVE DRAB | 155 or 116 | XF-62 | | |

*\* Armour and vehicles have varying shades of color due to condition, age, repair and weathering so lightening or darkening of colors is recommended where the modeller feels adventurous*

*\* When Painting Armour in UN White, it is advisable to use Tamiya Flat White XF-2*

*\* It is advisable to thin all paints by at least 10-30% when using free hand brushing (this depends on how light or dark the color being used is)*

*\* When requiring a GLOSS finish I recommend Airbrushing XTRACRYLIX XA1G*

*\* When requiring a FLAT/MATT finish I recommend Airbrushing XTRACRYLIX XA1F*

*\* Where Tamiya numbers are shown these are Acrylic only*

*\* Where Humbrol numbers are shown these are Enamels only*

# Appendix 2:
# IRISH CAVALRY CORPS UNIT DESIGNATIONS

Due largely to the relatively small size of the Irish Army and the limited number of units and types of units in the establishment, early naming and numbering conventions were relatively simple, straightforward, uncomplicated, and consistent.

Armoured car units (companies), and later, cavalry units (squadrons) were simply numbered sequentially, using an ordinal numbering system. Thus, armoured car companies were numbered 1st through 4th, and with the change in designation from the Armoured Car Corps to the Cavalry Corps, cavalry squadrons similarly were numbered 1st, 2nd, etc.

The numbering of the cyclist squadrons, although generally straightforward, does have some oddities that bear explanation. By 1939 the Volunteer Forces component of the Irish Army included nineteen cyclist squadrons, rather conventionally numbered 2 through 20. In 1940 and 1941 these volunteer cyclist squadrons were reduced in number to fourteen and integrated into the regular army, being numbered from 1 through 14. In 1942, four additional cyclist squadrons, the 41st through the 44th formed part of the 11th Cyclist Regiment stationed in the North Dublin area.

*Rolls-Royce A.R.R. -7 Moneygall without its Vickers armament. The markings are unusual inasmuch as not only does the car's name appear in the usual position on the front of the turret, but the car's number, A.R.R.-7, is prominently displayed on the turret scallop rather than on the front plate below the radiator. The rear tires seem to be underinflated, and the left front fender shows signs of minor damage. Close scrutiny of the tires reveals different tread patterns on each of the front tires, and yet a third pattern on the dual rear tires. Barely visible behind the turret is what appears to be part of a Peerless armoured car; the letter P, preceded by what might be part of the letter A, and followed by what appears to be an indistinguishable number can be seen when the image is magnified. Also, above the number 7 on Moneygall's turret there appears to be the outline of the top of a Peerless turret, and above the storage box on the rear of the Rolls-Royce the rear tire of the Peerless is visible. (Terry Ward)*

*A lineup of the various types of armoured vehicles in the National Army inventory in late 1923. Note the variety of colours; the two closest vehicles are Rolls-Royce cars whose colours differ markedly. The next six vehicles are Lancias (the closest of which is almost completely obscured by troopers); the fourth in line is much lighter in colour than the others, likely a grey or light greygreen. The last car is a Peerless in dark livery. (MA)*

*The* Fianna Fail *badge. The Gaelic inscription reads* Òglaigh na hÉireann *(Irish Defence Forces), while* Fianna Fail *refers to a legendary band of Celtic warriors. (Sean O'Sullivan)*

*The restored L 180 photographed at the Curragh on 8 May, 2005, in Battleship Grey livery. The AML 60 parked alongside is in the standard green livery used on the Panhard cars. (Terry Ward)*

**193**

After The Emergency, the 11th Cyclist Regiment was reorganized as the 11th Cavalry Squadron and became mechanized.

As the Motor Squadrons began to be formed beginning in 1939 they were numbered in accordance with the brigade to which they were assigned; thus 1 Motor Squadron was organic to 1st Brigade. Eventually, all seven wartime brigades had an attached Motor Squadron, the squadrons thus being numbered 1 through 7. These squadrons, however, are commonly referred to using cardinal rather than ordinal numbers.

A somewhat anomalous situation obtains with respect to the difference in numbering between the current Permanent Defence Force (PDF) cavalry squadrons and the Reserve Defence Force (RDF) cavalry squadrons. The PDF cavalry squadrons are designated by single-digit numbers, and

*A "hybrid" AML 60CS/90 photographed in 2006 preparatory to firing at the Glen of Imaal. The vehicle hull is one of the early AML 60CS vehicles, upgraded to AML 20 standard, that had returned from a U.N. assignment and was painted white. There is evidence of considerable rust on the rear panels, and the storage box visible on the left side has been sprayed with a grey primer. The turret is an AML 90 turret and is painted the standard green as on the other vehicles in the column. The turret was temporarily fitted to the older hull due to the AML 90 hull being out of service at the time. (Paul Murphy)*

*Despite the muddy environment, except for the wheels and tires this Piranha MRV's factory applied three-tone brown and black over green colour scheme remains surprisingly clean. (Irish Defence Forces)*

are referred to by ordinal numbers (1st, 2nd, and 4th) reflecting the same number as their parent brigade, whereas the RDF cavalry squadrons are designated by two-digit numbers expressed as cardinal numbers. The RDF squadron designations combine the number of the Reserve brigade they were associated with prior to the 1959 army reorganization with the number of the counterpart PDF cavalry squadron with which they are "twinned." Thus, 31 Reserve Cavalry Squadron (RCS) bases its designation on its association with 3 Brigade and with the 1st PDF Cavalry Squadron. Similarly, 54 RCS is based on the combination of 5 Brigade and 4th Cavalry Squadron, while 62 RCS is based on the former 6 Brigade and 2nd Cavalry Squadron. Parenthetically, the correct expression of these RCS numbers would be three-one, five-four, and six-two rather than thirty one, fifty four, or sixty two, reflecting a precise verbal breakout of the brigade and PDF cavalry squadron elements included in the designation.

*A VTT M3 in U.N. livery and markings, Lebanon, 2 January, 1990. This was one of the last patrols carried out by the VTTs supporting the 66th Irish Battalion prior to replacement by SISUs in February 1990. The UNIFIL registration plate has been bent to fit the contour of the glacis of the VTT, and the Panhard logo has been highlighted in red by the local Transport Sgt. (Brian Quinn)*

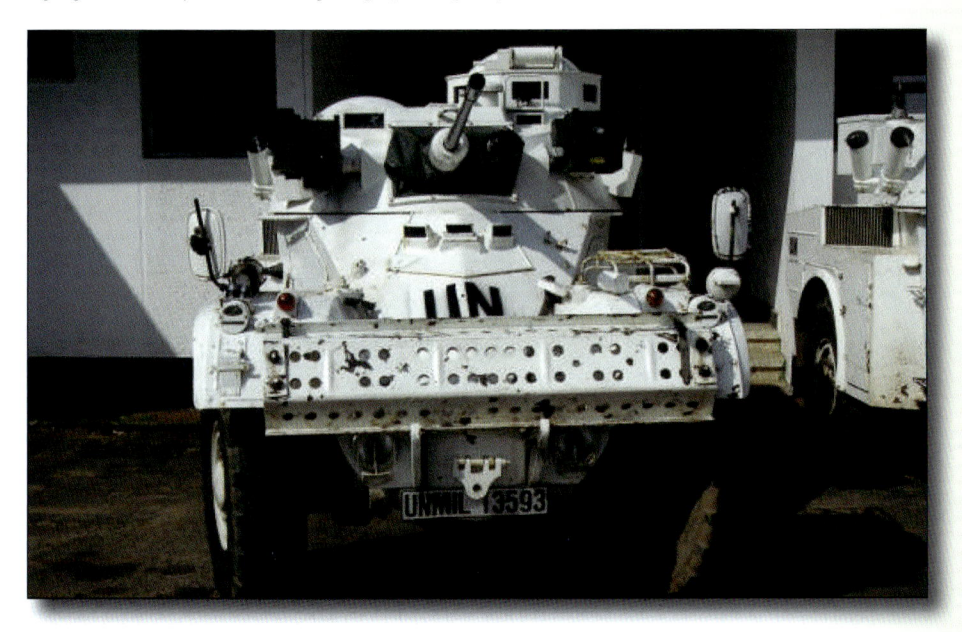

*An AML 20 in white U.N. livery at Camp Clara, Monrovia, on 12 October, 2004. The car has had its Irish registration replaced by a U.N. registration plate (UNMIL 13593). The vehicle would resume its original Irish registration number upon return to Ireland. (Mats Hjorter)*

**195**

*Above: A Scorpion, with a Mowag Piranha behind it, both displaying the three-tone camouflage scheme. (Paul Murphy)*

*A 4th Cavalry Squadron unit identification disc, or decal, illustrative of the badges applied to Irish Army vehicles until mid-2006. (Paul McMenamin)*

*An AML 20 returned from Liberia, in open storage, Curragh Camp, May 2009. The shamrock displayed on the vehicle was a popular, but not universal, marking applied by crews on Irish vehicles in U.N. service. (Ralph Riccio)*

# Appendix 3:

# CAVALRY CORPS UNIT INSIGNIA

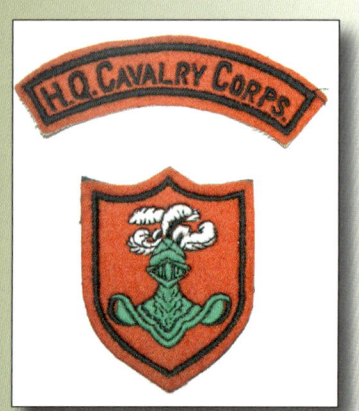

Headquarters, Cavalry Corps

1st Armoured Car Squadron

1 Motor Squadron
(1973 – early 1980s)

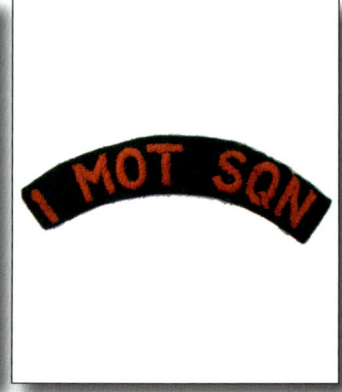

1 Motor Squadron shoulder tab
(1970-1974)

| | | | |
|---|---|---|---|
| 1st Cavalry Squadron (May 2006) | 2 Motor Squadron (1975 – early 1980s) | 3rd Cavalry Squadron (1981-1990) | 3rd Cavalry Squadron (2000-2005) |
| 4th Cavalry Squadron | 5 Motor Squadron (1968-1978) | 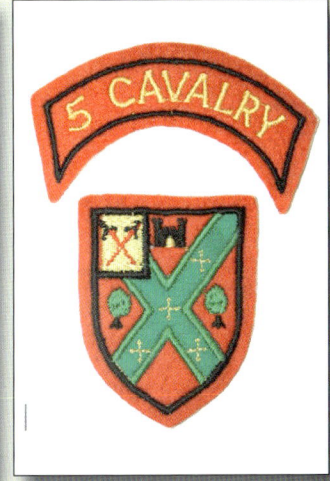 5 Motor Squadron (1968-1978) | 5th Cavalry Squadron |
| 5th Cavalry Squadron | 5th Cavalry Squadron (1979-2005) |  11 Motor Squadron (1968-1971) | 11th Cavalry Squadron |
| 11th Cavalry Squadron shoulder tab (1962-1968) |  31 Reserve Cavalry Squadron | 54 Reserve Cavalry Squadron |  62 Reserve Cavalry Squadron |

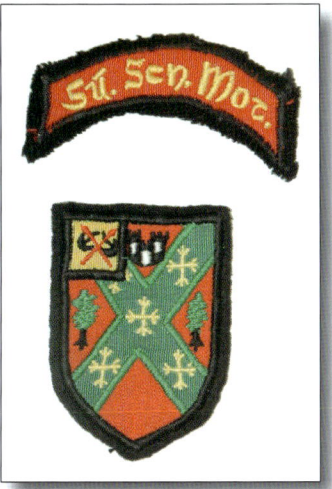

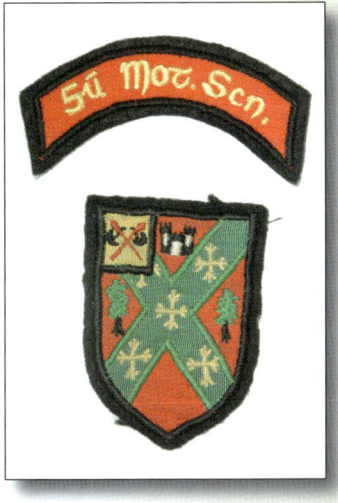

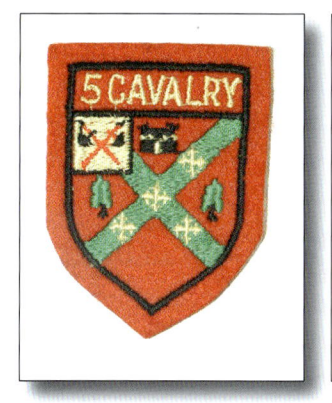

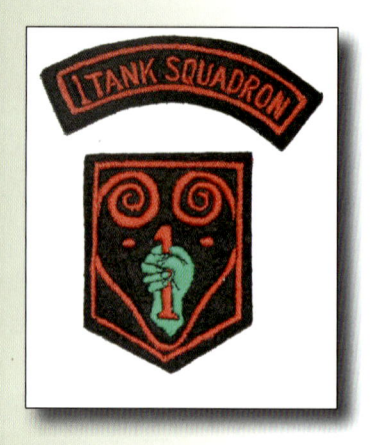

*1st Tank Squadron (1981-mid 1980s)*      *1st Tank Squadron (mid 1980s)*      *1st Armoured Cavalry Squadron*

# Appendix 4: MARKINGS AND COLOURS

Before describing the markings and colours of vehicles in Irish service, a brief note concerning markings on British vehicles in Ireland prior to 1922 is appropriate. The body of knowledge concerning such markings is limited primarily to what can be gleaned from period photographs. Of the Medium A and Mk V* tanks sent to Ireland in January 1919, by November many, if not all of them, had been christened with names; the Medium A tanks were named Fanny Adams, Fanny's Sister, Gofasta, and Golikell (which also bore the designation A 378 on the superstructure side). Gofasta and Golikell were thin disguises for the names Go Faster and Go Like Hell, respectively. One of the Mk V*s was named Malvern, likely a reference to Malvern, England. At least two of the Medium A tanks had white and red identification bands painted on their engine decks and the forward portion of their suspension assemblies, while another had the white and red bands on the suspension only. A photograph shows one of the Mk V*s also with identification bands on the forward portion of its suspension.

Armoured cars in British service in Ireland similarly often bore names. Two Jeffery Quads are known to have been named George and Mary, and a period photograph shows an Austin bearing the name May. A photograph also exists of a Rolls-Royce 1920 Pattern named Scorpion, purportedly in service with the RIC. Denis McCarthy confirms that six Rolls-Royces were assigned to the RIC so if indeed this car was one of the cars turned over to the Provisional Government, its name was either obliterated or changed at the time of the turnover.

Markings on early Free State vehicles varied immensely, although there were some identifiable patterns and conventions within some of the vehicle types. As mentioned in the text, all of the Rolls-Royce armoured cars bore descriptive names, prominently painted in an essentially consistent style, on the upper front of the turret, above the Vickers machine-gun port. The names could be commemorative of a person or event (such as Tom Keogh or Custom House), or could be somewhat more fanciful, such as The Big Fella (a reference to General Michael Collins). In a photograph from early July 1922 Custom House also was identified as AC-1 painted on the metal splash plate underneath the radiator, suggesting that it was one of the earliest Whippets turned over by the British.[1] Photographs also show the splash plates with what appear to be holdovers from the British special Allied Armies registration system adopted in 1918 which was a number/letter system that always included the letter C. The registration identification consisted of prominent, highly visible numbers, the characters measuring five inches high and one inch wide painted in yellow; the first four characters consisted of numbers, the first two of which consistently seem to be 10, plus two additional numbers. These were separated by a dash from the last two characters, which likely were the

---

1  Although Mutineer may have been turned over even earlier, it was in Republican hands in early July and not available when the AC numbers were assigned.

letters CK. The system appears to have been dropped in 1921, but implementation of the follow-on system of registering military vehicles in the County of Middlesex may have not been initiated or completed for vehicles based in Ireland. To add further to the lack of clarity with respect to registrations, during the 1920s and 1930s a limited number of "Board of Works" vehicles in the Curragh were registered in Kildare with the initial letter code IO. At some point after 1922, the Rolls-Royces were progressively numbered as ARR 1 through ARR 14 (ARR stood for Armoured Rolls Royce, and the number 13 was skipped, possibly due to superstition), and were registered with Dublin license plates running from YI 6450 through YI 6461. At least for some period both the names as well as the ARR numbers may have been present on the cars; a photograph shows Moneygall retaining its name, and having the identifier A.R.R.-7. painted on the turret side slope. Finally, with respect to the Rolls-Royces, some appear to have had various letter and number combinations painted on the metal splash plate below the radiator, but no pattern seems to be apparent. The Peerless cars do not appear to have been similarly named, but did receive numbers 1 through 7 preceded by the letters AP (for Armoured Peerless). A period photograph shows one of the Peerless cars used in the landing against Cork in August 1922 bearing the number H-337 on the rear bumper; this would appear to be its old British registration number. Both the Rolls-Royces and the Peerless machines were emblazoned with a rather prominent "sunburst" emblem applied quite liberally in the case of the Whippets (one on each side of the turret, and one on each side of the driver's compartment); the Peerless cars had the emblem displayed on the body sides. The emblem, painted in white, contained the Gaelic words Óglaiġ na h-Éirann (Armed Forces of Ireland) and stylized intertwined letters "FF" (for Fianna Fáil, a reference to the mythical warriors of pre-Christian Ireland).

Lancia armoured personnel carriers bore two types of identifying numbers. The older identification scheme, based on "Vehicle Classification Letters" was introduced in 1916; in the case of the Lancias, a three or four digit number was prefixed by the letter L, which stood for Lorry, but this system was discontinued in 1922. In 1922, most or all of the RIC vehicles were re-registered in Belfast with the Belfast County registration letters OI[2] followed by four digits, the first digit being a 9.[3] The Lancias inherited by the Free State initially bore these numbers as a holdover from service with the RIC. Several photos show Lancias bearing a dark-coloured diamond painted on the side or rear of the troop compartment, possibly used to identify them as belonging to the National Army; the dark diamond is also shown on the photograph of a tender impressed for military use. It is in the nature of soldiers, in the absence of any directives to the contrary, to christen vehicles (or aircraft) with names – indeed, they often adorn their vehicles even despite such directives. Some of the Lancias did in fact bear names, applied to various parts of the body, while many, if not most, bore no such individual identification. One photograph from the July 1922 fighting against the Republicans in Dublin shows Lancia OI 9173 already bearing the "sunburst" insignia on the armoured radiator plate; this vehicle also bears the name Ashtown (undoubtedly commemorating the failed ambush of Lord French on 19 December 1919) above the insignia. Another Lancia was named Handy Andy, the name being painted on the side of the troop compartment. Other names known to have been bestowed upon Lancias were Dublin Liz and Fernside. A photo taken aboard the Arvonia during the early August seaborne assault on Cork shows a Lancia with "G.H.Q. DEPOT. PORTOBELLO" painted in white on the body side; interestingly, this particular Lancia appears to be in a much darker paint scheme than normally seen. At some point the Lancias were assigned an AL letter/number code (AL for Armoured Lancia). A vintage photograph from 1922 shows four Lancias parked in a row, with the markings A.L. 47 through A.L. 50 prominently displayed on the sides of the bodies. Two Lancias converted for railway use bear relatively small numbers 47 and 51 within circles, painted on the lower part of the driver's compartment (the prominent markings on the body sides are absent). The highest AL number recorded is AL 51.

---

2    The OI prefix was the code assigned to vehicles registered in Belfast, according to the vehicle registration system introduced in the UK in 1904, and used in Ireland until 1987. For whatever the reason, it seems that all of the Lancias assigned to the RIC were registered as Belfast vehicles.

3    The initial digit 9 seems to have been used for vehicles assigned to the Dublin area; vehicles actually assigned to the Belfast area appear to have had a 1 as the initial digit.

Other than in the most generic of terms, the colour or colours of British vehicles in Ireland up to 1922, and of the vehicles when transferred to Irish service, is not subject to verification or confirmation. Informed sources hazard that the World War I colour used for British armoured vehicles was some shade of brown, ranging from an earthy medium to a dark chocolate, and that after the war an unspecified shade of dark green was adopted*. Unfortunately, there is no quick and easy, nor for that matter, any tedious and difficult way of determining when any changeover from browns to greens may have occurred, or which vehicles or classes of vehicles may have escaped the colour change. One source suggests that some of the Rolls-Royce cars were painted a light grey-green, and that the Lancia carriers, being police vehicles, were painted in light matte battleship grey.

Period photographs make it difficult, if not impossible, to determine the colours or shadings.

(* - see Warpaint Vol 1, by Dick Taylor, MMP Green series, for details of British colour schemes of the period.)

The Irish may have inherited vehicles of both colours (brown or green), and then may have repainted their vehicles in yet another colour. Photographs of the armoured cars sporting the Fianna Fail emblem suggest that the cars were repainted prior to application of the emblem, but that the names of the cars, painted on the turret above the machine-gun, were masked off, as the background on which the names are painted is darker than the colour of the rest of the vehicles. Photographs of the Lancia personnel carriers show significant variations in the colours; some are a light colour, while others are very dark. At least one photograph of a railway Lancia, the "Grey Ghost," dating back to 1922, shows what appears to be a three-tone camouflage scheme applied to the vehicle.

Sometime after 1922, but prior to 1939, armoured vehicles in Irish service were painted in widely varying shades of matt green. In September 1939 all brigades were ordered by the Chief of Staff to paint their vehicles in a camouflage scheme, but there was no specific instruction as to what colours or pattern were to be used. This naturally resulted in a situation in which each brigade conjured up its own camouflage scheme. Photographs show some vehicles with broad bands of light and dark colours, while at least one shows a Landsverk L 180 with a pattern of small dark splotches (orange, red, yellow, and black over grey), somewhat reminiscent of some German camouflage patterns of the times. This led to a decision in late 1941 to evaluate the various camouflage schemes to determine which was best. A board of officers was established, and after testing (which interestingly concluded that a disruptive camouflage scheme in and of itself immediately identified a vehicle as a military target, and that trucks filled with troops in battledress were less conspicuous than empty trucks because the troops in the truck bed broke up the stark outlines of the truck) recommended that all Army vehicles be painted in a two-tone matt grey scheme. Specifically, top surfaces were to be painted in dark grey, while side surfaces be painted a medium grey.

Due to the spirits and ingredients used in the matt grey paints, they were much less resistant to the elements than a gloss finish would have been, leading to serious problems with corrosion. In 1946 vehicles were repainted in a gloss finish using a grey-green finish referred to as Battleship Grey (occasionally also referred to as Panzer Grey), but as the exact shade was not specified, different shades emerged (essentially a repeat of the 1939 order to apply camouflage, but without providing any specific guidance). In March 1954 another board was convened to deal with the problem of paint quality. The result was that in early 1956, Quaker Grey 629 was adopted as the standard Army paint colour. It was similar to the grey-green already in use, and was to be applied in gloss to transport vehicles and armoured cars in peacetime, and in a matt finish in wartime. The matt finish was standard for tracked vehicles and artillery at all times.

Sometime in the 1960s, yet another shade, Olive Drab 298, was adopted for transport vehicles and armoured vehicles. Transport vehicles were given a gloss finish, while armoured vehicles were oversprayed with a matt varnish. The Ford MkVI armoured cars that were sent to the Congo in 1961 were shipped there in the olive drab livery; horizontal white bands were painted on the front of both front fenders, with the letters ONU painted in black on the right front band. It is not clear what was painted on the left band. Subsequently, the Fords were painted white overall, with prominent U.N. markings.

The Churchill tanks delivered in 1948 were in their original British dark green livery, and were identified by a prominent identification code (1A, 1B, 1C, and 1D) painted on the turrets. The Churchills subsequently were repainted in the standard Irish Army olive drab.

The AML armoured cars were delivered in a factory applied green referred to as Bronze Green, but over time vehicles were painted and repainted in varying shades of green, either at the unit, or later as awareness of environmental safety and health issues increased, by civilian contractor firms who had the requisite facilities. Finishes varied from gloss to semi-gloss or satin, although some finishes had a tendency to deteriorate to a matt finish. Of note is that vehicles that had been on UN duty returned to Ireland in the white UN livery and, on at least one occasion, due to a slippage in the painting schedule, an AML H 90 was in an operational status in Ireland still sporting its white paint scheme. There have also been instances of vehicles as recently as 2008 having been painted by hand (i.e. with a brush) at the unit level, in a light olive green finish.

In the 1997-98 timeframe an experimental paint scheme was applied to the FV 101 Scorpions. The matt green finish was oversprayed with matt brown and matt black (the same colour scheme as used on the current Piranha III vehicles). Although the colours used are consistent for all of the Scorpions, there is no standard pattern; whoever was responsible for painting the vehicles used a free-hand technique rather than a set or mandated pattern. Some of the schemes display relatively hard edges, whereas others have edges that are soft or "feathered." Interestingly, the three-tone scheme was applied only to the hulls and turret sides, but not to the turret roofs. Karl Martin speculates that this may have been to avoid smudging or otherwise degrading the optics.

Paint specifications for the Light Tactical Armoured Vehicle (LTAV) ordered in 2008 are Bronzegreen RAL 6031, Tar-black RAL 9021, and Leather-brown RAL 8027. All vehicle corners are to be painted black, with an even mix of colours throughout the vehicle in a matt finish. The paint used shall be water based. The specifications make no mention of Chemical Agent Resistant Coating (CARC) paints.

Generally speaking, vehicles on duty with UN peacekeeping forces are painted white, with prominent UN markings applied. Upon return to Ireland, they are then repainted green or in camouflage scheme, as appropriate to the vehicle type. Some instances may be noted where a vehicle that has been repainted may develop areas where the white UN livery shows through. Also, there is at least one instance of a vehicle (an AML 90) with an unintentional "two-tone" paint scheme, i.e., the hull in the UN white paint, and the turret in green; this was due simply to the painting schedule being somewhat out of phase. At least on some UN deployments, vehicles are assigned a UN registration plate that replaces the Irish registration plate or number.

The interior of armoured vehicles generally are painted in a gloss white finish, although parts of the interior surfaces of the Mowags are painted in green.

Until 1 August 2006, Irish Army vehicles displayed a five inch diameter circular disc with a unit identification badge (referred to in Irish as a decal). All Irish Army vehicles displayed such a badge, which was affixed to the vehicle by means of two screws.

# Appendix 5: VEHICLE REGISTRATION NUMBERS

Irish Army vehicle registration plates reflect Dublin area registrations.

Rolls-Royce armoured cars: ARR 1 through ARR 12; ARR 14

Leyland armoured cars: ZC 773 through ZC 776

Morris-Commercial armoured car (Ford Mk IV precursor): IP 2853

Ford Mk IV armoured cars: ZD 1189; ZD 1523 through 1528

Ford Mk V armoured cars: ZD 1736; ZD 1741 (remaining 12 numbers unknown)

Ford Mk VI armoured cars: ZD 1644, ZD 1759 through 1772, ZD 1775 through ZD 1778, ZD 1797, ZD 1811, ZD 1834, ZD 1839, ZD 1844, ZD 1854 (remaining three numbers unknown)

Dodge Mk VII and Mk VIII armoured cars: ZC 9483 through ZC 9487

Landsverk L 180 armoured cars: ZC 757; ZC 758; ZC 5837 through ZC 5842

Beaverette scout cars: ZD 3315 through 3324 (Mk III); ZD 3401 through 3420 (Mk IV)

Timoney Mk I armoured personnel carrier: Unknown

Timoney Mk II armoured personnel carrier: 8796 ZD

Timoney Mk III armoured personnel carrier: 6723 ZU

Timoney Mk IV armoured personnel carrier: 364 through 368 KZE

Timoney Mk VI armoured personnel carrier: ASI 124 through ASI 128

Unimog scout car: 2259 ZC through 2273 ZC (prototypes 2274 and 2275 ZC)

Panhard AML 60CS: NZH 7 through NZH 23

Panhard AML 60 HB: 318 NRI, 632 NRI, 633 NRI, 6456ZE, 6459ZE (remaining 10 numbers unknown)

Panhard AML 90: 190 AZI, 428 VZJ, 361 KZE, 362 KZE, 1371 ZD (remaining 15 numbers unknown)

Panhard VTT M3 armoured personnel carrier: 1364 ZD through 1380 ZD; 6147 ZH, 6154 ZH, 6157 ZH; 199 AZI (remaining 39 numbers unknown, but numbers 6147 ZH through 6157 ZH are likely)

SISU: 91-D-2347 and 91-D-2350

Mowag III H: Observed registrations for Mowags are in the 01-D 8XXXX and 04-D 4XXXX and 04-D-6XXXX series

Mowag CRV: Observed registrations are in 07- KE 6XXX series

Mowag MRV: Observed registrations are in 07-D 85XXX series Landsverk L 60 tanks: L601 and L602

Universal Carriers: ZD 3332, ZD 3429, ZD 3436, ZD 3454, ZD 3468, ZD 4627, ZD 4891 (Obtained from photographic observation; remaining 219 numbers unknown, but all likely in the ZD 3XXX and 4XXX series)

Churchill tanks: ZD 5052 through ZD 5055

Comet tanks: TYI 431 through TYI 434; TYI 496 through TYI 499

FV 101 Scorpion light tanks: 457 DZI through 460 DZI; 438 VZJ through 441 VZJ; 571 BZU through 574 BZU; SI 5361 and SI 5362

# Appendix 6: VEHICLE SERVICE DATES

| Rolls-Royce 1920 Pattern | 1922-1954 |
| Peerless | 1922-1932 |
| Lancia | 1922-1933 (?) |
| Vickers Mark D | 1929-1940 |
| Landsverk L 60 | 1935-1968 |

| | |
|---|---|
| Leyland | 1938-1980s (?) |
| Landsverk L 180 | 1937-1982 |
| GSR Morris Mk IV | 1940-1946 |
| GSR Ford Mk IV | 1940-1954 |
| Ford Mk V | 1940-1954 |
| Ford Mk VI | 1941-early 1970s (?) |
| Dodge Mk VII and VIII | 1942-1962 |
| Beaverette | 1944-1965 |
| Universal Carrier | 1940-1944 |
| Churchill | 1948-1969 |
| Comet | 1958-late 1970s |
| Ferret Mk II | 1962-1964 (on loan by UN to Irish contingent in the Congo) |
| SKPF m/42 | 1962-1964 (on loan by Sweden to Irish contingent in the Congo) |
| M 113 | 1962-1963 (on loan by UN to Irish contingent in the Congo) |
| Humber Pig | 1964-1965 (on loan by UN to Irish contingent in Cyprus) |
| Panhard AML 60 CS | 1964-1989 (converted to AML 127 in 1989) |
| Panhard AML 60 HB | 1970-?? (fourteen of 16 were scrapped by 2005; the fifteenth was scrapped after 2005, and one remains for historic purposes with the Cavalry Corps as of 2009) |
| Panhard AML 90 | 1970-2008 |
| Panhard AML 127 | 1989-199? (all were converted to AML 20 in the late 1990s) |
| Unimog | 1972-1987 |
| Panhard VTT M3 | 1972-2008 (46 of the 60 purchased were scrapped in 1996; 14 upgraded models were still believed to be in the inventory in a reserve status in 2009) |
| Timoney Mk I | 1973-1974 |
| Timoney Mk II | 1974-1977 |
| Timoney Mk III | 1974-1980 |
| Timoney Mk IV | 1978-1988 |
| Timoney Mk VI | 1983-1999 |
| Scorpion CVR (T) | 1980-2008 |
| SISU XA-180 | 1989-2001 (on loan by UN to Irish contingent in Lebanon; two SISUs were also purchased by Ireland in 1990 and as of 2009 were still in the Irish inventory) |
| RG-31 Nyala | 1996-2001 (on loan by UN to Irish contingent in Lebanon) |
| Mowag Piranha III H | 2001-present |
| Mowag Piranha II CRV/MRV | 2007-present |
| RG 32M | 2009-present |
| Vickers Mk D | 1929-1940 |
| Landsverk L60 | 1935-1968 |
| Universal Carrier | 1940-1965 |
| Churchill Mk VI | 1948-1981 (last operational until 1967; training until 1981) |
| Comet | 1958-late 1970s |
| Scorpion CVR(T) | 1980-present |

# Appendix 7: WEAPON CHARACTERISTICS

| Weapon | Caliber | Weight (kg) | Ammunition Type | Rate of fire | Muzzle velocity (m/s) | Range (m), max/effective |
|---|---|---|---|---|---|---|
| Vickers .303 | .303 | 15 | Ball, tracer | 450-600 | 844 | 4100/740 |
| Hotchkiss Mark I | .303 | 12 | Ball, tracer | --- | 844 | 3800/- |
| Madsen .303 | .303 | 9 | Ball, tracer | 450 | 844 | -/600 |
| Browning .30 caliber M1919A4 | .30 | 14 | Ball, tracer | 400-600 | 854 | 1370/- |
| AA52 MG (French) | 7.5mm | 9.75 | Ball, tracer | 900 | 830 | --- |
| MAG 80 GPMG | 7.62mm | 11 | Ball, tracer | 650-1000- | --- | --- |
| Browning M2 HB | .50 inch | 38 | Ball, tracer, | --- | 887 | 2000 |
| Madsen 20mm | 20mm | --- | AP-T, APHE, | --- | 780 | --- |
| G12 20mm | | 20mm | 83 | HE | 650 | 1050 |
| Hispano-Suiza Mk V | 20mm | 43 | HE | --- | 840 | --- |
| OTO M44 | | 30mm | --- | HEI-T, APDS-T | --- | --- |
| Ordnance QF 6-pdr | 57mm | --- | HE, AP | --- | 554 | 3700 |
| 60mm CS mortar | 60mm | --- | HE | --- | --- | --- |
| 60mm HB mortar | 60mm | --- | HE | 10 | --- | 2600/500 |
| Ordnance QF 75mm | 75mm | --- | HE, APCBC | --- | 625 | --- |
| L 23A1 | 76mm | 146 | HESH-T, HE, | --- | --- | 2200/- |
| Ordnance QF Mk IV | 76.2mm | --- | HE, APC, APCBC | --- | --- | ---/10,000 |
| GIAT F1 | 90mm | --- | HE, HEAT, smoke, | 760 (HEAT)/1100 | | |

# Appendix 8:

# PRESERVED VEHICLES

Considering the relatively modest number of armoured vehicles to have been in the Irish Army's inventory between 1922 and 1975, a significant number of vehicles have been preserved or restored and are located either in museums or in the hands of private collectors. The following is believed to be a complete list of surviving vehicles that saw service in the Irish Army between 1922 and 1975:

**Rolls-Royce 1920 Pattern Armoured Car**
Two ex-Irish Rolls-Royce 1920 Pattern armoured cars have survived. One (ARR1, Danny Boy, later Tom Keogh) is owned by a private collector in England, and the other (ARR2, Slievenamon) is maintained by the Irish Cavalry Corps at Curragh Camp, County Kildare, Ireland.

**Peerless Armoured Car**
The Irish Defence Forces Combined Vehicle Base Workshops have built a faithful replica of a Peerless armoured car, using a chassis and engine acquired in 1990. The project was completed in June 2009.

**Republican Improvised Armoured Car "Moon Car"**
As of December 2008, restoration of the "Moon Car" had begun by a member of the Rolls-Royce Enthusiasts Club (Northern Ireland), but further details, and status of the restoration project as of the publication date have not been forthcoming.

**Lancia Triota armoured personnel carrier**
Two Lancia armoured personnel carriers have survived. An ex-Irish Lancia Triota, previously owned by an English collector named Tony Oliver, is located at the Italian Army's Museo Storico

*Above: The restored A.R.R. 2 (Slievenamon/Sliabh na mBan) Rolls-Royce belonging to the Cavalry Corps. The car is still used on ceremonial occasions. (Matt McNamara)*

*Another view of A.R.R. 2, taken at the Curragh in 1967. Note the warning "No water" chalked on the armoured radiator door, and that the headlights have been reversed for some reason. The Vickers machinegun is also missing. (Peter Leslie)*

*A.R.R. 2 at Curragh Camp, 2 July, 2009. In view of its historic significance, this car continues to receive pride of place in the Cavalry Corps collection and continues to receive lavish attention to its preservation. (Terry Ward)*

*The reproduction of the Peerless armoured car AP 1, shown at its public debut at Curragh Camp on 2 July, 2009. This is not an original Irish Peerless, but is a faithful replica built by the Base Workshops at Curragh Camp. The front fenders have not been installed, and armament seems to be lacking as well. (Terry Ward)*

della Motorizzazione Militare in Rome. The vehicle was restored in 1978 by Fiat-IVECO's Defence Vehicles Division in Bolzano, and later ceded to the Italian Army's museum. It is painted in spurious British markings. Another Lancia Triota (OI 1399) has been restored by the Royal Ulster Constabulary and is located at the Ulster Folk and Transport Museum, Holywood, County Down, Northern Ireland. Although original plans were followed faithfully with respect to the configuration and appearance, in fact, the "armour" on the restored vehicle is sheet metal rather than plate. This machine originally would have been assigned to the Royal Irish Constabulary; following the 1922 partition of Ireland, Royal Irish Constabulary units remaining in Northern Ireland were redesignated as the Royal Ulster Constabulary.

### Leyland armoured car

Three of the four Leyland armoured cars have survived. One (ZC 773) is preserved by the Irish Cavalry Corps at Curragh Camp. A second (ZC 776) is awaiting restoration at the National Transport Museum, Howth, County Dublin. The third surviving Leyland (ZC 774) has been meticulously restored and is located at the Tank Museum, Bovington, Dorset, England.

### Landsverk L 180 armoured car

Five of the eight Irish Landsverk cars have survived. One (ZC 757) is preserved by the Irish Cavalry Corps at Curragh Camp. Car ZC 758 was presented to The Netherlands Army in November 1982; ZC 5838 was given to the National Transport Museum in Howth in 1988; and ZC 5837 was transferred to the Swedish Army in 1998. A fifth Landsverk (possibly ZC 5842) was acquired by a private collector in The Netherlands in 2005 and as of 2009 was being restored to the Dutch M38 Pantserwagen configuration.

*The Leyland at the National Transport Museum, Howth, as it appeared in 2008. Although in need of restoration, its overall appearance is remarkably good considering that is more than seventy years old. (Howth)*

*The Lancia Triota displayed at the Museo della Motorizzazione Militare, Rome, Italy. Although very colourful, the colours and markings are far from authentic. (Pignato)*

*The Landsverk L 180 armoured car at Howth in 2008. The vehicle is well preserved for its age, having been originally acquired by the Irish Army in 1938. (Howth)*

### Ford Mk VI

The number of Mk VIs to have survived is somewhat in question. Although two can be accounted for, the fate and whereabouts of the possible third and fourth are not clear. One (ZD 1844) has been preserved and is maintained by the Cavalry Corps at Curragh Camp. Car ZD 1760 was located at the Preston Isaac Museum (Cobbaton Combat Collection) in Devon, England, but was returned to Ireland to the National Museum at Collins Barracks, Dublin in 2006. ZD 1767 was sold to a collector in Shropshire, England, but its current (2009) status is unknown, and one, whose registration is not available, was sold to the defunct Grange Cavern Museum in Wales, and subsequently sold to a private collector, but further details are lacking.

### Beaverette Mk III

Only two ex-Irish Beaverettes are known to have survived. One (ZD 3319) is maintained by the Cavalry Corps at the Curragh; the turret and roof of this vehicle were cut off and the vehicle was used as a scout car. Another (ZD 3317) is located at the Preston Isaac Museum in Devon, England. ZD 3317 was issued to the British 5th Division in 1942, but was sold to Ireland after the war. In Irish service the turret and roof were cut off, as on the ZD 3319 Cavalry example. At least two other Irish Beaverettes were up for sale by a dealer during the 1970s, but their location and disposition are unknown.

### Ferret Mk II armoured car

A Ferret Mk II is maintained by the Cavalry Corps. Although not one of the actual machines used by the Irish contingent in the Congo, it is representative of the type used.

*Ford Mk VI ZD 1844 at Curragh Camp, 2 July, 2009. The armament was installed just prior to the parade, and is not painted in green as is the rest of the vehicle. (Terry Ward)*

*The restored Beaverette in Battleship Grey livery, maintained by the Irish Cavalry Corps. (Bob Cantwell)*

*The Cavalry Corps' Ferret at a parade on 2 July, 2009. (Terry Ward)*

*The National Transport Museum, Howth's Unimog scout car in a 2008 photograph. The Cavalry Corps also maintains a Unimog. (Howth)*

### Unimog scout car

One Unimog scout car (2269 ZC) is preserved at the National Transport Museum, Howth, and another (2259 ZC) is maintained by the Cavalry Corps at Curragh Camp. Two others (2262 ZC and one other, registration unavailable) are owned by private collectors in County Limerick and Clonmel but are not in running condition.

### Timoney Mk IV armoured personnel carrier

Two examples of the Timoney Mk IV have survived; one (365 KZE) is located at the National Transport Museum, Howth, which acquired it from the Irish Army in April 1996, and the other (368 KZE) is maintained by the Irish Cavalry Corps at Curragh Camp.

### Timoney Mk VI armoured personnel carrier

Three Timoney Mk VI APCs (ASI 125 and ASI 128, and another in the hands of a private collector in Clonmel, registration details unavailable) have survived. At one point all were repainted in a three-tone camouflage scheme similar to that used on the Scorpion, using standard commercial vehicle paint, although the scheme resembled that of the low reflectivity CARC (Chemical Agent Resistant Coating) paint used on the Mowags. ASI 125 has since been repainted overall green and is maintained at the Curragh; ASI 128, also maintained by the Cavalry Corps at the Curragh, retains the three-tone camouflage scheme.

### Panhard AML 60 armoured car

All of the AML 60 CS cars have been upgraded to AML 20 cars; none survive in their original configuration. Four AML 60 HB cars apparently have survived, all maintained by the Cavalry Corps at Curragh Camp. Both 318 RRI and 6459 ZE are in running condition; 6459 has been cosmetically reconfigured to resemble the earlier CS version. As of mid-2009 another HB car, with no registration number, was on static display at the camp, and a fourth (formerly registered as 632 NRI, apparently rescued from being used as a target, was in deplorable condition, also at Curragh Camp.

*One of two surviving examples of the Timoney Mk IV photographed at Howth in 2008. The other Mk IV is in possession of the Cavalry Corps. At Curragh Camp. The production Mk IV run amounted to only five vehicles. (Howth)*

*Timoney Mk VI (ASI 128) refurbished in a three-tone camouflage scheme. (Paul Murphy)*

*Timoney Mk VI (ASI 125) at Curragh Camp, 27 May, 2009, in solid green livery. (Roy Kinsella)*

*An AML 60 HB minus armament on static display at Curragh Camp, May 2009. It rests on the plinth on which the Landsverk L60 light tank, now at Collins Barracks, Dublin, formerly rested. (Ralph Riccio)*

*An AML 60 HB that has escaped destruction as a range target, photographed at Curragh Camp on 27 May, 2009. Although its registration plates have been removed, the numbers painted on its side identify it as 632 NRI. (Paul Murphy)*

Although AML 60 6459 ZE is an HB car, it has been modified by the Cavalry Corps to a CS configuration, as can be seen by the smooth CS-type gun tube. The photograph was taken on 27 May, 2009. (Ralph Riccio)

### Panhard VTT M3 armoured personnel carrier

At least eight Panhard M3s have survived. 6156 ZH belongs to Sean O'Sullivan, a private collector in County Limerick, Ireland, and is the only running VTT M3 in Ireland. A second is in the National Museum of Ireland, Collins Barracks, Dublin. Two are gate guardians at Collins Barracks, Dublin, and another two are gate guardians at Custume Barracks, Athlone. One is on static display at Curragh Camp, and one is in open storage at the Vehicle Base Workshops in Curragh Camp. One M3 apparently was illegally exported to the UK, where it was restored by RR Motor Services, Ltd in the 1990s and subsequently sold to an undisclosed client.

Panhard VTT M3 61256 ZH belonging to Sean O'Sullivan, a private collector in Ireland. The vehicle is in excellent condition and frequently participates in parades. (Sean O'Sullivan)

A Panhard VTT M3 in white U.N. livery. This vehicle is on display indoors at the National Museum of Ireland's Collins Barracks in Dublin. (Sean O'Sullivan)

*This rather profusely marked VTT M3 was photographed on 27 May, 2009 at Curragh Camp. It is on loan to the UNIFIL Veterans Reenactment Group. Open storage has left it to the mercy of the Irish weather. (Ralph Riccio)*

*The Scania SKPF m/42 that was acquired from Sweden in 1998. It has been painted in the standard Irish Army green livery. (Paul Murphy)*

### Scania SKPF m/42 armoured personnel carrier

In 1998 the Irish Army provided the Swedish Army a Landsverk L 180 armoured car in exchange for a Scania m/42. The Scania is maintained by the Irish Cavalry Corps at Curragh Camp.

### Landsverk L 60 light tank

Both of the L 60s in Irish service have survived. One (L-601) is on display at the National Museum of Ireland, Collins Barracks, Dublin, as of mid-2009, having been formerly a gate guardian at Curragh Camp; the second (L-602) is preserved in working condition by the Cavalry Corps, minus its armament.

### Churchill Mk VI tank

Two ex-Irish Churchills have survived. One (ZD 5054) is on static display at Plunkett Barracks, Curragh Camp, Ireland, and the other (ZD 5055) was donated to The North Irish Horse, a wartime British regiment from Northern Ireland, and is displayed at Dunmore Park, Belfast, Northern Ireland.

The restored Landsverk L 60 in running condition, 2 July, 2001. It is painted in Battleship Grey livery. (Terry Ward)

The Cavalry Corps L60 at Curragh Camp, May 2009, with the turret access hatch open. (Roy Kinsella)

Churchill Mk VI gate guardian at Plunkett Barracks, Curragh Camp. The track guards are not the correct configuration, but have been fabricated to replace the originals. (Bob Cantwell)

*The Churchill at Curragh Camp in July, 2009, showing considerably more weathering than the preceding photo. (Terry Ward)*

*The Churchill displayed at Dunmore Park, Belfast. The front track guards on the left side are completely missing, although the guards on the right side are relatively intact despite having been buried for some twenty years prior to being disinterred for presentation to the North Irish Horse by the Irish Defence Forces in 2003 or 2004. (David Dunne)*

*The Dunmore Churchill from the right side. The main gun is a dummy gun, as is the BESA machinegun (not visible). Despite its relatively recent restoration, the tank shows considerable signs of deterioration. (David Dunne)*

### Universal Carrier

The Irish Army maintains one Universal Carrier at Curragh Camp, and another (ZG 3469) is on display at the National Museum of Ireland, Collins Barracks, Dublin. A third Carrier has been salvaged by a private collector in Clonmel, but is not in running condition.

### Comet A34 tank

Four of the eight ex-Irish Comets have survived. One is preserved in running order by the Cavalry Corps at Curragh Camp, and three others have survived as gate guardians (two at Curragh Camp, and the other at Custume Barracks, Athlone, having been moved from Connolly Barracks, Longford, in March 2009 at an estimated cost of 14,000 Euros.)

### Diamond T 981 Recovery Vehicle

One Diamond T 981, ex-British Army, is in the possession of the Cavalry Corps. Although acquired in 2001, as of late May 2009 it was in open storage at Curragh Camp awaiting restoration.

*The restored Universal Carrier as maintained by the Irish Cavalry Corps at the Curragh, Jul 2009. As with many other vehicles in the Cavalry Corps collection, this carrier is painted in Battleship Grey. (Terry Ward)*

*Rear view of the Cavalry Corps carrier, the Curragh, May 2009. The large rear stowage locker and the small square panels welded to the upper edge of the hull tend to identify this as a Mk III version. (Ralph Riccio)*

*The Comet serving as a gate guardian at Ceannt Barracks, Curragh Camp. This is one of the four surviving Comets in Ireland. (Bob Cantwell)*

*One of the three Comets at Curragh Camp, May 2009. This is a Type B configuration, with the fishtail exhaust pipes mounted on the rear plate. (Ralph Riccio)*

*The restored Cavalry Corps Comet, 2 July, 2009. Despite its status as a decommissioned historic vehicle, this Comet is the heaviest and most heavily armoured combat vehicle in Ireland. (Terry Ward)*

The Diamond T 981 at Curragh Camp on 27 May, 2009. Although this is not the actual vehicle that was in Irish service, it is of the same type that served from 1951 through 1980. (Ralph Riccio)

# BIBLIOGRAPHY

Anon. Short History of the Royal Tank Corps. Wellington Works, Aldershot: Gale and Polden, Ltd., 1930.

Baker, Joe. My Stand for Freedom. Westport, County Mayo, Ireland: Westport Historical Society, 1988.

Becze, Csaba. Magyar Steel. Sandomierz, Poland: Mushroom Model Publications/STRATUS s.c., 2006.

Caidin, Martin, and Barbree, Jay. Bicycles in War. New York: Hawthorn Books, Inc., 1974.

Bishop, Chris. Encyclopedia of Weapons of World War II. Barnes & Noble Books, 1998.

Carroll, John, and Davies, Peter. The Complete Book of Tractors and Trucks. New York: Hermes House, Anness Publishing, Inc., 2002.

Coogan, Tim Pat, and Morrison, George. The Irish Civil War. London: Weidenfeld & Nicholson, 1998.

Cottrell, Peter. The Irish Civil War 1922-23. Botley, Oxford: Osprey Publishing, 2008.

Crow, Duncan, and Icks, Colonel Robert. Encyclopedia of Tanks. Secaucus, New Jersey: Chartwell Books, Inc., 1975.

Doyle, Tom. The Civil War in Kerry. Cork: Mercier Press, 2008.

Dunne, David. Armoured and Heavy Vehicles of the RUC 1922-2001. Hersham, Surrey: Ian Allen Publishing Ltd., 2007.

Fletcher, David. War Cars, British Armoured Cars in the First World War. London: Her Majesty's Stationery Office, 1987.

Fletcher, David. Mr. Churchill's Tank. The British Infantry Tank Mark IV. Atglen, Pennsylvania: Schiffer Publishing, Ltd., 1999.

Fletcher, David. Universal Carrier 1936-48. The 'Bren Gun Carrier' Story. Botley, Oxford: Osprey Publishing, 2005.

Fletcher, David. Sherman Firefly. Botley, Oxford: Osprey Publishing, 2008.

Forty, George. A Photo History of Armoured Cars in Two World Wars. Poole, Dorset: Blandford Press, 1984.

Foss, Christopher, and Dunstan, Simon. Scorpion Reconnaissance Vehicle 1972-94. Botley, Oxford: Osprey Publishing, 1995.

Harrington, Niall C. Kerry Landing, August 1922. Dublin: Anvil Books, Limited, 1992.

Hopkinson, Michael. Green Against Green: The Irish Civil War. Dublin: Gill & Macmillan Ltd., 2004.

Hoppe, Henry. Deutsche Fahrzeugraritäten (3)/German Military Vehicle Rarities (3), Tankograd Wehrmacht Special No. 4003. Erlangen: Tankograd Publishing – Verlag Jochen Vollert, 2005.

Ishizuka, Katsumi. Ireland and International Peacekeeping Operations, 1960-2000. London: Frank Cass Publishers, 2004.

Jane's Armour and Artillery 1990-91. Couldson, Surrey: Jane's Information Group, Ltd., 1991.

Kennedy, Mark. The LMS in Ireland. Hinckley, Leicestershire: Midland Publishing, 2000.

Lewin, Ronald. Man of Armour: A study of Lieut-General Vyvyan Pope and the development of armoured warfare. London: Leo Cooper, 1976.

MacCarron, Donal. Step Together! Ireland's Emergency Army 1939-46 As Told By Its Veterans. Dublin: Irish Academic Press, 1997.

MacCarron, Donal. The Irish Defence Forces Since 1922. Botley, Oxford: Osprey Publishing, 2004.

Martin, Karl. Irish Army Vehicles. Transport & Armour Since 1922. Dublin: Cahill Printers, Ltd., 2002.

Money, Robert R. Flying and Soldiering. London: Ivor Nicholson and Watson, 1936.

Neeson, Eoin. The Civil War 1922-23. Dublin: Poolbeg Press, Ltd., 1995.

Share, Bernard. In Time of Civil War: The Conflict on the Irish Railways 1922-23. Doughcloyne, Wilton, Cork: The Collins Press, 2006.

Sheehan, William. British Voices From the Irish War of Independence 1918-1921. Doughcloyne, Wilton, Cork: The Collins Press, 2005.

Sheehan, William. Fighting for Dublin: The British Battle for Dublin 1919-1921. Doughcloyne, Wilton, Cork: The Collins Press, 2007.

Taylor, Dick. Warpaint: Colours and Markings of British Army Vehicles 1903-2003. Volume 1. Sandomierz, Poland: Mushroom Model Publications/ STRATUS s.c., 2008.

Townshend, Charles. The British Campaign in Ireland 1919-1921. Oxford: Oxford University Press, 1975.

Walsh, Paul V. The Role of Armoured Fighting Vehicles in the Irish Civil War, 1922-1923. Paper presented to The Civil War Conference, Cathal Brugha Barracks, Dublin, 11-13 September, 1997.

Walsh, Paul V. The Irish Civil War, 1922-1923: A Military Study of the Conventional Phase, 28 June – 11 August, 1922. Paper presented to NYMAS, 11 December 1998.

White, B.T. Tanks and Other Armored Fighting Vehicles 1900-1918. New York: Blandford Press Ltd., 1970.

White, Gerry and O'Shea, Brendan. Irish Volunteer Soldier 1913-23. Botley, Oxford: Osprey Publishing, 2003.

Younger, Calton. Ireland's Civil War. London and Glasgow: Collins Clear-Type Press, 1970.

Clothier, John. The Moon Car. The Rolls-Royce Enthusiasts' Club, Bulletin 154.

English, Adrian J. Irish Army Orders of Battle, 1923-2004. Takoma Park, Maryland: Tiger Lily Publications LLC, 2005.

MacNamee, Captain Liam. The Cavalry Corps. An Cosantoir, January, 1976.

Magennis, Comdt. A.J. Cavalry in the Congo and Cyprus. An Cosantoir, January, 1976.

McCarthy, Denis J. Armour in the War Years. An Cosantoir, March, 1975.

McCarthy, Denis J., and English, Adrian J. Armoured Fighting Vehicles of the Army: No.1: The Peerless Armoured Car. An Cosantoir, August ,1975.

McCarthy, Denis J., and English, Adrian J. Armoured Fighting Vehicles of the Army: No. 2: The Rolls-Royce Whippet Armoured Car. An Cosantoir, December, 1975.

McCarthy, Denis, and Leslie, Peter. Armoured Fighting Vehicles of the Army: No. 2: Lancia Armoured Car. An Cosantoir, May, 1976.

McCarthy, Denis J. Armoured Fighting Vehicles of the Army, No. 4: The Vickers Medium Tank, Mk C. An Cosantoir, February 1977.

McCarthy, Denis J. Armoured Fighting Vehicles of the Army, No.5: Landsverk L-60 Tank. An Cosantoir, September 1977.

McCarthy, Denis J. Armoured Fighting Vehicles of the Army, No. 6: Landsverk L-180 Armoured Car. An Cosantoir, August 1978.

McCarthy, Denis J. Armoured Fighting Vehicles of the Army, No7: The Leyland Armoured Car. An Cosantoir, February 1980.

McCarthy, Denis J. Armoured Fighting Vehicles of the Army, No. 8: Ford Mk IV & Ford Mk V. An Cosantoir, May 1981.

McCarthy, Denis J. Armoured Fighting Vehicles of the Army, No 9: Ford Mk VI. An Cosantoir, July 1981.

McCarthy, Denis J. Armoured Fighting Vehicles of the Army, No. 10: Universal Carriers. An Cosantoir, November 1981.

McCarthy, Denis J. Armoured Fighting Vehicles of the Army, No11: Dodge Armoured Cars Mk VII & Mk VIII. An Cosantoir, April 1984.

McCarthy, Denis J. Armoured Fighting Vehicles of the Army, No. 12: Beaverette Armoured Cars. An Cosantoir, January 1982.

McCarthy, Denis J. Armoured Fighting Vehicles of the Army, No 13: Churchill Tank. An Cosantoir, May 1982.

McCarthy, Denis J. Armoured Fighting Vehicles of the Army, No 14: The Comet Tank. An Cosantoir, March 1983.

McCarthy, Denis J. Armoured Fighting Vehicles of the Army, No. 15: Panhard Armoured Cars. An Cosantoir, October 1983.

McCarthy, Denis J. Armoured Fighting Vehicles of the Army, No 16: The Unimog Scout Car. An Cosantoir, October 1984.

McCarthy, Denis J. Armoured Fighting Vehicles of the Army, No. 17: Scorpion CVR(T). An Cosantoir, January 1985.

McCarthy, Denis J. Irish Armoured Carrier. An Cosantoir, October, 1975.

McCarthy, Denis J. The Timoney Vehicles. An Cosantoir, October, 1976.

Ogorkiewicz, R.M. A Novel Irish Armoured Carrier. International Defence Review, 4/1975, pages 578-580.

O'Shea, Lt Col Brendan. Punching Above Our Weight: Living, Learning and Leading the Peacekeeping Revolution. Óglaigh na hÉireann, Defence Forces Review, 2008.

The Irish Times newspaper articles 13, 18, and 22 April 1922; 20 May 1922; 20 and 27 September 1922.

Walsh, Paul V. British Use of Armored Vehicles During the 1916 Easter Rebellion in Ireland. AFV News, Jan-Apr 2000, Volume 35, No. 1.

Walsh, Paul V. Tanks in Ireland 1919-1922. Tank IV, Twenty Five, August 2001.

Letter, 7 December 1922, from Governor General T.M. Healy to Duke of Devonshire, dealing with supply of equipment to the Irish Free State.

Document, No. 129, untitled, from Duke of Devonshire to Governor General T.M. Healy, 9 March 1923, dealing with supply of equipment to the Irish Free State.

Copy of telegram, undated, from Duke of Devonshire to Governor General of the Irish Free State, dealing with supply and payment of equipment to the Irish Free State.

Document, Ref. No. TC/T/238, 2 Armoured Squadron, Cavalry Corps, McDermott Barracks, Curragh Command, 31st January, 1936, Subject: Landsverk Light Tank.

Document, Chief of Staff (Ceann Foirne): Test of Armour – Ford Armd Cars, 14 February, 1961.

Document, Director, Cavalry Corps, 3 September, 1965, Subject: Beaverettes.